CROSSCURRENTS

CROSSCURRENTS

Themes for Developing Writers

Janet Madden and Sara M. Blake
El Camino College

Harcourt Brace Jovanovich College Publishers
Fort Worth Philadelphia San Diego New York Orlando Austin San Antonio
Toronto Montreal London Sydney Tokyo

Publisher	Ted Buchholz
Executive Editor	Bill McLane
Acquisitions Editor	Michael Rosenberg
Development Editor	Christine Caperton
Design/Project Editor	Publications Development Company
Permissions Editor	Barbara McGinnis
Production Manager	Ken Dunaway
Cover Design Supervisor	John Ritland
Cover Painting	Gloria Ross
Cover Design	Nancy Turner
Composition	Publications Development Company

Address Editorial Correspondence to: 301 Commerce Street, Suite 3700, Fort Worth, TX 76102

Address Orders to: 6277 Sea Harbor Drive, Orlando, Fl 32887 1-800-782-4479, or 1-800-433-0001 (in Florida)

Acknowledgments start on page 325.

Printed in the United States of America

Library of Congress Cataloging-in-Publication Data

Madden, Janet.
    Crosscurrents : themes for developing writers / Janet Madden and Sara M. Blake.
      p.   cm.
    Includes index.
    ISBN 0-03-055852-2
    1. College readers. 2. English language—Rhetoric. I. Blake, Sara M. II. Title.
PE1417.M37   1992
808'.0427—dc20   91-42627
                                     CIP

2 3 4 5 016 9 8 7 6 5 4 3 2 1

To Muireann,
Taidgh,
Curtis,
and Julia

To The Instructor

This developmental reader reflects the interconnectedness of reading, critical thinking and writing. In reading and writing activities provided in the text, students are asked to look critically at the lives they lead, at the forces which surround them and at the cultural influences that shape their lives. The text, therefore, includes topics from popular culture, and readings are sensitive to and representative of the ethnic diversity of today's student population. All materials in this text—readings, activities, writing assignments and the annotated bibliography project—have been classroom developed and tested.

The book is organized into seven chapters. The first chapter addresses the critical reading, thinking, and writing concerns that form the basis of the rest of the book. The next five chapters are composed of readings, each chapter centered around a different theme. The final chapter is designed to familiarize students with the rudiments of library research through a controlled research project.

The first chapter focuses on critical reading and writing. In addition to the usual written explanation of the writing and reading processes, this chapter is activity rich, providing students with the opportunity and challenge of reading actively, using a dictionary, recording reactions in a journal, analyzing sample student essays, and writing a summary. Students will also be encouraged to keep a Writer's Notebook, which includes sections for a reader response journal, a personal spelling/grammar log, and all stages of writing.

The reading selections are arranged thematically, and ordered from inner directed topics to outer directed topics. All of the topics are of immediate concern to students. The first chapter, composed of personal narratives detailing memorable experiences of individuals, is designed to prompt students to examine their own lives and write autobiographical essays (generally the easiest mode for beginning writers). The second chapter focuses on the concept of the hero, with essays on types of heroes, on unsung heroes, on the need for heroes today. Students can use the ideas raised in these selections to examine their own heroes and the heroes in their communities. While still dealing essentially with portraits of individuals, the writing assignments in this chapter will move the students from the intensely personal narrative to an essay form that, though it may incorporate narrative, is more outer directed. The third chapter introduces students to the trickster figure in folklore, myth, and fairy tale. The culturally diverse readings in this section provide students with the materials to explore an archetype common to all cultures. The chapter moves from the more familiar figure of trickster as it appears in the character of Jack in "Jack and the Beanstalk" to its less familiar manifestations. By tracing this figure through a number of cultures, this chapter underscores cultural similarities. The writing assignments in this chapter invite students to consider and analyze cultural myths. The fourth chapter deals with advertising, asking students to look critically at ad strategies and at the portrayal of different groups in advertising. Students can then apply their insights to advertisements that they find in magazines or on television. The final chapter of reading selections invites students to examine television—television dads, MTV, cartoons, ethnic portrayals. Student writing assignments in this chapter center on analysis of television format and content and incorporate the element of argument.

The final chapter acquaints students with techniques of library research through a controlled research project. This project requires students to prepare an annotated bibliography on a subject that is related to ideas raised in the reading chapters. For example, after reading a selection in the television chapter, a student might want to investigate the effect of television violence on children. In locating sources for the project, students will learn to use the library. In preparing the annotated bibliography, students must draw on critical reading skills to find the thesis and major points of a source, on high level critical thinking skills to evaluate the usefulness of a source, and on critical writing skills to produce a summary of the source. Students will also gain experience with bibliographic form—their first introduction to MLA style.

Apparatus for each chapter of readings includes a chapter introduction which ends in a prereading question and a postreading question. Each selection is preceded by a headnote, a question for the student to consider before reading, and two items for the student to keep in mind or look for while reading. Selections are followed by a reader-response journal question which asks students to respond to a selection immediately after reading it. Some questions encourage students to find a personal connection with the text through freewriting; others ask them to practice another prewriting skill, such as listing or charting information included in the selection. For each reading, extensive questions for discussion have been provided. While some questions are text and language centered, others ask students to make personal connections and draw on personal experience to offer judgments on the authors' assertions. Finally, a variety of detailed suggestions for writing topics has been included at the end of each chapter.

While developing this book, we benefited from the thoughtful comments of colleagues who reviewed the manuscript: Leslie Bradley, Penn State University; Lawrence Carlson, Orange Coast College; Marcia Curtis, University of Massachusetts at Amherst; Krystan Douglas, University of New Mexico; Hilde Dubebbert, Southern Illinois University at Edwardsville; and Philip A. Tetreault, Dean Junior College.

We also received invaluable support and guidance from the staff of Harcourt Brace Jovanovich—Ted Bucholtz, publisher; Michael Rosenberg, acquisitions editor; Christine Caperton, development editor; Barbara McGinnis, literary permissions editor; Ken Dunaway, production manager; and John Ritland, design supervisor of the cover. We also thank Nancy Land of Publications Development Company for shepherding our book through text design, composition, and production.

J.M./S.M.B.

CONTENTS

xi

4.   The Trickster   145

5. Advertising   193

Prereading   193

Postreading   194

1

EFFECTIVE READING
AND WRITING

EFFECTIVE READING

Every day we read instructions, news reports, signs, billboards, magazine articles, and books. We read for many different reasons—for information, for enjoyment, for safety, for work—because our society is based on the assumption that people can and do read. Each type of reading demands different skills which extend beyond just the ability to decipher the words on the page.

College reading requires a number of skills. Like the activity of reading instructions, college reading is, on one level, reading for information. But college reading also requires constant assessment. You need to think about who is writing, to whom the author is writing, for what purpose the author is writing, and even whether you agree with the author's opinions. By reading the information contained in this chapter and working through the exercises, you will learn and practice specific techniques for college reading.

1. Before you begin to read a selection that your instructor has assigned, check to see if any important information for better understanding the reading is provided for you. For example, many editors and authors introduce a chapter or a reading with information telling about the content, about the author, where the piece originally appeared, and so on. Always read

1

this information because it may help you interpret or find the main points of the reading itself. In this book, for example, each selection includes a note about the piece and its author, a question to consider before you read, and two things to keep in mind or watch for as you read.

2. If your assigned reading is reasonably brief, read the entire selection through completely so that you have an overall idea of the content. This first reading should be for information. Then, read the piece again. This time, you will need to employ additional skills discussed in this chapter.

3. The first section of a piece of writing is the INTRODUC-TION. It will vary in length depending upon the scope of the selection. In the introduction, the author must not only present the subject of the writing, but also must attract the reader's interest and attention. There are a number of strategies for beginning an essay: using a startling statistic, making an unusual comparison, telling a story, using a series of vivid examples, defining terms or concepts. Always look at the way that the reading selection begins. What strategies does the author use, both to introduce the subject and to capture the reader's attention? How effective are they?

4. One of the most important aspects of college reading is finding the author's main point, which is called the THESIS. The thesis may be expressed in a sentence or two, often at the end of the introduction, or it may be only suggested and not actually written out. In this case, the author expects the reader to be able to figure out the point of the reading.

5. The majority of any piece of reading is based, one way or another, on proving or illustrating the thesis. This supporting information is referred to as the DEVELOPMENT. The author may use various techniques for developing the thesis: telling one long story or a series of small stories, showing how things are alike or different, showing and/or explaining how to do something or how something works, giving reasons in favor of or against something, using a number of examples and/or facts, defining what something is or what something

means. Watch closely to see which strategy or strategies a writer uses to develop the essay's major point or points.

6. Closely related to the development of a piece of writing is the author's PURPOSE. You, the reader, will need to determine this purpose. For example, is the writer trying to get you to change your mind about something, trying to teach you how to do something, trying to show you what something means?

7. Other important considerations for the reader include the question of AUDIENCE, or the people for whom the piece is written. You also need to pay attention to the author's TONE, which indicates how the author feels about the subject. Is the author writing out of anger or sorrow or is the writer trying to be funny or merely give information?

8. At the end of a piece of writing, the writer makes a final impression on the reader and ties the essay together in what is called the CONCLUSION. Sometimes the writer may refer back to the opening of the essay to bring the essay to a close. At other times, writers may pose a question, predict a consequence, provide a solution, or call for action. Notice which strategy or strategies a writer uses to close the essay.

9. Finally, you should always pay attention to the TITLE of a piece of writing. Titles often give clues about content as well as about the opinion the author holds toward the subject. After you have finished reading a selection, go back and consider the title once more.

EFFECTIVE READING ACTIVITY:
BUGS BUNNY SAYS THEY'RE YUMMY

Use the questions below to help you read effectively the selection "Bugs Bunny Says They're Yummy" which follows.

1. Before you read "Bugs Bunny Says They're Yummy," look at the material that appears before the actual reading itself.

What information *about* this reading is provided for the reader? What do you expect to find in the reading?

2. Read the selection over once quickly, then go back and refer to the reading to answer questions 3 through 9.

3. After her initial explanation of why she is appearing before the Senate, Kurth introduces her topic with a description of a family incident. What is the incident and how does it lead in to the topic of the essay?

4. Kurth's THESIS does not appear in one particular sentence. Choose the thesis that you think best reflects the point of the selection:

   A. Television ads aimed at children should be banned.

   B. Television ads aimed at children are objectionable.

   C. Television ads aimed at children are deceptive.

   All of these ideas appear in some form in the reading, but B is the best answer. If you chose B, why did you select it? If you chose A or C, look over the essay once more and see if you can explain why B might be a better answer.

5. Kurth identifies two types of objectionable ads aimed at children. What are the two types?

6. What method(s) does Kurth use to develop her thesis?

7. What is Kurth's purpose in testifying before the Senate?

8. Before her closing remarks thanking the Committee for letting her speak, Kurth concludes her discussion of advertising. What strategy does she use in her conclusion?

9. Look at the title of the selection. A title should interest or intrigue the reader, provide a key to the content, and/or reveal the author's attitude toward the subject matter. How effective is the title of this piece?

BUGS BUNNY SAYS THEY'RE YUMMY

Dawn Ann Kurth

About the Reading

Eleven-year-old Dawn Ann Kurth testified before a 1972 Senate subcommittee on television advertising. The following piece is a transcript of her statement about false and deceptive television ads directed at children.

Before You Read

Children are a particularly good audience for television advertising. They generally watch television for concentrated periods of time, such as Saturday mornings or weekday afternoons, so they are easily targeted by marketers of children's products. Furthermore, children are relatively gullible; not only do they usually believe the ad claims they see and hear, but very young children often fail to differentiate between advertisements and television shows. Can you think of something you saw advertised as a child that failed to live up to what you perceived as its television promises?

As You Read

1. Remember that this piece is a transcript of testimony and was not originally written as an essay. Yet, it contains all of the elements of an essay: an introduction, development, a conclusion. Try to identify these different elements as you read.

2. Kurth uses many examples of specific advertising slogans to demonstrate what she considers to be deceptive advertising practices. Consider how these examples help

convince the reader of the problem which Kurth is trying to illustrate.

Mr. Chairman:

1   My name is Dawn Ann Kurth. I am 11 years old and in the fifth grade at Meadowlane Elementary School in Melbourne, Florida. This year I was one of the 36 students chosen by the teachers out of 20,000 5th-through-8th graders to do a project in the Talented Student Program in Brevard County. We were allowed to choose a project in any field we wanted. It was difficult to decide. There seem to be so many problems in the world today. What could I do?

2   A small family crisis solved my problem. My sister Martha, who is 7, had asked my mother to buy a box of Post Raisin Bran so that she could get the free record that was on the back of the box. It had been advertised several times on Saturday morning cartoon shows. My mother bought the cereal, and we all (there are four children in our family) helped Martha to eat it so she could get the record. It was after the cereal was eaten and she had the record that the crisis occurred. There was no way the record would work.

3   Martha was very upset and began crying and I was angry too. It just didn't seem right to me that something could be shown on TV that worked fine and people were listening and dancing to the record and when you bought the cereal, instead of laughing and dancing, we were crying and angry. Then I realized that perhaps here was a problem I could do something about or, if I couldn't change things, at least I could make others aware of deceptive advertising practices to children.

4   To begin my project I decided to keep a record of the number of commercials shown on typical Saturday morning TV shows. There were 25 commercial messages during one hour, from 8 to 9 A.M., not counting ads for shows coming up or public service ads. I found there were only 10 to 12 commercials during shows my

parents like to watch. For the first time, I really began to think about what the commercials were saying. I had always listened before and many times asked my mother to buy certain products I had seen advertised, but now I was listening and really thinking about what was being said. Millions of kids are being told:

5   "Make friends with Kool-Aid. Kool-Aid makes good friends."

6   "People who love kids have to buy Fritos."

7   "Hershey chocolate makes milk taste like a chocolate bar." Why should milk taste like a chocolate bar anyway?

8   "Cheerios make you feel groovy all day long." I eat them sometimes and I don't feel any different.

9   "Libby frozen dinners have fun in them." Nothing is said about the food in them.

10   "Cocoa Krispies taste like a chocolate milk shake only they are crunchy."

11   "Lucky Charms are magically delicious with sweet surprises inside." Those sweet surprises are marshmallow candy.

12   I think the commercials I just mentioned are examples of deceptive advertising practices.

13   Another type of commercial advertises a free bonus gift if you buy a certain product. The whole commercial tells about the bonus gift and says nothing about the product they want you to buy. Many times, as in the case of the record, the bonus gift appears to be worthless junk or isn't in the package. I wrote to the TV networks and found it costs about $4,000 for a 30-second commercial. Many of those ads appeared four times in each hour. I wonder why any company would spend $15,000 or $20,000 an hour to advertise worthless junk.

14   The ads that I have mentioned I consider deceptive. However, I've found others I feel are dangerous.

15   Bugs Bunny vitamin ads say their vitamins "taste yummy" and taste good.

16   Chocolate Zestabs say their product is "delicious" and compare taking it with eating a chocolate cookie.

17   If my mother were to buy those vitamins, and my little sister got to the bottles, I'm sure she would eat them just as if they were candy.

18   I do not know a lot about nutrition, but I do know that my mother tries to keep our family from eating so many sweets. She says they are bad for our teeth. Our dentist says so too. If they are bad, why are companies allowed to make children want them by advertising on TV? Almost all of the ads I have seen during children's programs are for candy, or sugar-coated cereal, or even sugar-coated cereal with candy in it.

19   I know people who make these commercials are not bad. I know the commercials pay for TV shows and I like to watch TV. I just think that it would be as easy to produce a good commercial as a bad one. If there is nothing good that can be said about a product that is the truth, perhaps the product should not be sold to kids on TV in the first place.

20   I do not know all the ways to write a good commercial, but I think commercials would be good if they taught kids something that was true. They could teach about good health, and also about where food is grown. If my 3-year-old sister can learn to sing, "It takes two hands to handle a whopper 'cause the burgers are better at Burger King," from a commercial, couldn't a commercial also teach her to recognize the letters of the alphabet, numbers, and colors? I am sure that people who write commercials are much smarter than I and they should be able to think of many ways to write a commercial that tells the truth about a product without telling kids they should eat it because it is sweeter or "shaped like fun" (what shape *is* fun, anyway?) or because Tony Tiger says so.

21   I also think kids should not be bribed to buy a product by commercials telling of the wonderful free bonus gift inside.

22   I think kids should not be told to eat a certain product because a well-known hero does. If this is a reason to eat something, then, when a well-known person uses drugs, should kids try drugs for the same reason?

23   Last of all, I think vitamin companies should never, never be allowed to advertise their product as being delicious, yummy, or in any way make children think they are candy. Perhaps these commercials could teach children the dangers of taking drugs or teach children that, if they do find a bottle of pills, or if the

medicine closet is open, they should run and tell a grown-up, and never, never eat the medicine.

24   I want to thank the Committee for letting me appear. When I leave Washington, the thing that I will remember for the rest of my life is that some people *do* care what kids think. I know I could have led a protest about commercials through our shopping center and people would have laughed at me or thought I needed a good spanking or wondered what kind of parents I had that would let me run around in the streets protesting. I decided to gather my information and write letters to anyone I thought would listen. Many of them didn't listen, but some did. That is why I am here today. Because some people cared about what I thought. I hope now that I can tell every kid in America that when they see a wrong, they shouldn't just try to forget about it and hope it will go away. They should begin to do what they can to change it.

25   People will listen. I know, because you're listening to me.

USING A DICTIONARY

A dictionary can be a useful tool not only for helping you find the correct spelling of a word, but also for helping you to understand what you read and to pronounce new words you encounter in your reading. By using a desk-style dictionary to work through the items that follow, you'll learn what a dictionary can do for you.

Some good desk dictionaries are listed below:

The American Heritage Dictionary of the English Language
Webster's New Collegiate Dictionary
Webster's New World Dictionary
The Random House College Dictionary

1. Pronunciation

    A. Look up the word *indefatigable*. Copy down the pronunciation, which usually appears in parentheses directly after the main entry for a word.

    B. To decode pronunciation marks, look for key words at the bottom of the page or locate a pronunciation key at the beginning of your dictionary.

    C. Look at the pronunciation you copied down for *indefatigable*. Under each letter that has a pronunciation mark over it and under any unfamiliar symbols, jot down the word from the pronunciation key which explains the sound of the letter. Keys to pronouncing letters and vowel sounds differ from one dictionary to another. For example, many dictionaries use a schwa (ə) to indicate the sound of the letter "a" in the word *ago*; other dictionaries will use **a** or **uh** to show how to pronounce this same sound.

    D. In every word of more than one syllable, one portion of the word is emphasized more than others. In pronouncing the word *student*, for example, we stress the first syllable (*stu*dent); in *exam*, we stress the last syllable (ex*am*). Some dictionaries indicate a stressed syllable by an accent mark (´) after the syllable to be stressed, some by a stress mark before the syllable to be stressed, and others by placing the stressed syllable in **bold type**. Find the syllable in the word *indefatigable* which should be stressed and underline it.

    E. Finally, pronounce the word aloud, being careful to use the correct sounds and stress the appropriate syllable.

    F. To practice what you have just learned, use your dictionary as you did above to pronounce these words: *schism, indecorous, indictment, banal.*

    G. Sometimes a word has more than one pronunciation. The first pronunciation listed in the dictionary is the more common or preferred one. Write down the two pronunciations for the word *harass*. Circle the most common or preferred pronunciation.

2. Meanings

One word may have several meanings. When you look up an unfamiliar word that you have encountered in conversation or in your reading, you need to find the definition that is appropriate to its use or context.

A. Look up the word *cardinal* and copy the one definition that explains the word's meaning in the following sentence:

> One of the *cardinal* rules of my health club is "No pain, no gain."

B. Look up each underlined word and record the dictionary definition that best fits the word as it is used in the sentence:

1. His professor would have to be pretty *credulous* to believe that story.

2. Mario spent an *inordinate* amount of time styling his hair each morning.

3. With a sinking feeling, Keisha *submitted* her essay to Dr. "Doom" Carroway.

3. Common Abbreviations and Foreign Phrases

When you encounter an unfamiliar abbreviation or foreign phrase, you may be able to find its meaning in your dictionary.

A. Look up the meaning of the following abbreviations:

i.e. e.g. lb. GNP

B. Look up the meaning of the following foreign phrases:

ipso facto   joie de vivre

4. Names of People and Places

In some dictionaries, names of famous people are found in a separate section of Biographical Names and place names are found in a section of Geographical Names; in others, names of people and places are included with the other entries.

A. Look up the following names:
Martin Van Buren, Simon Bolivar, Anne Bradstreet.

B. Look up the following place names:
Persia, Timbuktu, Ghana.

Now that you have worked through this section, you can see that there are other reasons to use a dictionary than just to find out how to spell a troublesome word. The dictionary contains a great deal of information that can help you become a more discerning reader.

However, just knowing how to use the dictionary alone will not always provide you with the key to understanding a writer's words. Understanding what you read involves both knowing the basic definition for words and also considering the way in which a particular word is used in a selection. Sometimes you can figure out the meaning of a word from its *context* without having to look it up; many times the context must be considered in conjunction with dictionary definitions to help you choose the appropriate meaning. Still other times, however, you will have to decode the author's meaning by analyzing closely the emotional associations of various words and the way certain words are placed together. As you practice critical reading, your interpretive skills should improve.

The activity that follows gives you some practical experience with interpreting what you read. First you will need to read the article "Children Who Dress for Excess"; then, using your dictionary to help you, work through the questions which follow the reading selection.

CHILDREN WHO DRESS
FOR EXCESS

Ron Harris

About the Reading

The following article, which appeared in the *Los Angeles Times* on November 12, 1989, was written by *Times* staff writer Ron Harris. Harris explores the growing trend toward expensive name-brand clothing and its harmful effect on children.

Before You Read

Designer clothing has become almost a necessity in our culture, or at least it is perceived as a necessity for children who desperately want to fit in with their peers in the neighborhood and at school. What do you think of the practice of buying children expensive name-brand clothing?

As You Read

1. This selection begins with a striking *anecdote*. Notice, however, the almost matter-of-fact tone that the author uses to relate the horror of the incident while the emotional words are reserved for the description of the shoes. Consider how this subtle treatment underscores the message of the piece.

2. Harris points out a number of reasons that contribute to the problem he describes in this piece. As you come across these reasons, consider whether you agree or disagree, and whether you can think of additional reasons.

1   BALTIMORE—When 15-year-old Michael Thomas left home for school last May, he couldn't have been prouder. On his feet, thanks to his mother's hard work, were a pair of spanking new Air Jordans—$100 worth of leather, rubber and status that to today's youth are the Mercedes-Benzes of athletic footwear.

2   The next day it was James David Martin, 17, who was strolling down the street in Thomas' new sneakers, while Thomas lay dead in a field not far from his school. Martin was arrested for murder.

3   For the Baltimore school system, Thomas' death was the last straw. He was the third youngster to have been killed over his clothes in five years. Scores of others had been robbed of name-brand sneakers, designer jogging suits, leather jackets and jewelry.

4   This fall, the school board instituted an exclusionary dress code. Devised by parents, students and educators, it prohibits leather skirts and jackets, jogging suits, gold chains and other expensive items.

5   Clothes, said board president Joseph Smith, had just gotten out of hand.

6   Across the nation, parents, school officials, psychologists and even some children agree.

7   They say that today's youngsters, from New York's poverty-ridden South Bronx to Beverly Hills, have become clothes fixated. They worry over them, compete over them, neglect school for them and sometimes even rob and kill for them.

8   This obsession with clothing, say those who study it, is fueled by the visual media and advertising, is nurtured by overindulgent parents and is reinforced by youthful peer pressure and the child's overriding desire to fit in.

9   And, they note, the clothing industry is using advertising to court today's youngsters at a younger age and with much greater intensity.

10   "All of these people understand something that is very basic and logical, that if you own this child at an early age, you can own this child for years to come," said Mike Searles, president of Kids 'R' Us, a chain of specialty children's stores. "Companies are saying, 'Hey, I want to own the kid younger and younger and younger.'"

11   Thus, as early as age 4, many of today's children embark on a frenetic quest for the right clothes with the right style and the right name in order to maintain the right look.

12   For schoolchildren, clothes no longer represent just good grooming; they have become symbols of status, indicators of wealth and a passport into the mainstream of today's childhood.

13   "We've seen that to today's kids, the clothes and footwear are a sense of who they are," said Betty Richardson, vice president of marketing for Reebok. "They represent what they think to be special and what they think to be important to them."

14   And what *is* important, youngsters say, are name brands—Nike, Reebok, L.A. Gear, Guess, Bugle Boy, Jimmy Z, Cavarrichi, Edwins, Benetton, Esprit, Public Image, Gitano, Jordache, Ultra Pink and dozens more.

15   They wear the names like badges of honor. Show up for school without them, students say, and they may be ridiculed, scorned and sometimes even ostracized by their classmates.

16   "When people look at you and you're not wearing something that has a name brand, they'll comment on it," said Aime Lorenzo, an 11th grader at Beach High School in Miami.

17   "People will tease you and talk about you, say you got on no-name shoes or say you shop at K mart," said Darion Sawyer, 10, of Tench Tillman Elementary School in Baltimore. Children have developed derisive nicknames for non-name brands—"bo bos, no names, and fish heads."

18   One group of Miami sixth-graders have even developed a sarcastic couplet: "Bo bos cost $1.99. Bo bos make your feet feel fine."

19   Youngsters, naturally, try to avoid such taunting. Jessica Hoffman, 11, spent three hours earlier this year trying to decide what to wear for her first day at Walter Reed Junior High School in Los Angeles.

20   "It sounds stupid," she said, "but what I was worried about was whether people would like what I was wearing."

21   Schoolmate Tim Baca picked out his first-day outfit three days before school started.

22   "I think there are very few people who dress for themselves," Shelly Ann Gouldborne, a Miami High School student, said of her contemporaries.

23   Educators complain that because of such attention to attire, schools from the elementary level to high school have become fashion shows as students try to either outdo each other or just keep up with rapidly changing trends.

24   "I've seen kids come in with wallets and purses that must be well over $100, and I can't figure out why a kid would spend that much money," said Alan Joseffberg, counselor at Fairfax High School in Los Angeles. "And they all have to have a label on their jeans."

25   Robert Davis, a teacher at a middle school in one of Miami's poorer neighborhoods, said as a class exercise he and his class priced the clothes one student was wearing. It came to $180.

26   "And that was just for one day," he said.

27   In many cases, students are so concerned about what they and their classmates are wearing, they forget what they came to school for, educators said. Teasing and arguments over clothes, particularly at the elementary level, result in fights and disruptions. On the high school level, counselors report that more and more students are working, often so they can keep up their wardrobes.

28   "Everybody is spending huge amounts on clothes and the kids who can't afford it—instead of doing homework and studying—are taking jobs after school just to buy designer jeans," said Patrick Welsh, a high school English teacher in Washington, D.C. "It's crazy."

29   In response, scores of public schools, mainly in Eastern cities, have voluntarily adopted school uniforms to cut down on competition. Paradoxically, educators say, in the current fashion climate, dressing students alike allows them greater freedom to be individuals.

30   But elsewhere, parents complain that their children are pressing to keep up.

31   "My daughter wants the $60 pair of jeans, but we're a $30 household," said Pat Anderson, who lives in Geneva, Ill., just outside Chicago. "Maybe if we had a $300,000-a-year income, that

would be fine. But we're on a limited budget and there's no way we can afford this stuff."

32   "Money is always a battle," said Char Christian, who lives in the Chicago suburb of Hinsdale. "I am torn trying to determine the difference between what she needs and what she wants."

33   "It's awful," said Lissa Thompson of Orange County, the mother of two daughters. "It bothers me that children who are so young—7 and 9—are aware of things that are so unimportant. Don't get me wrong, I like nice clothes too, but I think there's a time and a place to be a kid. This is no time for them to be preoccupied with what you put on every day."

34   Psychologists say that an interest in trends and fashion, particularly at the older ages, is just a part of growing up.

35   "Some of this whole clothes business has to do with a normal developmental process," said Maryland psychologist Andrea Vanderpool, "but I think it takes on a more dangerous kind of aura when you see the lengths that these kids have to go to to look like everybody else and how the kids who don't look like everybody else are treated."

36   For clothing models, children look increasingly to the visual media—television, video and even movies. And, advertising executives say, there is no group more susceptible to advertising than youngsters.

37   Nancy Shalek, president of Shalek Advertising Agency, which has handled accounts for a number of children's clothing lines, is also a mother who is concerned about the effect of advertising on today's youth.

38   "Advertising at its best is making people feel that without their product, you're a loser," she said. "Kids are very sensitive to that. If you tell them to buy something, they are resistant. But if you tell them they'll be a dork if they don't, you've got their attention. You open up emotional vulnerabilities and it's very easy to do with kids because they're the most emotionally vulnerable."

39   Peer pressure can also be a powerful force.

40   One result is readily apparent in the shopping cycle. Stores say the two biggest shopping periods for school clothes are the week before school begins and the week after school begins.

41   "The kids go to school and they find out somebody is wearing Reebok instead of Nike or acid-washed jeans instead of tapered," Searles said. "So the desire to fit in drives to more purchases that are totally peer-related."

42   But, observers say, parents can also unwittingly add pressure.

43   Prof. Carol Seefeld of the University of Maryland's Institute for Child Study sees too many acquisitive, success-sodden adults chasing after too few superficial advantages for their children.

44   "It's the Reagan 'You are what you spend' mentality," she said. Seefeld said that parents too often have a need to turn their kids into pint-size status symbols.

45   "I have parents who tell me they buy $50 Nikes for their kids because the kids really want them. I know developmentally that a 4-year-old doesn't know labels unless it is drummed into him. That's why you end up with pre-adolescents demanding $100 outfits."

46   She adds that adolescent pressure and advertising aimed at kids can hardly be blamed for the huge amount of money being spent on status items for newborns—$300 strollers, $40 name-brand sneakers, $10 designer booties, $80 coveralls.

47   Child, a magazine devoted to the nation's newest customers, said a couple can spend $60,000 in the first two years of a baby's life. In interviews for this story, some parents admitted spending as much as $4,000 a year to outfit older children.

48   "It's a very strong sign of the times when our generation is more materialistic, where greed and consumption are high on the list," said Lydia Caffery, an editor with the Tobe Report, a fashion industry trade publication. "The children learn it from their parents—who has the nicest car on the block, who's redecorating the living room."

49   A related problem, observers say, is that today's parents are no longer the countervailing voice against their children's desire for unchecked consumption. Consequently, the relationship between parent and child has changed.

50   "When I grew up, you wore what you were given," said Searles of Kids 'R' Us. "Now, the relationship we see is that parents have

veto rights as opposed to selection rights. They can say no, but the child is the one who says yes."

51 "A lot of parents don't have the control because this society is so confusing that they try to appease their kids any way they can," psychologist Vanderpool said. "A lot of it comes from the fact that parents are more confused today in terms of what's right and what's wrong."

52 For many youngsters, designer labels are mainly a way of letting other students know that what they're wearing had high price tags.

53 Yes, students must have name-brand sneakers to be in step, agreed three pupils at Burrville Elementary in Washington, D.C., "and they have to cost more than $40," chimed in one. The others nodded in agreement.

54 In city after city, when students were asked whether they would wear expensive name-brand clothes without the designer label, they said no. The reason? "People wouldn't know what it costs."

55 "They see it as a way of stating their own personal conviction and commitments," Shalck said. "'I'm making a commitment to $60 or $100 versus $19.99. This is who I am.'

56 "Or they see it as a sign of how much your parents care for you. Sometimes, it's 'I feel good about my ability to control my parents because I made them pay 70 bucks for this.'"

57 Teens shun discount stores. Linnea Chastain in Chicago refers to them as "loser stores." One Chicago mother said her daughter and son won't even sit in the car in a discount store parking lot. A mother in Detroit said her son actually hid in the restroom when he spotted a classmate as they were shopping in K mart.

58 Parents, educators and psychologists are disturbed that the emphasis on clothes reflects heightened class consciousness among youngsters. And they are saddened that children judge individual worth largely on something so superficial.

59 "On one hand, who am I to say that a parent who can afford to buy his 16-year-old a Corvette, shouldn't," said Burrville Elementary Principal Walter O. Henry. "But . . . where do we draw the line? When we start letting children dictate to us, then we've lost them. Simply because parents are able to buy whatever their

children want, doesn't necessarily mean that it's the best thing for them."

60   Lorie Lawson, a Baltimore custodian, agrees. A single parent, Lawson shelled out $1,000 a year to keep her 10-year-old son in the latest clothes, and only stopped this year when her son's elementary school went to uniforms.

61   "I spoiled him rotten," she said. "I bought him Nike. I bought him Reebok. I bought him BMW sweat shirts. Every day, it was something he just had to have. And the more I got, the more he wanted.

62   "It ruined him. His grades went down. He couldn't concentrate in school for trying to pay attention to what everybody had on.

63   "It did something to him and it did something to me. I see what it means for a person to be addicted to cocaine."

CRITICAL READING ACTIVITY: "CHILDREN WHO DRESS FOR EXCESS"

1. The title of the article contains a type of word play called a *pun*. One type of pun involves substituting a word for another word with a similar sound but a different meaning. What word do we usually expect to hear after *Dress for* _____?

2. What does Harris mean when he describes Air Jordans as "the Mercedes-Benzes of athletic footwear" (paragraph 1)? What qualities do the shoes and the automobiles share?

3. In paragraph 4, Harris states that the Baltimore school system instituted an "exclusionary dress code." Look up the word *exclusion*. From the definition of *exclusion*, explain what is meant by an "exclusionary dress code."

4. In the first sentence of paragraph 7, Harris writes that today's youngsters have become "clothes fixated." Instead of looking up the word *fixate*, read the second sentence in the paragraph and write your own definition of *fixated*.

5. In paragraph 9, advertisers are said "to court" youngsters. We usually think of "courting" and "courtship" in terms of marriage. Ask yourself what similarities there might be between the behavior of the advertisers and male-female courtship. Without looking up the definition of the verb *court*, explain what Harris means by "the clothing industry is using advertising to court today's youngsters . . . ."

6. In paragraph 15, Harris notes that children are "sometimes even ostracized by their classmates" if they do not wear designer-label clothing. Use your dictionary to write a definition of *ostracize*.

7. The word *derisive* appears in paragraph 17. Use your dictionary to look up the pronunciation of this word (the pronunciation usually appears right after the entry word and is often set off by \ \). Copy the pronunciation as it is given. Refer to the pronunciation guide in your dictionary to decode what you have copied and pronounce the word *derisive* aloud.

8. Draw on your own knowledge or use your dictionary to answer the following questions:

   A. What is a *couplet* (paragraph 18)?

   B. What are *contemporaries* (paragraph 22)?

   C. What number equals a *score* (paragraphs 3, 29)?

   D. What does *susceptible* mean (paragraph 36)?

   E. What does *acquisitive* mean (paragraph 43)?

   F. What does *superficial* mean (paragraphs 43, 58)?

   G. What do you do if you *shun* something or someone (paragraph 57)?

9. Carefully read the first sentence of paragraph 49. Without looking in the dictionary, explain what is meant by a *countervailing voice*.

10. Explain in your own words the following phrases found in the article:

    A. "success-sodden adults" (paragraph 43)

    B. "heightened class consciousness" (paragraph 58)

11. In paragraph 8, Harris asserts that the clothing obsession is "nurtured by overindulgent parents." We usually think of parents "nurturing" children. How does a person "nurture" an obsession? What does Harris mean?

12. In discussing the adoption of school uniforms in Eastern cities, Harris writes, "Paradoxically, educators say, dressing students alike allows them greater freedom to be individuals" (paragraph 29). Rewrite Harris' sentence in your own words. You need to be sure you understand what a *paradox* is.

13. In one sentence, write down what you think is the main idea (also called the *thesis*) of the article.

14. List three reasons given in the article which suggest why children have become so concerned about their clothing.

15. From your reading of the article, what would you say is Harris' position on the issue of designer label clothing for children? What do you think he would say parents and schools should do, if anything?

EFFECTIVE WRITING

Just as there are many kinds of reading, so there are many kinds of writing. We write letters, make lists of things we have to do, leave notes for others, write memos, keep diaries—the list could go on and on. We write for many different reasons: because we are required to write at work or at school, because we need to communicate with others, or just because we enjoy writing. While each type of writing requires a slightly different emphasis, the skills you acquire in doing any kind of writing can help you with other kinds.

Like leaving a note for a friend or writing a memo at work, the writing you do in college must communicate your ideas effectively on paper. Like keeping a diary or writing creatively, college writing requires original thinking on your part. Coming up with ideas for responding to writing assignments is much like making a list of things to do or to buy at the store; it necessitates generating material for a future purpose.

The material in this section will show you some techniques that will enable you to draw on the writing skills you already possess for help with your course writing assignments. You will get a chance to respond to sample journal questions and to examine sample essays by students responding to writing assignments. Finally, you will learn how to write a summary and be provided with a model for keeping a Writer's Notebook, a notebook which will help you organize your ideas, collect all stages of your writing, and record your growth as a writer.

Keeping a Journal

Each reading selection in this book is followed by a journal question. These journal questions encourage you to make a personal connection with the material you have just read or to think further about some aspect of the reading selection. In some cases, the journal question requires you to be creative, in others, to be analytical, and in still others, to be introspective.

The two journal questions that appear below correspond to the two selections in this chapter: "Bugs Bunny Says They're Yummy" and "Children Who Dress for Excess." If you have not read these pieces already, read each one. Then answer the journal questions which follow.

"Bugs Bunny Says They're Yummy"
Journal: Think for a few minutes about ads you have seen or heard. You need not limit yourself to ads on television or to ads directed at children. Describe one ad that you find objectionable and explain your objection(s).

"Children Who Dress for Excess"
Journal: List as many designer labels as you can think of in two or three minutes. How many of these designer labels can be found on clothing items in your home? Why do you (or do you not) buy clothing with designer labels?

Keep in mind that there are no right or wrong answers to journal questions; they are merely intended to get you thinking. Here are some sample student responses to these same journal questions.

Sample Student Responses to "Bugs Bunny" Topic

Student A:

The ad which I choose to be objectionable is the Home Club commercial that shows a man trying to build a fence before the dog next door breaks off his chain. The dog in the commercial happens to be a Pit Bull dog, and Home Club is exploiting on the recent press coverage of pit bull attacks. By showing the dog as mean and vicious, the Home Club is furthering the idea to the public that pit bulls are mean and ferocious, making them appear as a threat to all. The pit bull dog itself is not mean and an attack dog by nature, instead it is the owner who makes the dog what it is, not the dog by its own. With this commercial, the public will continue to look down on the breed of pit bull, and not the owners, who are responsible for the moods of the dogs.

Student B:

Ads that I object to are Lite beer commercials aimed at young adults, or basically the beach goers. I see Lite beer advertising on t.v. about beach activities or I see ads at the beach, sponsoring volleyball or other types of beach associated sports. It is ridiculous because you aren't even allowed to drink at the beach. It is against the Law to drink alcohol of any type at the beach. I don't understand why they have alcohol mixed with water sports or beach sports or sports period. You'll drown or flounder if

you are under the influence of alcohol. I'm
sure you don't see a pro-volleyball player
down a quart of vodka and go rip it up against
the opposing team, and win with a stunning
victory. Or a professional water skier
drinking a twelve-pack of Lite beer and then
water skiing. It just can't be done. Today
most people are concerned about their health
and wouldn't even think of putting some
alcohol into their system. I'm really sure
drinking alcohol is what kept them at the top
of their profession.

Sample Student Responses to "Dressed for Excess" Topic

Student A:

   guess, yes, reebok, Nike, gitano, Jimmy Z,
L.A. gear, public image, esprit, Jordache,
Air Jordan
   In my house I have about five different
label brands. There's no really particular
reason why I buy them its just because
usually the only thing I can find that I like
happens to be name brand. Not all the time do
I buy name brands. Depending on the mood I'm
in, sometimes I admit I might buy something
outragously expensive. I usually do this when
I just get in a fight with friends
or family. I feel girls dress for girls,
not guys as much for guys because girls
constantly compete with one another, you
can't deny it everyone does it.

Student B:

   Guess, Esprit, Air Jordan, LA Gear,
Quicksilver, Billabong, Jimmy Z, Cavarichia,
Liz Claiborne, Bongo.
   I have very little brand name clothing
because I think it's too expensive. The
few things I do have are things my mother

```
has bought me or things I found on sale that
I liked. My sister and brother have alot of
brand name things cause they have to be "in."
```

Writing an Essay

Very few individuals can sit down at a computer or with a pen and paper and dash off an essay that accurately reflects their thoughts on a topic. Most of us go through certain steps when we write: *prewriting, planning, drafting, revising,* and *editing.* First we have to generate ideas about our topic; then we need to plan what point we'll make and how we'll structure our essay. Once we're ready to write the essay itself, most of us begin by putting all of our thoughts into the essay structure on which we have decided; then we go back and revise for organization, smoothness, and logical relationship between ideas; finally, we edit for grammar and mechanics. In responding to a writing topic assigned by an instructor, students must also be sure they understand the nature of the assignment and what elements the teacher wants them to focus on.

The assignment that appears next is based on the selection "Bugs Bunny Says They're Yummy," which appears earlier in this chapter. Read the assignment carefully, and answer the questions which follow it.

> **Assignment:**   In "Bugs Bunny Says They're Yummy," Dawn Ann Kurth discusses objectionable advertising practices aimed at children. Write an essay of your own in which you discuss objectionable advertisements. You need not limit yourself to advertisements aimed at children or to television ads. Be sure to use specific examples to illustrate your objections.

1. What will the topic of your essay be?
2. In what way might your essay be different in focus from Kurth's?

3. Where might you come up with "specific examples" to illustrate your objection?

If you have read the assignment carefully, you may have answered the questions something like this:

1. The topic of the essay will be types of ads or advertising practices that I object to.
2. My essay won't be limited to ads directed at children or those on TV; I can choose ads directed toward other groups or just toward people in general, and I can discuss ads on radio, in magazines and on billboards as well as on TV.
3. I can find specific examples by using ads themselves and telling what's so bad about them.

Once you are sure you have understood the assignment, you will need to think carefully about your topic and how you might approach it. There are a number of strategies for *prewriting*, the term which describes methods for generating ideas before you begin to write. Some of the most common are *listing, brainstorming, clustering*, and *freewriting*. Prewriting activities are designed merely to get ideas out of your head and onto paper. These ideas need not be in any particular order or spelled correctly or expressed grammatically. No idea is "wrong." You will go back later and choose which ideas will eventually turn up in your paper.

Listing, as the name implies, means quickly putting down in a list ideas that you might use to develop your topic. *Brainstorming*, is even less structured than listing because you don't follow any format. You merely write ideas all over your paper as they occur to you. Sometimes it helps to put the topic you are brainstorming in a circle in the middle of your paper. *Clustering* is similar to brainstorming, but it is a bit more structured because it stresses relationships between ideas. The topic is placed in a circle in the middle of the page; then lines are drawn from idea to idea to indicate their interrelationship. *Freewriting* refers to continuous writing, writing without stopping to mentally or physically edit your ideas. From the time you start freewriting until you finish (usually five to ten minutes), you should not lift your pen from the paper or reread what you have written so far. If you get stuck for something to say, merely repeat your topic over and over or write something like "I can't think of anything else to say." The main thing is to continue writing, without stopping.

Once your ideas are on paper, you can then go back and look them over to see which ones you might want to use to develop your essay and/or to get ideas about how you might want to group these ideas to make a point. As you decide which ideas to use and how to arrange them, you are leaving the prewriting stage and entering the *planning* stage of writing. One particularly effective method for structuring a writing plan is *outlining*, but a more informal plan will also work.

In looking over prewriting for this assignment, for example, you might come up with several different ideas for structuring an essay. For example, you might write about ads that are demeaning to men and women and ads that mislead children. Or you might decide to discuss misleading ads and dangerous ads. Then you can go back to your prewriting and pull out those specific examples that illustrate your objections.

If you choose to discuss misleading and dangerous ads, for example, as Dawn Kurth did, your *outline* might look like this:

Thesis: Many ads are objectionable.

I. Some ads are misleading.
   A.
   B.
   C.
II. Some ads are dangerous.
   A.
   B.
   C.

Or you might have a more informal *plan for writing* that looks something like this:

Thesis: Many ads are objectionable.

Major idea: Some ads are misleading.
    Supporting example:
    Supporting example:
    Supporting example:

Major idea: Some ads are dangerous.
    Supporting example:
    Supporting example:
    Supporting example:

Drawing on the ideas in the Kurth essay and on your own observations, respond to this assignment by completing a plan for writing that provides specific examples of misleading and dangerous ads for one of the patterns just illustrated. You might use specific ads, such as a television ad for a particular product. Or you might target types of ads and then illustrate these types of ads by referring to specific advertisements. Compare your plan for writing with those of your classmates so that you get a good sense of the many possibilities for developing a single thesis.

The next stage after *planning* is writing a first, or rough, *draft.* The first version of an essay is considered rough because its primary aim is to get the ideas down on paper. The writer will go back later to *revise* the essay in order to make it read smoothly and to check to be sure that the essay communicates ideas as effectively as possible. Finally, the writer will check for grammar and mechanics—a step referred to as *editing.* The following is a rough draft of a student essay on the topic of objectionable advertising.

Rough Draft

The Military: Is It for Real?
By Holly Peck

Have you ever thought about joining the military? Did you think, "If I join, I will come out as someone important"? Don't let yourself believe that if you join the military you will come out as someone important.

The advertisements for the military are deceptive. These advertisements glamorize the military and don't let you in on the details until after you sign your life over to the Government.

The Government glamorizes the military by presenting advertisements that convey such things as, "Join the Navy, See the World". True, perhaps if you join the Navy you will see the world, but is it the part of world you want to see? Do they give you a choice of where you want to go? No, they don't. Another advertisement the Government conveys is, "It's Not Just a Job, It's an Adventure". What's so adventurous about spending fifteen months cooking in a mess hall in the Aleutian Islands? Or worrying about where they are going to send you next? Sure they train you, but you don't necessarily get a choice of what you want to be trained in. It is usually what they want.

The military misleads you into job and school opportunities. The most advertised school opportunity they talk about is the G.I. Bill. The advertisement tells you that when you're in the military you will get the G. I. Bill. What

they don't tell you is that the money that goes
toward this G. I. Bill is taken out of your
checks, which aren't very big in the first
place. Also, the only way you will get any of
this money back is if you go to college after
you get out of the military. Otherwise, you
don't get any of this money back at all. Another
advertisement is the commercial with the man
wearing a combat uniform, then he is walking
down the street in a three piece suit carrying a
briefcase. Just because you are or were in the
military doesn't mean that you will have a job
as soon as you get out. You still have to fill
out applications just like everyone else. Most
places won't look on an application and say,
"Hire this person. He was in the military for
four years." They would most likely look at an
application to see what kind of experience you
have for this certain job. Also, how much
college education you have. These advertisements
make it seem like you can get a job anywhere you
want.

Don't listen to these advertisements that
glamorize the military and don't let you in on
the details until after you sign your life over
to the Government. In the long run, you will
still have to prove yourself to the rest of the
world.

Revising an essay is at least as important as coming up with good material to put in it. Student writers often forget that they are writing for a reader; revising creates a bridge between the writer's ideas and the reader's understanding. Therefore, when you revise, the first step is reading your essay objectively—as if you were someone else reading it for the first time; look for strengths and weaknesses.

A strength of the student essay just shown is its clear thesis and good specific examples. In order to make the essay as effective as possible, this student followed a process like the one suggested in the checklist below.

Checklist for Revision

1. Does the essay have a clear, identifiable, and interesting introduction?

2. Does the essay have a clear thesis?

3. Are major ideas clearly expressed? Are they logically arranged and developed? Do they clearly relate to the thesis?

4. Does the essay provide sufficient specific examples to support the thesis and major ideas in the essay? Do all of the examples clearly develop the major ideas?

5. Are sentences written clearly? Has the writer avoided sentence-level errors, such as fragments and run-ons, which interfere with the presentation of ideas?

6. Does the essay have a clear and identifiable conclusion which effectively ends the essay without raising new ideas?

After checking over her essay and conferencing with her instructor, the student decided where and how she might make changes in her rough draft, and also considered what elements she wanted to retain. In addition to revising her essay, the student has edited to correct problems in spelling, capitalization, and grammar. Notice the changes that the writer has made in this draft.

Revised and Edited Draft

The Military: Is It For Real?
By Holly Peck

Have you ever thought about joining the
military? Did you think, "If I join, I will
come out as someone important"? Don't let
yourself believe that if you join the military
you will come out as someone important. The
advertisements for the military are deceptive.
These advertisements glamorize the military and
don't let you in on the details until after you
sign your life over to the government.

The Government glamorizes the military in its
advertisements. One ad, for example, says,
"Join the Navy. See the World." True, perhaps
if you join the Navy you will see the world,
but is it the part of the world you want to
see? Do they give you a choice of where you
want to go? No, they don't. Another advertising
message the Government conveys is, "It's Not
Just a Job. It's an Adventure." What's so
adventurous about spending fifteen months
cooking in a mess hall in the Aleutian Islands
or worrying about where they are going to send
you next? The Government also emphasizes the
training you get. Sure the military trains you,
but you don't necessarily get a choice of what
you want to be trained in. It is usually what
the government needs.

The military ads also mislead the public
about job and school opportunities. The most
advertised school opportunity is the G.I. Bill.
The advertisement tells you that when you're in
the military you will get G.I. Bill benefits.

What it doesn't tell you is that the money that
goes toward this G.I. Bill is taken out of your
checks, which aren't very big in the first
place. The military deducts one hundred dollars
each month for the first year and applies it to
the G.I. Bill. True, the government pays the
remainder of the college fund, but, the only way
you will get any of your money back is if you go
to college after you get out of the military.
Otherwise, you don't get any of this money back
at all. Another advertisement shows a man
wearing a combat uniform; then he is walking
down the street in a three-piece suit and
carrying a briefcase. Just because you are or
were in the military doesn't mean that you will
have a job as soon as you come out, as this ad
implies. You still have to fill out applications
just like everyone else. Most employers won't
look on an application and say, "Hire this
person. He was in the military for four years."
They will most likely look at an application to
see what kind of experience you have for this
certain job. The employers will also look to see
how much college education you have. These
advertisements make it seem like you can get a
job anywhere you want.

   If you are considering entering military
service, beware of these advertisements that
glamorize the military and don't let you in on
the details until after you sign your life over
to the Government. In the long run, you will
still have to prove yourself to the rest of the
world.

As you can see, writing is a *continuous* process. You may need (as professional writers do) to work through several drafts of an essay before you and your instructor are satisfied that it communicates your ideas as effectively as possible.

ANALYZING ESSAYS

Look carefully at the three student essays that follow. All of these essays were written in response to the writing assignment about objectionable advertising. After you have read the essays, use the questions to help you determine which one most successfully responds to the assignment.

Essay A

Deceptive Advertisements

"Hey look, they are advertising for a new product. I wonder if it really works like it does on television?" This is the question that many of us ask ourselves before buying a product that we have seen advertised on television commercials. Many of the ads of television are very entertaining, but they are also very deceptive. For example, the commercials about the health spas and the many brands of cold medicine never really seem to hold true once we have tried them.

How often have we seen a famous body builder or model on television looking very sexy trying to talk us into joining their health spa? They are telling us that it is fun not hard work. They also exclaim without using words that if you join, you will have a body like theirs. I feel that this is false advertising. The people that do these commercials are actors who have been picked by a director that wants a certain look. Those models don't work out regularly. The bodies that they have came from dieting or they were just born with them. Exercise doesn't build a perfect figure, it just helps you stay in shape along with a good food diet. The professional body builders that they get to do those commercials have been training their bodies to look like that for the past five or ten years. The T.V. ad makes you believe that it only took a short time.

Next, the advertisements for the cold medicines mislead many people more so than the health spas. Every cold medicine commercial has this one famous saying, "so take . . . and get rid of that cold." This is a false statement. There aren't any cures for the common cold and no cures for the symptoms. The only thing that helps a cold is rest and time given until it is gone. Every time I see a co-tylenol commercial it reminds me how dumb advertisement companies think the public really is. First they show a woman in bed looking like she is getting ready to die. Then her husband gives her some co-tylenol and in a few seconds, she is up and wants to go out for the evening. This doesn't and will probably never happen in real life.

The advertisements that companies use to sell their products aren't real. They use people who aren't real to try and get us to buy their products. When we look at a commercial, we have to remember that those people are actors who are being paid to say those things. By going to the spa two times a week, we will not develop that kind of shape over night. Also, cold remedies are false. There isn't any cures for the common cold. Advertisement companies should give the public more credit. They should try telling the truth about how their product really works.

Essay B

Objectionable Ads

   Advertisers today will do anything to entice
the viewer to watch their ads. Advertisers use
every gimmick from flying dogs to opera singers
to get our undivided attention. But sometimes
they go too far. Many ads today are
objectionable. Ads are often unrealistic and
are demoralizing to groups and individuals.

   Ads are often unrealistic. Some advertisers
will use the super-natural to sell their items.
Parkay uses their talking tupperware to show
how much enjoyment one can have using Parkay
margarine. Aunt Jemima Syrup uses their
human-like talking bottle to sing the praises
of the product, and special effects to display
the smooth texture of their syrup. The most
unrealistic ad these days is for the dogfood
called "Mighty Dog." This advertisement gives
off the impression that if your dog eats Mighty
Dog, your dog will be able to fly like Superman
and save female poodles from disaster.

   Ads can also be demoralizing to groups and
individuals. Advertisers often exploit a weak
spot in an individual or group just to grab a
viewer's attention. In Ray Charles' Pepsi
commercial, the writer plays with Ray's
blindness and has him drink the wrong soda.
During a Nut & Honey commercial, the gay
community is ridiculed when an answer of one
male cowboy to another implies he is making
homosexual overtures. Finally, in Joe Piscapo's

Miller Lite commercial, the Asian community is shamed with Joe's ridiculous karate imitation.

In conclusion, advertisers today are going way overboard just to get a point across. Their advertisements are giving people of all ages the wrong ideas about a product and are often ruining the images of people. Unrealistic ads too often use false objects to sell a product and never reveal a product's true content. Ads today are also heartless and will embarrass a group's belief or handicap just to sell their insignificant product.

Essay C

Objection!

Consumers today are being bombarded by advertisements on radio, on T.V., in magazines and in newspapers. These ads try to sell us everything from toothpaste to vacation retreats. However, we should not take all of these ads at face value. Many are just plain misleading, and others are even dangerous.

Some ads mislead the public. T.V. ads for Dow bathroom cleanser, for example, would have consumers believe that, with a touch of a button, they will have a clean bathtub. On the commercial, tiny scrubbing bubbles "make soap scum disappear." These ads fail to show the housewife on her knees sloshing the product around the tub with a sponge as tears stream down her face from the chemical fumes. A recent magazine ad for G.I. Joe action figures and vehicles showed these toys set up on an elaborate and realistic battle scape. The child who actually gets these toys, however, will be disappointed if he expects them to look as realistic on the stained tan shag carpet in his bedroom, especially when he discovers the motorized tank will not move on carpet. Most misleading of all are ads for children's cereals. One cereal, Lucky Charms, claims to be "part of a nutritious breakfast." The cereal is about one third tiny marshmallows dyed with food coloring. While marshmallows probably won't kill anyone, they are hardly "nutritious."

Even more objectionable than misleading ads are those that can be dangerous. Virginia Slims cigarettes, famous for their "You've come a long way, Baby" slogan, attempt to get women to smoke in order to show how independent they are. By showing their independence, of course, these women may contract lung cancer. Budweiser beer commercials encourage blue collar workers to treat themselves to a few beers after a hard day's work, saying, "After all, you've earned it." If they do decide to treat themselves to a few beers every day after work, they will soon have liver damage—that is, if they survive the drive home. Some of the most dangerous ads today are those for fad diet products, especially those featuring a powdered base that, mixed with water, is supposed to be the purchasers' only food source. A number of deaths have been reported among users of these so-called nutritionally complete food substitutes.

To be sure, not all advertisements are misleading or dangerous, but a significant number of them are. Consumers should be wary of any product that looks or sounds too good to be true. And, we should all use common sense to evaluate the possible dangers of using a product that is going to make us look better or feel better about ourselves.

Questions for Essay Analysis

1. Notice the overall structure of the essays. Does each one have a clear thesis, an identifiable introduction and conclusion?

2. All of the essays have broken objectionable ads into two parts, with each part providing the focus for one of the body paragraphs. Essays B and C illustrate types of objections while Essay A focuses on two specific types of advertisements. Which of these two strategies for organization seems most effective?

3. Look closely at the introductory paragraphs. Which two essays open with general remarks about advertising? Which one opens with a question?

   All of the introductory paragraphs contain a sentence which indicates how the essay will be developed (that is, what two major ideas will be discussed). Identify these sentences. How do these sentences help the reader?

   Underline the thesis in each essay. Does each introduction contain an easily identifiable thesis?

4. Notice the beginning of the body paragraphs. Most of the body paragraphs begin with a *topic sentence;* as a thesis gives the main idea for an essay, a topic sentence states the main idea for the paragraph. Which essay contains a body paragraph which does not begin with a clearly stated topic sentence? Is the topic of this paragraph clear even without the topic sentence? Why or why not?

5. Look at the development of the body paragraphs. What vivid examples are included in each of the essays? Choose the one best example in each essay. Why do you think that this example is so good?

   Pick out the least powerful example in each essay. What is lacking in these examples?

   Which essay, in your opinion, makes the most effective use of examples to develop the ideas in each body paragraph?

6. Conclusions are often the hardest part of an essay to write. Look at the strategies used in each of these conclusions.

What common elements can you identify? To what extent does each conclusion tend to repeat what has been said in the body paragraphs? Which conclusion or conclusions do you think most effectively wrap up the essay?

7. Certain words and phrases, known as *transitions*, help to show the reader logical relationships between ideas and to emphasize the organization of an essay. Common transitions include words like *also, however, next,* and *finally,* and phrases such as *for example, in addition, in conclusion,* and *even more.* Locate as many transitions as you can in the essays.

   A. According to what criteria are the examples in paragraph 2 of Essay B arranged (by chronology, or time, by importance—least to most, most to least)? What transitions stress this arrangement of ideas?

   B. Which two essays use transitions to begin their conclusions? What transitions do they use?

   C. What phrase is used in Essay C to indicate that the author objects more strongly to harmful ads than to misleading ads?

8. Look at the titles of these essays. Which title do you think is best? Why?

9. Now that you have considered the various components of each essay, which essay is the best response to the assignment? Why did you choose this one?

WRITING A SUMMARY

A *summary* is a shortened or condensed version, in your own words, of something you have read. In college, you may be asked on an essay examination to write a summary of a particular episode described in your history text, or you might be asked to report on a book read outside of class. In the workplace, you may be expected to prepare a summary of a lengthy technical report or market analysis. The summary is also an important element in writing a research paper, something you will most likely be required to write in college.

Not only an important writing skill, summary writing is also a valuable learning tool. The most common kind of summary writing in college requires you to read the work of someone else, to be able to pick out the most essential idea, and to put these ideas into your own words. The summary, therefore, becomes a tool for understanding what you read; it forces you to read critically, differentiating between main ideas and minor points. Summary writing also forces you to write clearly because you cannot waste any words.

The first aim of the summary is *brevity*: your job as a summary writer is to convey in as few words as possible the information contained in the piece of writing. Because the summary is concerned with stating the ideas of someone else, the second aim of the summary is *objectivity*. This is not the place to respond to a writer's ideas but to demonstrate your understanding of them. The third aim of the summary, *completeness* is the most crucial. Both objectivity and brevity will follow from your ability to isolate and concentrate on the *main idea* contained in the selection you are summarizing.

Method for Writing a One-Paragraph Summary

1. Read the passage carefully and answer the following questions.

    A. What is the topic of the passage?

    B. What is the author's purpose in writing? Does the author describe something, analyze a problem, give information, review a book or movie, try to persuade the reader to adopt his point of view or take some action, state a personal opinion or grievance, give instructions for completing a task, or compare different products or viewpoints?

2. What point is the author trying to make? Which are major ideas used to develop this point and which are minor supporting ideas and examples? Underline the major ideas.

3. Now reread. Go back and break up the piece of writing into sections or stages of thought, labeling each section. The

author's use of paragraphing may be helpful in identifying the different stages of thought.

4. On a separate sheet of paper, write a one-sentence restatement in your own words of the main idea of the passage. Include in this sentence the title and author of the piece you are summarizing.

5. Next, give a one-sentence summary of each of the stages of thought you identified and combine these sentences with the one-sentence restatement of the main idea.

6. Read over what you have written to make sure you have eliminated less important information and left out minor details. Use as few words as possible to convey the major ideas.

7. Read over your summary and revise it. First, be sure you have followed the organizational pattern of the original. Next, insert transitions where necessary and combine sentences so as to eliminate choppiness and repetition. If you have taken a key word or phrase directly from the text, be sure to enclose it in quotation marks (" "). Finally, check for correct grammar, spelling, and punctuation.

8. As a final test, ask yourself if someone who had not read the piece would get a clear and correct idea of its contents by reading your summary.

To practice writing a summary, follow the steps just outlined to summarize the article "Children Who Dress for Excess," which appears in this chapter. Then compare your answer with the student sample that follows.

Sample Summary

In "Children Who Dress for Excess," Ron Harris discusses the problem of children who are obsessed with wearing expensive name-brand clothing—even to the point of killing for costly clothes. Harris cites several reasons for this clothing fixation. Advertising directed toward kids make them feel that they must wear the proper clothes to be worthwhile people. This feeling is reinforced by peer pressure; in some cases, students who wear no name clothes are "ridiculed, scorned and sometimes even ostracized by their classmates." The problem is worsened by parents who buy their children everything they ask for. Some schools have begun to try to correct this problem by adopting "exclusionary" dress codes or requiring students to wear uniforms, and educators at other schools wish parents would learn to say "no" to their kids. Though a lot of parents seem upset by their kids' emphasis on material goods, in most cases the kids learned this behavior from their parents.

KEEPING A WRITER'S NOTEBOOK

As you read the selections in this book, write journal responses, and compose essays, you will find yourself accumulating a lot of materials. You might find it helpful to create a writer's notebook to organize your materials, to preserve all stages of your writing, and to help you keep track of and correct spelling and/or grammatical errors that recur in your writing. In order to set up a writer's notebook, you will need a one-inch three-ring binder (either plastic or cardboard is ideal in terms of weight and cost) and a pack of section dividers.

Your instructor may specify a particular arrangement for setting up the notebook. If not, you may wish to create a section for each of the following:

1. Journal—for all journal entries
2. Spelling log—record all spelling errors on returned papers and write each word correctly
3. Grammar log—record all nongrammatical sentences marked on returned papers, note the rule for correcting your error, and include a corrected version of each sentence
4. Writing assignments—include *all* pieces of writing, from prewriting to finished drafts of essays
5. Annotated research project—include all materials pertaining to the Annotated Bibliography Assignment

2

AUTOBIOGRAPHY

Autobiography, telling the story of one's own life, is far more than a record of an individual's life, experiences, and perceptions. Story-telling is one of the most vital ways that we have of making connections with life around us. From an early age, using the phrase "tell me a story" becomes a way for us to gain knowledge about the world as well as about individuals and their experiences, especially those closest to us.

Real stories from real people—our family and friends at first, the lives of strangers, later—help to provide us with models by which we can understand our own lives, and which we can use in learning how to tell our own stories, thus sharing our lives with others. In the selections in this chapter, a variety of individuals relate their memorable experiences.

PREREADING

Before you begin reading the selections in this chapter, think about how often you tell stories about your life or listen to the life stories of your friends and relatives. Write down the qualities of stories you like to hear or find especially memorable. Have you ever encouraged any of these people to record their stories? Have you ever thought of recording some aspect of your own life story? Do you think that others, apart from your family and friends, would be interested in your life experiences?

POSTREADING

After you have read the selections in this chapter, look over your Prereading responses. Have the readings in this chapter made you feel differently about creating some form of autobiography? How valuable do you think that autobiographies are?

SALVATION

Langston Hughes

About the Reading

Langston Hughes was one of the most influential figures in the history of American literature. Well known for his poetry and fiction, he was also an expert in folklore and jazz. He was particularly important for his role in the 1920s during the African-American literary movement known as the Harlem Renaissance. "Salvation," a portion of Hughes' autobiography, *The Big Sea* (1940), relates Hughes' experience of disillusionment in his early adolescence.

Before You Read

One of the most painful aspects of growing up is the discovery that the world is imperfect. Most of us can remember a moment in which we learned that adults didn't know everything or that we no longer believed in something. Can you think of a time when you learned this painful lesson?

As You Read

1. This essay is written in *chronological order*, a pattern in which events are related in the order they took place. An important element of essays organized in this pattern is the use of *transitions*, words such as "then" or "finally." Watch how Hughes uses words like these to help the reader move smoothly through the various stages of his experience.

2. Hughes' main idea—waiting for something to happen and ultimately experiencing disappointment when it does not—is introduced early and is reinforced throughout the essay. In fact, the essay can be cleanly divided into two parts. Notice how almost every paragraph in the first part of the essay

is followed by a reminder that the child is still sitting and waiting. After the dramatic "So I got up" the essay proceeds rapidly to its conclusion.

———————

1   I was saved from sin when I was going on thirteen. But not really saved. It happened like this. There was a big revival at my Auntie Reed's church. Every night for weeks there had been much preaching, singing, praying, and shouting, and some very hardened sinners had been brought to Christ, and the membership of the church had grown by leaps and bounds. Then just before the revival ended, they held a special meeting for children, "to bring the young lambs to the fold." My aunt spoke of it for days ahead. That night I was escorted to the front row and placed on the mourners' bench with all the other young sinners, who had not yet been brought to Jesus.

2   My aunt told me that when you were saved you saw a light, and something happened to you inside! And Jesus came into your life! And God was with you from then on! She said you could see and hear and feel Jesus in your soul. I believed her. I had heard a great many old people say the same thing and it seemed to me they ought to know. So I sat there calmly in the hot crowded church, waiting for Jesus to come to me.

3   The preacher preached a wonderful rhythmical sermon, all moans and shouts and lonely cries and dire pictures of hell, and then he sang a song about the ninety and nine safe in the fold, but one little lamb was left in the cold. Then he said, "Won't you come? Won't you come to Jesus? Young lambs, won't you come?" And he held out his arms to all us young sinners there on the mourners' bench. And the little girls cried. And some of them jumped up and went to Jesus right away. But most of us just sat there.

4   A great many old people came and knelt around us and prayed, old women with jet-black faces and braided hair, old men with

work-gnarled hands. And the church sang a song about the lower lights are burning, some poor sinners to be saved. And the whole building rocked with prayer and song.

5   Still I kept waiting to see Jesus.

6   Finally all the young people had gone to the altar and were saved, but one boy and me. He was a rounder's* son named Westley. Westley and I were surrounded by sisters and deacons praying. It was very hot in the church, and getting late now. Finally Westley said to me in a whisper: "Goddamn! I'm tired o' sitting here. Let's get up and be saved." So he got up and was saved.

7   Then I was left all alone on the mourners' bench. My aunt came and knelt at my knees and cried, while prayers and songs swirled all around me in the little church. The whole congregation prayed for me alone, in a mighty wail of moans and voices. And I kept waiting serenely for Jesus, waiting, waiting—but he didn't come. I wanted to see him, but nothing happened to me. Nothing! I wanted something to happen to me, but nothing happened.

8   I heard the songs and the minister saying: "Why don't you come? My dear child, why don't you come to Jesus? Jesus is waiting for you. He wants you. Why don't you come? Sister Reed, what is this child's name?"

9   "Langston," my aunt sobbed.

10   "Langston, why don't you come? Why don't you come and be saved? Oh, Lamb of God! Why don't you come?"

11   Now it was really getting late. I began to be ashamed of myself, holding everything up so long. I began to wonder what God thought about Westley, who certainly hadn't seen Jesus either, but who was now sitting proudly on the platform, swinging his knickerbockered legs and grinning down at me, surrounded by deacons and old women on their knees praying. God had not struck Westley dead for taking his name in vain or for lying in the temple. So I decided that maybe to save further trouble, I'd better lie, too, and say that Jesus had come, and get up and be saved.

12   So I got up.

*drunkard's

13   Suddenly the whole room broke into a sea of shouting, as they saw me rise. Waves of rejoicing swept the place. Women leaped into the air. My aunt threw her arms around me. The minister took me by the hand and led me to the platform.

14   When things quieted down, in a hushed silence, punctuated by a few ecstatic "Amens," all the new young lambs were blessed in the name of God. Then joyous singing filled the room.

15   That night, for the last time in my life but one—for I was a big boy twelve years old—I cried. I cried, in bed alone, and couldn't stop. I buried my head under the quilts, but my aunt heard me. She woke up and told my uncle I was crying because the Holy Ghost had come into my life, and because I had seen Jesus. But I was really crying because I couldn't bear to tell her that I had lied, that I had deceived everybody in the church, and I hadn't seen Jesus, and that now I didn't believe there was a Jesus any more, since he didn't come to help me.

Journal Entry

We have all done things simply because "everyone" else was doing them, from getting a particular haircut to behaving self-destructively. Tell about something you did just because everyone else was doing it. How did you feel afterward? Were you glad you did what you did?

Questions for Discussion

1. In paragraph 2, Hughes says that his aunt told him that "when you were saved you saw a light. . . ." His aunt uses the word "light" as a *metaphor*, a figure of speech in which a word or phrase ordinarily used to describe one thing is applied to something else. How does Hughes' failure to perceive that she is speaking metaphorically help to set the *tone* (or attitude) for the entire essay?

2. The thesis in this piece is in two sentences. What are they?

3. Note the last sentence in each paragraph. How do these sentences help remind the reader of the thesis?

4. Look at paragraphs 3 and 4. Underline the verbs. How do these words help to give the reader a vivid picture of the scene in the church?

5. In paragraph 3, Hughes describes the sermon as "wonderful" and "rhythmical." Define *rhythm* and look carefully at this paragraph and the following paragraph, in which Hughes attempts to recreate the rhythm of the sermon. How is rhythm important to this essay?

3. Paragraph 5, like paragraph 12, is a one-sentence paragraph. How do these paragraphs affect the reader's response to the essay?

4. In paragraph 6, Hughes includes a comment by Westley. What point does Hughes make by including this comment? This episode takes place almost precisely halfway through the essay; how is its placement particularly effective?

5. What thoughts and emotions go through Hughes' mind as he sits alone on the bench? Why does Hughes finally pretend to experience something which he has not experienced?

6. Look carefully at the final paragraph of the essay, paying special attention to the punctuation of the sentences. How can you account for the length of the essay's final sentence? What impact does the sentence have on the reader? In your own words, describe why the boy cries.

7. What would you consider to be Hughes' purpose in writing this essay? Is religion the important theme, or does the theme take in something larger than just this particular experience?

8. Why does Hughes title the piece "Salvation?" From what or for what is he saved?

9. What lesson or moral can be learned from this story?

THE DARE

Roger Hoffmann

About the Reading

In this piece, which originally appeared in the *New York Times*, Roger Hoffmann retells an incident from his adolescence when he allowed peer pressure to outweigh his own safety. In describing his experience, Hoffmann explores the desire for acceptance that all of us have felt both as children and as adults.

Before You Read

Dares are an important part of growing up. Almost everyone remembers daring or being dared; almost everyone remembers that learning how to say "no" to a dare indicated a certain level of maturity. Think back to your childhood. What was your response to the childhood challenge "I dare you"?

As You Read

1. Although Hoffmann begins his essay explaining "the secret to diving under a moving freight train," for much of the first part of the essay he does not talk about the dare itself. Watch how he approaches his subject from several angles, emphasizing the power of the dare, the circumstances which led up to the dare, and his adult perceptions of the social and cultural meanings of dares.

2. Notice that after Hoffmann has given the reader the background to his acceptance of the dare, the essay changes considerably. From paragraph 5, even the sentences become shorter and more direct as Hoffmann adopts a *process* approach to his topic. Look for the details he uses as he

provides a step-by-step "how-to" guide for diving under a moving freight train.

———————————

1   The secret to diving under a moving freight train and rolling out the other side with all your parts attached lies in picking the right spot between the tracks to hit with your back. Ideally, you want soft dirt or pea gravel, clear of glass shards and railroad spikes that could cause you instinctively, and fatally, to sit up. Today, at thirty-eight, I couldn't be threatened or baited enough to attempt that dive. But as a seventh grader struggling to make the cut in a tough Atlanta grammar school, all it took was a dare.

2   I coasted through my first years of school as a fussed-over smart kid, the teacher's pet who finished his work first and then strutted around the room tutoring other students. By the seventh grade, I had more A's than friends. Even my old cronies, Dwayne and O.T., made it clear I'd never be one of the guys in junior high if I didn't dirty up my act. They challenged me to break the rules, and I did. The I-dare-you's escalated: shoplifting, sugaring teachers' gas tanks, dropping lighted matches into public mailboxes. Each guerrilla act won me the approval I never got for just being smart.

3   Walking home by the railroad tracks after school, we started playing chicken with oncoming trains. O.T., who was failing that year, always won. One afternoon he charged a boxcar from the side, stopping just short of throwing himself between the wheels. I was stunned. After the train disappeared, we debated whether someone could dive under a moving car, stay put for a 10-count, then scramble out the other side. I thought it could be done and said so. O.T. immediately stepped in front of me and smiled. Not by me, I added quickly, I certainly didn't mean that I could do it. "A smart guy like you," he said, his smile evaporating, "you could figure it out easy." And then, squeezing each word for effect, "I . . . DARE . . . you." I'd just turned twelve. The monkey clawing my back was Teacher's Pet. And I'd been dared.

4   As an adult, I've been on both ends of life's implicit business and social I-dare-you's, although adults don't use those words. We provoke with body language, tone of voice, ambiguous phrases. I dare you to: argue with the boss, tell Fred what you think of him, send the wine back. Only rarely are the risks physical. How we respond to dares when we are young may have something to do with which of the truly hazardous male inner dares—attacking mountains, tempting bulls at Pamplona—we embrace or ignore as men.

5   For two weeks, I scouted trains and tracks. I studied moving boxcars close up, memorizing how they squatted on their axles, never getting used to the squeal or the way the air felt hot from the sides. I created an imaginary, friendly train and ran next to it. I mastered a shallow, head-first dive with a simple half-twist. I'd land on my back, count to ten, imagine wheels and, locking both hands on the rail to my left, heave myself over and out. Even under pure sky, though, I had to fight to keep my eyes open and my shoulders between the rails.

6   The next Saturday, O.T., Dwayne and three eighth graders met me below the hill that backed up to the lumberyard. The track followed a slow bend there and opened to a straight, slightly uphill climb for a solid third of a mile. My run started two hundred yards after the bend. The train would have its tongue hanging out.

7   The other boys huddled off to one side, a circle on another planet, and watched quietly as I double-knotted my shoelaces. My hands trembled. O.T. broke the circle and came over to me. He kept his hands hidden in the pockets of his jacket. We looked at each other. BB's of sweat appeared beneath his nose. I stuffed my wallet in one of his pockets, rubbing it against his knuckles on the way in, and slid my house key, wired to a red-and-white fishing bobber, into the other. We backed away from each other, and he turned and ran to join the four already climbing up the hill.

8   I watched them all the way to the top. They clustered together as if I were taking their picture. Their silhouette resembled a round-shouldered tombstone. They waved down to me, and I dropped them from my mind and sat down on the rail. Immediately, I jumped back. The steel was vibrating.

9   The train sounded like a cow going short of breath. I pulled my shirttail out and looked down at my spot, then up the incline of

track ahead of me. Suddenly the air went hot, and the engine was by me. I hadn't pictured it moving that fast. A man's bare head leaned out and stared at me. I waved to him with my left hand and turned into the train, burying my face into the incredible noise. When I looked up, the head was gone.

10   I started running alongside the boxcars. Quickly, I found their pace, held it, and then eased off, concentrating on each thick wheel that cut past me. I slowed another notch. Over my shoulder, I picked my car as it came off the bend, locking in the image of the white mountain goat painted on its side. I waited, leaning forward like the anchor in a 440-relay, wishing the baton up the track behind me. Then the big goat fired by me, and I was flying and then tucking my shoulder as I dipped under the train.

11   A heavy blanket of red dust settled over me. I felt bolted to the earth. Sheet-metal bellies thundered and shook above my face. Count to ten, a voice said, watch the axles and look to your left for daylight. But I couldn't count, and I couldn't find left if my life depended on it, which it did. The colors overhead went from brown to red to black to red again. Finally, I ripped my hands free, forced them to the rail, and, in one convulsive jerk, threw myself into the blue light.

12   I lay there face down until there was no more noise, and I could feel the sun against the back of my neck. I sat up. The last ribbon of train was slipping away in the distance. Across the tracks, O.T. was leading a cavalry charge down the hill, five very small, galloping boys, their fists whirling above them. I pulled my knees to my chest. My corduroy pants puckered wet across my thighs. I didn't care.

Journal Entry

Describe something you or someone you know has done on a dare. What happened as a result of acting on the dare? Did it have the expected or hoped-for consequences or did it have unexpected consequences?

Questions for Discussion

1. In paragraph 4, Hoffmann uses the *allusion,* or reference, "tempting bulls at Pamplona." To what is he referring? What does he intend the reader to understand by using this allusion?

2. In paragraph 2, Hoffmann refers to each rule breaking as a "guerrilla act." What is a guerrilla act? What effect does this word choice have on the reader?

3. The first two lines of the essay give the reader advice on how to dive "under a moving freight train" and survive. Do you think that Hoffmann expects readers to attempt this stunt? Why do you think he opens his essay this way?

4. Why, according to Hoffmann, does he feel the need to "break the rules"?

5. In paragraph 3, Hoffmann refers to "playing chicken." Describe the game and explain the part it plays in growing up.

6. A *figure of speech* makes an imaginative comparison. What does Hoffmann mean in paragraph 3 when he says, "The monkey clawing my back was Teacher's Pet"?

7. What does Hoffmann mean in paragraph 4 by "life's implicit business and social I-dare-you's"? Is this paragraph unified with the rest of the essay? Why or why not? Why do you think Hoffmann includes this paragraph about adult behavior?

8. Paragraphs 9 through 11 are filled with specific details of Hoffmann's experience. Identify and underline the details which help you to picture in your mind what Hoffmann is experiencing. How effective are these details?

9. Hoffmann doesn't come right out and tell *how* he felt after his experience. Reread paragraph 12. How do you think he was feeling—scared, excited, relieved, proud?

FROM "LAKOTA WOMAN"

Mary Crow Dog with Richard Erdoes

About the Reading

Lakota Woman, the book from which this excerpt is taken, is the autobiography of Mary Crow Dog, a Sioux woman who grew up on a South Dakota reservation and later joined the movement for Native American pride which gained power in the 1960s and 1970s. In this selection from the second chapter of *Lakota Woman*, Mary describes family members, mostly women, who were influential in her life on the reservation, where she lived with her grandparents.

Before You Read

Experts on the American family tell us that one of the most stressful elements of life in America today is our loss of the love and support of extended families—grandparents, aunts, uncles, cousins—as we become an increasingly faster paced and more mobile society. How has your family been influenced by the American trend of moving away from one's birthplace in search of better jobs or educational opportunities?

As You Read

1. In this piece, Mary gives many specific examples of knowledge she gained from various family members. Notice how each member of her family contributes to her education, particularly in educating her about her Sioux heritage. Pay special attention to the section about the turtle woman and the lessons that Mary draws from the life and death of this remarkable relative.

2. Even though there are really two authors of this piece, Mary Crow Dog, whose story is told, and Richard Erdoes,

author of a number of books on Native Americans, it appears to be told in one "voice." One of the distinctive characteristics of this "voice" is the repeated use of short sentences. As you read, notice what information is contained in these short sentences and how these sentences affect your reading of the selection.

――――――――――

1   Our cabin was small. It had only one room which served as our kitchen, living room, dining room, parlor, or whatever. At night we slept there, too. That was our home—one room. Grandma was the kind of woman who, when visitors dropped in, immediately started to feed them. She always told me: "Even if there's not much left, they gonna eat. These people came a long ways to visit us, so they gonna eat first. I don't care if they come at sunrise or at sundown, they gonna eat first. And whatever is left after they leave, even if it's only a small dried-up piece of fry bread, that's what we eat." This my grandmother taught me. She was Catholic and tried to raise us as whites, because she thought that was the only way for us to get ahead and lead a satisfying life, but when it came to basics she was all Sioux, in spite of the pictures of Holy Mary and the Sacred Heart on the wall. Whether she was aware of how very Indian she had remained, I cannot say. She also spoke the Sioux language, the real old-style Lakota, not the modern slang we have today. And she knew her herbs, showing us how to recognize the different kinds of Indian plants, telling us what each of them was good for. She took us to gather berries and a certain mint for tea. During the winter we took chokecherries, the skin and the branches. We boiled the inside layers and used the tea for various sorts of sicknesses. In the fall she took us to harvest chokecherries and wild grapes. These were the only sweets we had. I never discovered candy until much later when I was in school. We did not have the money for it and only very seldom went to town.

2   We had no shoes and went barefoot most of the time. I never had a new dress. Once a year we would persuade somebody to drive us to the Catholic mission for a basement rummage sale. Sometimes we found something there to put on our feet before it got cold, and maybe a secondhand blouse or skirt. That was all we could afford. We did not celebrate Christmas, at least not the kind of feast white people are used to. Grandma would save a little money and when the time came she bought some crystal sugar—it looked like small rocks of glass put on a string—some peanuts, apples, and oranges. And she got some kind of cotton material, sewing it together, making little pouches for us, and in each put one apple, one orange, a handful of peanuts, and some of that crystal sugar which took forever to melt in one's mouth. I loved it. That was Christmas and it never changed.

3   Grandma had been to mission school and that had influenced her to abandon much of our traditional ways. She gave me love and a good home, but if I wanted to be an Indian I had to go elsewhere to learn how to become one. To grandma's older sister, Mary, for instance, the one who is married to Charlie Little Dog. I call them grandfather and grandmother, too, after the Sioux manner. He is a hundred and four years old now and grandma Little Dog about ninety-eight. They are very traditional people, faithful to the ancient rituals. They still carry their water from the river. They still chop wood. They still live like the Sioux of a hundred years ago. When Charlie Little Dog talks, he still uses the old words. You have to be at least sixty or seventy years old to understand what he is talking about—the language has changed that much. So I went to them if I wanted to hear the old tales of warriors and spirits, the oral history of our people.

4   I also went to grand-uncle Dick Fool Bull, the flute maker, who took me to my first peyote meeting, and to people like the Bear Necklaces, the Brave Birds, Iron Shells, Hollow Horn Bears, and Crow Dogs. One woman, Elsie Flood, a niece of grandma's, had a big influence upon me. She was a turtle woman, a strong, self-reliant person, because a turtle stands for strength, resolution, and long life. A turtle heart beats and beats for days, long after the turtle itself is dead. It keeps on beating all by itself. In

traditional families a beaded charm in the shape of a turtle is fastened to a newborn child's cradle. The baby's navel cord is put inside this turtle charm, which is believed to protect the infant from harm and bad spirits. The charm is also supposed to make the child live to a great old age. A turtle is a strength of mind, a communication with the thunder.

5   I loved to visit Aunt Elsie Flood to listen to her stories. With her high cheekbones she looked like grandma. She had a voice like water bubbling, talking with a deep, throaty sound. And she talked fast, mixing Indian and English together. I had to pay strict attention if I wanted to understand what she told me. She always paid her bills, earning a living by her arts and crafts, her beautiful work with beads and porcupine quills—what she called "Indian novelties." She was also a medicine woman. She was an old-time woman carrying her pack on her back. She would not let a man or younger woman carry her burden. She carried it herself. She neither asked nor accepted help from anybody, being proud of her turtle strength. She used turtles as her protection. Wherever she went, she always had some little live turtles with her and all kinds of things made out of tortoiseshell, little charms and boxes. She had a little place in Martin, halfway between Rosebud and Pine Ridge, and there she lived alone. She was very independent but always glad to have me visit her. Once she came to our home, trudging along as usual with the heavy pack on her back and two shopping bags full of herbs and strange things. She also brought a present for me—two tiny, very lively turtles. She had painted Indian designs on their shells and their bottoms. She communicated with them by name. One she called "Come" and the other "Go." They always waddled over to her when she called them to get their food. She had a special kind of feed for them, leaving me whole bags of it. These small twin turtles stayed tiny. They never grew. One day the white principal's son came over and smashed them. Simply stomped them to death. When she heard it my aunt said that this was an evil sign for her.

6   The turtle woman was afraid of nothing. She was always hitch-hiking, constantly on the road thumbing her way from one place to the other. She was a mystery to some. The Indians held her in

great respect, saying that she was "wakan," that she was some sort of holy person to whom turtles had given their powers. In the summer of 1976 she was found beaten to death in her home. She was discovered under the bed, face down and naked, with weeds in her hair. She had never hurt anyone or done an unkindness to anybody, only helped people who needed it. No Indian would have touched a single hair on her head. She died that way. I still grieve for her. Her death has never been investigated. The life of an Indian is not held in great value in the State of South Dakota. There is no woman like her anymore.

7   So many of my relations and friends who were ever dear to me, or meant something to me, or meant something to the people, have either been killed or found dead of some out-of-the-way road. The good Indians die first. They do not grow old. This turtle aunt of mine was one of the traditionally strongest women of her generation. To bring back what knowledge she had is going to take time. It will take another generation or two to bring it back.

Journal Entry

Think about an older person—perhaps a family member, a neighbor, a teacher, a coach, or a youth leader—who taught you an important lesson about life. Tell about the person and the lesson you learned from that person.

Questions for Discussion

1. In paragraph 2, the authors use a figure of speech (that is, a descriptive tool) called a *simile* to describe a sweet treat that the grandmother made at Christmas. A *simile* is a comparison which uses the word *like* or *as*. For example, if we say someone eats like a pig, *like a pig* is a simile which compares the person's eating habits to those of a pig. Identify and underline the simile in paragraph 2. What is gained here by the use of simile?

Try your hand at composing a simile. Complete the following similes by adding a word or words:

She walked like a (an) _____.

The teacher's voice was like a (an) _____.

The airport lights sparkled like _____.

2. Another type of figurative language appears in paragraph 6. When she refers to the way turtle woman dies, Mary explains that "No Indian would have touched a single hair on her head." What is the literal meaning of the phrase "touched a single hair on her head"? What do the authors mean by this expression?

When figurative language like the example just given becomes familiar to a lot of people, we tend to use it in our own speech. A much used—usually overused—figure of speech is called a *cliche*. If you and your classmates fill in the same missing word or words in the examples below, you will know they are cliches. If most of you come up with different answers, chances are you are creating new figures of speech.

a) She was as pretty as a _____.

b) He was as strong as an _____.

c) The river wound through the valley like a _____.

d) Ricardo would give you the shirt off his _____.

3. This piece focuses on familial relationships. What family members are mentioned in this short piece? Why is having such a close extended family so important to Mary?

4. Knowledge is an important idea developed in this selection. What knowledge does Mary gain from her family? Several times she mentions the loss of knowledge. What types of knowledge have been lost to family members and so to Mary?

5. The majority of this piece is devoted to Aunt Elsie Flood, a turtle woman. What does it mean to be a "turtle woman"? Why do you think Mary found this relative to be so influential? What characteristics of this woman does the girl admire?

6. When one event described in a piece of writing is similar to another event which occurs later in the piece, the first event is said to *foreshadow* (or foretell) the second. In this selection, what event foreshadows the murder of the turtle woman? What clues alert the reader that the two are somehow connected? What similarities are there between the two incidents?

7. Many times people tell stories not just to amuse or update their listeners but to make a point which goes beyond just the story itself. Parents, for example, tell their children stories to illustrate important life lessons. What terrible lesson(s) does Mary find in the turtle woman's brutal murder?

THE STRUGGLE TO BE AN ALL-AMERICAN GIRL

Elizabeth Wong

About the Reading

In "The Struggle to Be an All-American Girl," which first appeared in the *Los Angeles Times*, Elizabeth Wong recalls her childhood rejection of Chinese culture and her resistance to the language that she considered "a source of embarrassment." Her ultimate success, a "cultural divorce," separated her from the heritage she spurned as a ten-year-old; at the age of twenty, she has a different view of growing up "American."

Before You Read

In today's United States, we hear a great deal about "multi-culturalism," "cultural diversity," and "cultural pluralism." All of these terms refer to the belief that we need to recognize that America is made up of many different ethnic groups and that each of these groups has its own heritage, culture, and language. What do you know about your own cultural heritage?

As You Read

1. Elizabeth Wong titles her essay "The Struggle to Be an All-American Girl." As you read the essay, look carefully for evidence of her "struggle"—notice her negative descriptions of Chinese school and contrast those with her approval of Anglo-American culture.

2. Much of the second part of this essay is concerned with Wong's feelings about the Chinese language as a "source of embarrassment." Notice how many specific examples she gives of what she finds to be embarrassing qualities of Chinese language and culture.

1   It's still there, the Chinese school on Yale Street where my brother and I used to go. Despite the new coat of paint and the high wire fence, the school I knew 10 years ago remains remarkably, stoically the same.

2   Every day at 5 P.M., instead of playing with our fourth- and fifth-grade friends or sneaking out to the empty lot to hunt ghosts and animal bones, my brother and I had to go to Chinese school. No amount of kicking, screaming, or pleading could dissuade my mother, who was solidly determined to have us learn the language of our heritage.

3   Forcibly, she walked us the seven long, hilly blocks from our home to school, depositing our defiant tearful faces before the stern principal. My only memory of him is that he swayed on his heels like a palm tree, and he always clasped his impatient twitching hands behind his back. I recognized him as a repressed maniacal child killer, and knew that if we ever saw his hands we'd be in big trouble.

4   We all sat in little chairs in an empty auditorium. The room smelled like Chinese medicine, an imported faraway mustiness. Like ancient mothballs or dirty closets. I hated that smell. I favored crisp new scents. Like the soft French perfume that my American teacher wore in public school.

5   There was a stage far to the right, flanked by an American flag and the flag of the Nationalist Republic of China, which was also red, white and blue but not as pretty.

6   Although the emphasis at the school was mainly language—speaking, reading, writing—the lessons always began with an exercise in politeness. With the entrance of the teacher, the best student would tap a bell and everyone would get up, kowtow, and chant. "Sing san ho," the phonetic for "How are you, teacher?"

7   Being ten years old, I had better things to learn than ideographs copied painstakingly in lines that ran right to left from the tip of a *moc but*, a real ink pen that had to be held in an awkward

way if blotches were to be avoided. After all, I could do the multiplication tables, name the satellites of Mars, and write reports on "Little Women" and "Black Beauty." Nancy Drew, my favorite book heroine, never spoke Chinese.

8   The language was a source of embarrassment. More times than not, I had tried to disassociate myself from the nagging loud voice that followed me wherever I wandered in the nearby American supermarket outside Chinatown. The voice belonged to my grandmother, a fragile woman in her seventies who could outshout the best of the street vendors. Her humor was raunchy, her Chinese rhythmless, patternless. It was quick, it was loud, it was unbeautiful. It was not like the quiet, lilting romance of French or the gentle refinement of the American South. Chinese sounded pedestrian. Public.

9   In Chinatown, the comings and goings of hundreds of Chinese on their daily tasks sounded chaotic and frenzied. I did not want to be thought of as mad, as talking gibberish. When I spoke English, people nodded at me, smiled sweetly, said encouraging words. Even the people in my culture would cluck and say that I'd do well in life. "My, doesn't she move her lips fast," they would say, meaning that I'd be able to keep up with the world outside Chinatown.

10   My brother was even more fanatical than I about speaking English. He was especially hard on my mother, criticizing her, often cruelly, for her pidgin speech—smatterings of Chinese scattered like chop suey in her conversation. "It's not 'What it is,' Mom," he'd say in exasperation. "It's 'What *is* it, what *is* it, what *is* it!'" Sometimes Mom might leave out an occasional "the" or "a," or perhaps a verb of being. He would stop her in mid-sentence: "Say it again, Mom. Say it right." When he tripped over his own tongue, he'd blame it on her: "See, Mom, it's all your fault. You set a bad example."

11   What infuriated my mother most was when my brother cornered her on her consonants, especially "r." My father had played a cruel joke on Mom by assigning her an American name that her tongue wouldn't allow her to say. No matter how hard she tried, "Ruth" always ended up "Luth" or "Roof."

12   After two years of writing with a *moc but* and reciting words with multiples of meanings, I finally was granted a cultural divorce. I was permitted to stop Chinese school.

13   I thought of myself as multicultural. I preferred tacos to egg rolls; I enjoyed Cinco de Mayo more than Chinese New Year.

14   At last, I was one of you; I wasn't one of them.

15   Sadly, I still am.

Journal Entry

Make two columns in your journal. First, in the left column, list all of the ways in which you and your family acknowledge your particular ethnic and cultural identity (or identities). Do you speak a native language other than English? Celebrate special national or religious holidays? If you and your family celebrate customs of another culture in addition to those in which your family has religious or ethnic roots, list those holidays and customs in the right column. After you have looked over your lists, tell how you feel about the traditions and customs you have grown up with. Do you intend to carry on any of these family traditions? If you intend to make changes (or have already made them) what are they?

Questions for Discussion

1. Why does Wong's mother want her children to learn Chinese? Why do the children resist?

2. Why do the children resent the grandmother and criticize the mother? If your parents speak another language, or if you know someone in this situation, are family reactions the same as those described in this essay?

3. In paragraph 6, Wong uses the word *kowtow*. What does it mean to kowtow? She also describes the chant "Sing san ho" as the "phonetic" for "How are you teacher?" What does *phonetic* mean?

4. The word *ideograph* appears in paragraph 7. An ideograph refers to Chinese writing. Look up the *suffix* "-graph" in your dictionary. Use that information to define ideograph.

5. In paragraph 8, Wong describes the Chinese language as "pedestrian" and "public." What do these words mean? Why does she describe the language in this way, and what does this description about the Chinese language suggest about English?

6. Paragraphs 13 through 16 are extremely short. How do these short paragraphs highlight the information contained in them? Why does Wong choose to end her essay in this way?

7. What does it mean to be "All-American"? What kinds of things do we label as "All-American"? What do you think Wong understands by the phrase "All-American"?

8. Is it important for children to be taught about their ethnic and cultural background? If you think they should be taught about their ethnic heritage, what kinds of things do you think are important for them to learn. If you think this information is unimportant, why do you think so?

9. Based on your observations and/or experiences, how common is Wong's story? Why do you suppose that she changes her mind when she grows up about the value of Chinese culture?

DADDY TUCKED THE BLANKET

Randall Williams

About the Reading

This essay, which originally appeared in the *New York Times*, focuses on a subject that makes many people uncomfortable— those American families who live in poverty in the midst of an affluent society. More precisely, Randall Williams examines the psychological effects of poverty on an adolescent boy who learned that "being poor is a humiliating experience for a young person trying hard to be accepted."

Before You Read

Although America likes to think of itself as a "classless" society, many Americans believe that we are profoundly affected by the idea of "upper class," "middle class," or "lower class." In fact, some would argue that by coining terms such as "lower middle class" and "upper middle class" we reveal our deep-seated anxieties and prejudices about class. What class do you consider yourself to be a part of? How "class-conscious" do you think you are?

As You Read

1. An important quality of this essay is Williams' use of the *first person narrative* —telling of his experiences using the "I" pronoun. As you read his essay, consider how his use of the first person influences the reader's response to his story. Watch especially how he uses *direct address* (speaking directly to the reader) in sentences such as "I tell you this to show that we weren't shiftless."

2. Williams uses a number of *anecdotes,* or short, episodic stories, in the course of his essay. Notice how he uses this device to involve the reader in his painful real-life experiences of growing up poor in America.

———————

1   About the time I turned 16, my folks began to wonder why I didn't stay home any more. I always had an excuse for them, but what I didn't say was that I had found my freedom and I was getting out.

2   I went through four years of high school in semirural Alabama and became active in clubs and sports; I made a lot of friends and became a regular guy, if you know what I mean. But one thing was irregular about me: I managed those four years without ever having a friend visit at my house.

3   I was ashamed of where I lived. I had been ashamed for as long as I had been conscious of class.

4   We had a big family. There were several of us sleeping in one room, but that's not so bad if you get along, and we always did. As you get older, though, it gets worse.

5   Being poor is a humiliating experience for a young person trying hard to be accepted. Even now—several years removed—it is hard to talk about. And I resent the weakness of these words to make you feel what it was really like.

6   We lived in a lot of old houses. We moved a lot because we were always looking for something just a little better than what we had. You have to understand that my folks worked harder than most people. My mother was always at home, but for her that was a full-time job—and no fun, either. But my father worked his head off from the time I can remember in construction and shops. It was hard, physical work.

7   I tell you this to show that we weren't shiftless. No matter how much money Daddy made, we never made much progress up the social ladder. I got out thanks to a college scholarship and because I was a little more articulate than the average.

8   I have seen my Daddy wrap copper wire through the soles of his boots to keep them together in the wintertime. He couldn't buy new boots because he had used the money for food and shoes for us. We lived like hell, but we went to school well-clothed and with a full stomach.

9   It really is hell to live in a house that was in bad shape 10 years before you moved in. And a big family puts a lot of wear and tear on a new house, too, so you can imagine how one goes downhill if it is teetering when you move in. But we lived in houses that were sweltering in summer and freezing in winter. I woke up every morning for a year and a half with plaster on my face where it had fallen out of the ceiling during the night.

10   This wasn't during the Depression; this was in the late 60's and early 70's.

11   When we boys got old enough to learn trades in school, we would try to fix up the old houses we lived in. But have you ever tried to paint a wall that crumbled when the roller went across it? And bright paint emphasized the holes in the wall. You end up more frustrated than when you began, especially when you know that at best you might come up with only enough money to improve one of the six rooms in the house. And we might move out soon after, anyway.

12   The same goes for keeping a house like that clean. If you have a house full of kids and the house is deteriorating, you'll never keep it clean. Daddy used to yell at Mama about that, but she couldn't do anything. I think Daddy knew it inside, but he had to have an outlet for his rage somewhere, and at least yelling isn't as bad as hitting, which they never did to each other.

13   But you have a kitchen which has no counter space and no hot water, and you will have dirty dishes stacked up. That sounds like an excuse, but try it. You'll go mad from the sheer sense of futility. It's the same thing in a house with no closets. You can't keep clothes clean and rooms in order if they have to be stacked up with things.

14   Living in a bad house is generally worse on girls. For one thing, they traditionally help their mother with the housework. We boys could get outside and work in the field or cut wood or

even play ball and forget about living conditions. The sky was still pretty.

15 But the girls got the pressure, and as they got older it became worse. Would they accept dates knowing they had to "receive" the young man in a dirty hallway with broken windows, peeling wallpaper and a cracked ceiling? You have to live it to understand it, but it creates a shame which drives the soul of a young person inward.

16 I'm thankful none of us ever blamed our parents for this, because it would have crippled our relationships. As it worked out, only the relationship between our parents was damaged. And I think the harshness which they expressed to each other was just an outlet to get rid of their anger at the trap their lives were in. It ruined their marriage because they had no one to yell at but each other. I knew other families where the kids got the abuse, but we were too much loved for that.

17 Once I was about 16 and Mama and Daddy had had a particularly violent argument about the washing machine, which had broken down. Daddy was on the back porch—that's where the only water faucet was—trying to fix it and Mamma had a washtub out there washing school clothes for the next day and they were screaming at each other.

18 Later that night everyone was in bed and I heard Daddy get up from the couch where he was reading. I looked out from my bed across the hall into their room. He was standing right over Mama and she was already asleep. He pulled the blanket up and tucked it around her shoulders and just stood there and tears were dropping off his cheeks and I thought I could faintly hear them splashing against the linoleum rug.

19 Now they're divorced.

20 I had courses in college where housing was discussed, but the sociologists never put enough emphasis on the impact living in substandard housing has on a person's psyche. Especially children's.

21 Small children have a hard time understanding poverty. They want the same things children from more affluent families have. They want the same things they see advertised on television, and they don't understand why they can't have them.

22   Other children can be incredibly cruel. I was in elementary school in Georgia—and this is interesting because it is the only thing I remember about that particular school—when I was about eight or nine.

23   After Christmas vacation had ended, my teacher made each student describe all his or her Christmas presents. I became more and more uncomfortable as the privilege passed around the room toward me. Other children were reciting the names of the dolls they had been given, the kinds of bicycles and the grandeur of their games and toys. Some had lists which seemed to go on and on for hours.

24   It took me only a few seconds to tell the class that I had gotten for Christmas a belt and a pair of gloves. And then I was laughed at—because I cried—by a roomful of children and a teacher. I never forgave them, and that night I made my mother cry when I told her about it.

25   In retrospect, I am grateful for that moment, but I remember wanting to die at the time.

Journal Entry

Think about the terms "upper," "middle," and "lower" class. In your journal, make three columns and list all of the characteristics you associate with each of these terms. Then write about yourself. Do you and your family neatly fit into a particular class? How do you feel about being described as belonging to a particular class?

Questions for Discussion

1. From the first paragraph of this essay, Williams writes in very short paragraphs. Look closely at paragraphs such as paragraph 2 or paragraph 19. What is the effect of these short paragraphs on the reader?

2. In paragraph 10, Williams says "This wasn't during the Depression; this was in the late 60's and early 70's." Why does Williams compare historical time periods? What does he expect his reader to understand by this comparison?

3. Williams ends paragraph 20 with a sentence fragment. Why does he use the fragment?

4. Williams uses the dash (—) several times in the course of this essay. Look carefully at the sentences which use this device in paragraphs 5, 17, 22, and 24. Why does Williams use this punctuation? Can you find anything in common among sentences in which Williams uses the dash?

5. How does Williams show how little money his father had for himself? How does he show the way his parents argued?

6. What details does Williams include to illustrate the poor condition of the houses he lived in?

7. Why does Williams say that he is "grateful" for the painful incident with which he ends his essay?

8. Consider the title of this essay, relating it to the anecdote about the relationship between Williams' parents. What do you think is the significance of the title?

9. In paragraph 7, Williams says that he "got out thanks to a college scholarship . . ." What does "got out" refer to?

10. What is the *thesis* (main idea) of this essay? If it is stated, where does it appear? If you believe that the thesis is suggested, rather than stated, write a one-sentence thesis for the essay.

FROM "HALFWAY TO DICK AND JANE"

Jack Agueros

About the Reading

Jack Agueros' "Halfway to Dick and Jane: A Puerto Rican Pilgrimage" comes from his book *The Immigrant Experience: The Anguish of Becoming American* (1971). The "anguish" of the book's title is expressed in this selection, as Agueros recalls his experiences growing up in an immigrant neighborhood.

Before You Read

Many people are concerned that American education is in crisis and that many students, especially minority and/or "English-as-a-Second-Language" students, are at risk of dropping out. Consequently, questions of how to keep students in school and how to make education more meaningful have become primary not just to educators but to many Americans. This selection begins with the statement "Junior high was a waste." Think back on your education. Was there any period of your education that you felt was "a waste"? Why did you feel that way?

As You Read

1. In the first paragraph, Agueros says that he came back to the neighborhood school in part because he "couldn't cut the mustard . . . with the 'American' kids." As you read the essay, watch carefully for ways in which Agueros indicates how important it is for him to be accepted by his friends in the neighborhood—and shows that he and his neighborhood friends are becoming increasingly alienated from mainstream "American" life and values.

2. As you read this essay, notice how many times Agueros uses words or phrases such as "Sunday words," "home-mades," "*motto,*" or "skin-popping," which he encloses in quotation marks. This device of quotation marks stresses the special use of these words—perhaps a foreign word or a slang phrase. Consider what these words and phrases contribute to the essay.

———————

1   Junior high school was a waste. I can say with 90 per cent accuracy that I learned nothing. The woodshop was used to manufacture stocks for "homemades" after Macy's stopped selling zipguns. We went from classroom to classroom answering "here," and trying to be "good." The math class was generally permitted to go to the gym after roll call. English was still a good class. Partly because of a damn good, tough teacher named Miss Beck, and partly because of the grade-number system (7–1 the smartest seventh grade and 7–12, the dumbest). Books were left in school, there was little or no homework, and the whole thing seemed to be a holding operation until high school. Somehow or other, I passed the entrance exam to Brooklyn Technical High School. But I couldn't cut the mustard, either academically or with the "American" kids. After one semester, I came back to PS 83, waited a semester, and went on to Benjamin Franklin High School.

2   I still wanted to study medicine and excelled in biology. English was always an interesting subject, and I still enjoyed writing compositions and reading. In the neighborhood it was becoming a problem being categorized as a bookworm and as one who used "Sunday words," or "big words." I dug school, but I wanted to be one of the boys more. I think the boys respected my intelligence, despite their ribbing. Besides which, I belonged to a club with a number of members who were interested in going to college, and so I wasn't so far out.

3   My introduction to marijuana was in junior high school in 1948. A kid named Dixie from 124th Street brought a pack of

joints to school and taught about twelve guys to smoke. He told us we could buy joints at a quarter each or five for a dollar. Bombers, or thicker cigarettes, were thirty-five cents each or three for a dollar. There were a lot of experimenters, but not too many buyers. Actually, among the boys there was a strong taboo on drugs, and the Spanish word "*motto*" was a term of disparagement. Many clubs would kick out members who were known to use drugs. Heroin was easily available, and in those days came packaged in capsules or "caps" which sold for fifty cents each. Method of use was inhalation through the nose, or "sniffing," or "snorting."

4   I still remember vividly the first kid I ever saw who was mainlining. Prior to this encounter, I had known of "skin-popping," or subcutaneous injection, but not of mainlining. Most of the sniffers were afraid of skin-popping because they knew of the danger of addiction. They seemed to think that you could not become addicted by sniffing.

5   I went over to 108th Street and Madison where we played softball on an empty lot. This kid came over who was maybe sixteen or seventeen and asked us if we wanted to buy Horse. He started telling us about shooting up and showed me his arms. He had tracks, big black marks on the inside of his arm from the inner joint of the elbow down to his wrist and then over onto the back of his hand. I was stunned. Then he said, "That's nothing, man. I ain't hooked, and I ain't no junky. I can stop anytime I want to." I believe that he believed what he was saying. Invariably the kids talking about their drug experiences would say over and over, "I ain't hooked. I can stop anytime."

6   But they didn't stop; and the drug traffic grew greater and more open. Kids were smoking on the corners and on the stoops. Deals were made on the street, and you knew fifteen places within a block radius where you could buy anything you wanted. Cocaine never seemed to catch on although it was readily available. In the beginning, the kids seemed to be able to get the money for stuff easily. As the number of shooters grew and the prices went up, the kids got more desperate and apartment robbing became a real problem.

7   More of the boys began to leave school. We didn't use the term drop out; rather, a guy would say one day, after forty-three truancies, "I'm quitting school." And so he would. It was an irony, for what was really happening was that after many years of being rejected, ignored, and shuffled around by the school, the kid wanted to quit. Only you can't quit something you were never a part of, nor can you drop out if you were never in.

8   Some kids lied about their age and joined the army. Most just hung around. Not drifting to drugs or crime or to work either. They used to talk about going back at night and getting the diploma. I believe that they did not believe they could get their diplomas. They knew that the schools had abandoned them a long time ago—that to get the diploma meant starting all over again and that was impossible. Besides, day or night, it was the same school, the same staff, the same shit. But what do you say when you are powerless to get what you want, and what do you say when the other side has all the cards and writes all the rules? You say, "Tennis is for fags," and "School is for fags."

Journal Entry

Tell about a time when, because of your gender, your age, your religion, your ethnicity, your economic status, or your language, you felt that some opportunities available to others simply were not available to you. Try to describe both how you felt and why you think you felt as you did.

Questions for Discussion

1. In paragraph 1, Agueros uses the *cliche* (an expression that has become dull with overuse) "I couldn't cut the mustard." What does this expression mean?

2. In paragraph 2, Agueros says "I dug school, but I wanted to be one of the boys more." Do you think that the need for

acceptance by his friends is unique to the circumstances in Agueros' life? Why or why not?

3. Although this piece begins with an analysis of school, by paragraph 3 Agueros is discussing his introduction to drugs. What connection is there between these topics?

4. The title of this piece is "Halfway to Dick and Jane: A Puerto Rican Pilgrimage." To what does "Dick and Jane" refer? Look up the exact meaning of "pilgrimage." How is "Halfway to Dick and Jane" related to the idea of a "pilgrimage"? What do you think Agueros intends the reader to understand by this title?

5. In paragraph 3, Agueros writes "Actually, among the boys there was a strong taboo on drugs . . . ." By paragraph 6, however, he writes that "the drug traffic grew greater and more open." How do you account for this apparent contradiction? What do you think has been responsible for the change in attitude?

6. Consider the *tone* (mood) of the essay. Can you find any changes in tone? If so, note where such changes occur. How does the author's use of a particular tone (or tones) affect the reader?

7. What would you consider the thesis of this essay? Where does the thesis appear?

8. In paragraph 7, Agueros uses the word "irony." Use a dictionary to define *irony*; what does Agueros mean?

9. In the final paragraph of the essay, Agueros describes the boys of his neighborhood as "powerless" since "the other side has all the cards and writes all the rules." Who is "the other side"?

10. Does it seem that American education has changed a great deal since Agueros' school days? Why or why not?

FROM "MOMMY, WHAT DOES 'NIGGER' MEAN?"

Gloria Naylor

About the Reading

Gloria Naylor, author of *The Women of Brewster Place* and *Mama Day*, writes novels that concentrate on the lives of African-American women. Her essay "Mommy, What Does 'Nigger' Mean?", in which she writes of a child's introduction to prejudice, originally appeared in the *New York Times*.

Before You Read

From childhood on, we learn that name calling can be an effective weapon for hurting others. Think back to your own childhood—can you remember incidents in which you discovered the power of name calling, either because you yourself name-called or because you were called a name? How might you define the power of name calling? Why does name calling hold such power?

As You Read

1. The first sentence of this piece introduces the topic—a grown-up's childhood memory of being called "nigger." Watch carefully how Naylor develops her subject as she moves outward from the specific childhood incident at school to the use of the same word in the black community, where it has a very different meaning. Watch how Naylor structures the entire piece as a *definition*, not only of the term "nigger" but of black culture.

2. Notice how Naylor uses grammar and gender as organizing principles for this essay. In paragraph 4, for example, she explains the singular use of "nigger," while in paragraph 8,

she discusses the plural. By paragraph 9, she introduces the female counterpart, "girl." Along the way, she discusses possessive adjectives and direct address. Consider why she has chosen to discuss her subject in this way.

———————

1   I remember the first time I heard the word nigger. In my third-grade class, our math tests were being passed down the rows, and as I handed the papers to a little boy in back of me, I remarked that once again he had received a much lower mark than I did. He snatched his test from me and spit out that word. Had he called me a nymphomaniac or a necrophiliac, I couldn't have been more puzzled. I didn't know what a nigger was, but I knew that whatever it meant, it was something he shouldn't have called me. This was verified when I raised my hand, and in a loud voice repeated what he had said and watched the teacher scold him for using a "bad" word. I was later to go home and ask the inevitable question that every black parent must face—"Mommy, what does 'nigger' mean?"

2   And what exactly did it mean? Thinking back, I realize that this could not have been the first time the word was used in my presence. I was part of a large extended family that had migrated from the rural South after World War II and formed a close-knit network that gravitated around my maternal grandparents. Their ground-floor apartment in one of the buildings they owned in Harlem was a weekend mecca for my immediate family, along with countless aunts, uncles and cousins who brought along assorted friends. It was a bustling and open house with assorted neighbors and tenants popping in and out to exchange bits of gossip, pick up an old quarrel or referee the ongoing checkers game in which my grandmother cheated shamelessly. They were all there to let down their hair and put up their feet after a week of labor in the factories, laundries and shipyards of New York.

3   Amid the clamor, which could reach deafening proportions— two or three conversations going on simultaneously, punctuated

by the sound of a baby's crying somewhere in the back rooms or out on the street—there was still a rigid set of rules about what was said and how. Older children were sent out of the living room when it was time to get into the juicy details about "you-know-who" up on the third floor who had gone and gotten herself "p-r-e-g-n-a-n-t!" But my parents, knowing that I could spell well beyond my years, always demanded that I follow the others out to play. Beyond sexual misconduct and death, everything else was considered harmless for our young ears. And so among the anecdotes of the triumphs and disappointments in the various workings of their lives, the word nigger was used in my presence, but it was set within contexts and inflections that caused it to register in my mind as something else.

4   In the singular, the word was always applied to a man who had distinguished himself in some situation that brought their approval for his strength, intelligence or drive:

5   "Did Johnny really do that?"

6   "I'm telling you, that nigger pulled in $6,000 of overtime last year. Said he got enough for a down payment on a house."

7   When used with a possessive adjective by a woman—"my nigger"—it became a term of endearment for husband or boyfriend. But it could be more than just a term applied to a man. In their mouths it became the pure essence of manhood—a disembodied force that channeled their past history of struggle and present survival against the odds into a victorious statement of being: "Yeah, that old foreman found out quick enough—you don't mess with a nigger."

8   In the plural, it became a description of some group within the community that had overstepped the bounds of decency as my family defined it: Parents who neglected their children, a drunken couple who fought in public, people who simply refused to look for work, those with excessively dirty mouths or unkempt households were all "trifling niggers." This particular circle could forgive hard times, unemployment, the occasional bout of depression—they had gone through all of that themselves—but the unforgivable sin was lack of self-respect.

9   A woman could never be a "nigger" in the singular, with its connotation of confirming worth. The noun girl was its closest equivalent in that sense, but only when used in direct address and regardless of the gender doing the addressing. "Girl" was a token of respect for a woman. The one-syllable word was drawn out to sound like three in recognition of the extra ounce of wit, nerve or daring that the woman had shown in the situation under discussion.

10   "G-i-r-l, stop. You mean you said that to his face?"

11   But the word was used in a third-person reference or shortened so that it almost snapped out of the mouth, it always involved some element of communal disapproval. And age became an important factor in these exchanges. It was only between individuals of the same generation, or from an older person to a younger (but never the other way around), that "girl" would be considered a compliment . . . There must have been dozens of times that the word "nigger" was spoken in front of me before I reached the third grade. But I didn't "hear" it until it was said by a small pair of lips that had already learned it could be a way to humiliate me. That was the word I went home and asked my mother about. And since she knew that I had to grow up in America, she took me in her lap and explained.

Journal Entry

Tell about a time when you were called a "bad" name or when you called someone else a "bad" name. What provoked the name calling? How did you feel about it at the time? Afterwards?

Questions for Discussion

1. This selection begins with an *anecdote*, or brief story, in which two children hurt each other's feelings. What does the speaker do that results in the boy calling her a

"nigger"? Why does she tell on him? What is the teacher's response?

2. In paragraph 1, Naylor uses the words *nymphomaniac* and *necrophiliac.* Look up these words in the dictionary. Why do you think Naylor, writing as an adult looking back on this incident, chooses these two words?

3. In paragraph 2, Naylor describes her grandparents' home as a "mecca." Mecca is a place; what are the characteristics of Mecca? How does her reference to Mecca, with a little "m," add to the description of her grandparents' home?

4. In paragraph 3, Naylor explains that in her home "the word nigger was used in [her] presence, but it was set within contexts and inflections that caused it to register in [her] mind as something else." What do the words *contexts* and *inflections* mean?

5. List all of the different ways in which the word *nigger* is used in Naylor's discussion. Give the meaning for each different way the word is used.

6. Paragraph 3 says that in Naylor's family, discussions of everything "[b]eyond sexual misconduct and death," were "considered harmless" for children to overhear. In your family, what kinds of things are considered appropriate or inappropriate for children to hear?

7. Explain the last sentence of the selection. How does this ending serve to pull the reader out of a discussion of African-American culture and back into considerations of the larger American culture?

8. Does the title prepare the reader for the contents of the piece that follows? Do you think this is an effective title? Why or why not?

SUGGESTIONS FOR WRITING

Assignment 1

Write an essay in which you describe a childhood experience that left you feeling frustrated or disappointed. In your essay, be sure that you describe what you expected, then how your expectations were not met, and finally how you felt as a result.

Strategies for Prewriting and Planning: In deciding which incident to write about, be sure to focus on one that you remember because of a sense of disappointment—perhaps something you were promised but you never received, or something you secretly hoped for that never materialized. Once you have chosen the incident, write a one-sentence summary of the experience and how you felt. Then spend ten or fifteen minutes trying to recapture the experience—all of the details and all of your feelings. Do not worry about grammar or order of ideas, spelling, or anything other than just getting your ideas flowing. Read over what you have written and select the most important or most vivid details. As you draft the actual essay, use these details to make your story come alive for the reader. Because this is a story, the most logical way to tell it is from beginning to end, in chronological order.

Assignment 2

Write an essay about a memorable experience. Focus on one small but important incident that has left a lasting impression on you. It may be something sad, happy, exciting, puzzling, funny, embarrassing, scary, or strange. This incident may have happened when you were a child, or it may have happened last week or today.

Strategies for Prewriting and Planning: Try the following strategy to help you come up with a topic. Complete sentences like the ones below for each emotion that you think you might wish to write about:

I can't help laughing when I remember the time I _____

_____.

I've never been as scared as I was when _____

_____.

The most embarrassing moment of my life was when I _____

_____.

After you have chosen a topic, write the experience in one sentence. This will be your thesis. Then, write supporting details about the experience that will give your reader a clear picture of it. Show, don't tell. Instead of saying "I was so scared," for example, say, "My heart pounded. My stomach churned. I shivered uncontrollably." Be sure your details are limited to those that support your thesis. If you are talking about a frightening experience on a camping trip, for instance, the fact that you took a lot of pictures of the beautiful scenery is irrelevant.

Assignment 3

Write an essay about a family incident that made you feel differently about yourself. It may have been something you overheard or found out. Or it may have been an event, such as the death of a loved one, a family move, the birth of a child or sibling, a marriage or divorce. Focus on the *change* in your thinking that resulted from the family incident.

Strategies for Prewriting and Planning: List family incidents that you particularly remember. Then, choose the most promising and brainstorm the incident or incidents. Look over your brainstorming results and decide which incident most changed you. Use this one as your subject. Write in *one* sentence what the incident was and how it changed you. Then, try to recreate the experience for your reader, and reflect on the change it made in you. You might wish to organize this essay in three sections: how you were before the incident, what the incident was, and how you were changed by it.

Assignment 4

Write an essay in which you describe how peer pressure caused you to act in a way you otherwise would not have acted. You might wish to reread "The Dare," "Halfway to Dick and Jane," or "Salvation" in preparing to write this essay.

Strategies for Prewriting and Planning: Your peers are people of your own age and social group, so try to think of a time when you were influenced by this group to take an unwise or uncharacteristic action. This action may have been positive or negative. For example, you may have been pressured to take drugs, or you might have been led to join a team or get involved in a community activity. In your essay, describe your attitude before being influenced by others, explain how you were pressured to behave a certain way, and tell how you acted as a result of this pressure and how your actions changed your life.

3

HEROES

Originally defined as a man of great strength and courage, favored by the gods (in some cases, the child of a human and a god), heroes have provided human culture with ideals and models that have occupied a special place in the imagination and have played an important role in every culture since ancient times. Hero-tales—stories about heroic figures and their great deeds—are some of the world's oldest and best-loved stories; today, people still look to stories about heroes for inspiration.

Modern American culture has redefined hero-figures—while heroes of the past were exclusively male and often demonstrated their heroic qualities in battle, today, "hero" refers to a central figure of any important event or period who is honored for his or her outstanding qualities. Today, heroes may be politicians, sports figures, labor leaders, or entertainers. We have also developed a vocabulary to explain different types of heroes, such as "reluctant heroes," "unsung heroes," "unlikely heroes," "accidental heroes," even "anti-heroes."

PREREADING

Who do you think of when you hear the word "hero"? Think of all the qualities you consider heroic. How would you define or describe a hero?

POSTREADING

After reading the selections in this chapter, what revisions would you make in your earlier definition of a hero? How have you changed your criteria for heroism or for evaluating heroic qualities?

FROM "WHY KIDS NEED HEROES"

Denise Fortino

About the Reading

Denise Fortino's "Why Kids Need Heroes" first appeared in *Parents* magazine in November 1984; the author's research on this topic included interviews with noted educators and psychologists who have also researched and written about the need children have for heroic role models. One expert she interviewed for her article and quotes from extensively is Mark Gerzon. Gerzon himself has written about the changing imagery of heroism for young people today in his book *A Choice of Heroes*.

Before You Read

Almost all children intensely admire someone they've never met, sometimes to the point of making that individual a personal hero. The people children look up to might be sports figures, entertainers, personalities who have done something newsworthy, or historical figures. Children also tend to look up to adults they know—a teacher or clergyman, someone in the neighborhood, the older siblings of their friends. How important do you think hero figures are for children? What do you remember about your childhood heroes? How did your ideas about heroes or admiration of heroes themselves change as you grew up?

As You Read

1. The opening of this selection makes an important distinction between heroes and celebrities. Notice how this argument is sustained throughout the essay as the reader is constantly reminded of the disadvantages of substituting media/celebrity heroes for real-life heroes.

2. Expert opinions, as well as *allusions*, or references, are very important to this essay. Watch how, in almost every paragraph, Fortino refers to or quotes from specialists in child development or mentions publications relevant to her topic. She also uses extensive allusions to well-known media/celebrity figures as well as to real-life heroes.

———————

1   More than simply reflecting our values and visions, "the hero images embedded in our culture have a tremendous power to *shape* our behavior," says Mark Gerzon. We absorb styles of conduct and thinking from a variety of sources—and media personalities are prime among them. "That's why it's healthy to see more choices of heroes projected on the TV or movie screen today," he continues. "The richer our wellspring of models to draw from, the more dimensions we can explore in ourselves and tolerate in others.

2   "Still, it's unhealthy when almost *all* our exposure to the heroic is filtered through the media alone," Gerzon believes. In fact, there is a good deal of modern-day confusion between heroes and celebrities as if the two were interchangeable. And, of course, they're not. The first are meant to be durable and real; the second are too often overnight sensations who are superseded year after year. Younger kids often can't discern the difference, and the older kids, who do, may end up feeling cheated and disillusioned. As each short-lived superstar fades, his or her successors cease to have the same kind of credibility and influence because the sham of their immortal hero status has been exposed. This leads children to feel they can't really count on anyone— that the people they've been admiring merely help publishers sell their magazines or adorn their record covers.

3   "Today children often have far more exposure to media heroes than they do to 'real-life' role models from the community or neighborhood," Gerzon observes. "And it's much harder to have a growing, trusting relationship with an electronic image than

with another human being. My eight-year-old son, for instance, does not know the neighborhood grocer or postman or town officials or any such people a boy his age would have been well-acquainted with 50 or 100 years ago. Yet he is 'intimately' familiar with Michael Jackson and Luke Skywalker, and thinks the guys who play on the Dallas Cowboys' football team 1,500 miles away are the 'living end.' This is a very different constellation of male figures from those in the past: a trend that becomes undesirable if and when these larger-than-life heroes impoverish or rule out the possibility of more personal ones."

Boys' and Girls' Heroes

4   Do boys need to rely on heroes more than girls do as sources of identity while growing up? While no one has gathered statistics, it is true that boys are more often called upon to prove themselves through performance. For example, even today, they're often still judged by how well they can kick and throw a ball. So they may have a greater *dependence* on athletes, if only as models to imitate. The baseball/football trading card ritual is still very common among elementary school-age boys; girls, however, have no equivalent for this practice, nor are they rated for their physical accomplishments the same way. Despite today's increasingly "nonsexist" child rearing, girls are still evaluated more on the basis of how they relate to other people than as solitary, achieving individuals.

But Where Are the Heroes . . .

5   Yet even the most imposing characters chosen by boys or girls often don't pass muster with parents who may well wonder what happened to the heroes with *real* stature. Where have all the "heroic" heroes gone? After all, TV/movie celebrities are simply not in the same league as, say, Albert Schweitzer, Eleanor Roosevelt, Charles Lindbergh, Martin Luther King, Jonas Salk—pioneers, selfless people with crusades, daring-in-the-face-of-adversity types. Dr. David Elkind, former professor and chairman of the Eliot Pearson Department of Child Study at Tufts University and author of *The Hurried Child* (Addison-Wesley), observes that even in much of children's current

fiction, heroes have become less admirable. Or rather, they are concerned more with overcoming personal obstacles than socially significant ones; they are noticeably busier healing *themselves* than helping others. Does this mean our society's values have changed? Does it mean that we despair of finding such models in our own time?

6   One mother suggests that heroes of the old-fashioned variety are on the wane largely because adults in public life have toppled from their pedestals. A major blow to adult authority was dealt by the political and social events of the last fifteen years or so, maintains Marie Winn, author of *Children Without Childhood* (Pantheon). Since then there has been a public erosion of confidence in the benevolence of elected officials and other figures who had formerly stood *in loco parentis* to our own fathers and mothers, and such shaken faith naturally filters down to children.

7   Again, the media may be largely responsible for disillusionment with even the best-intentioned politicians; their mistakes and slips of the tongue are magnified by TV's constant scrutiny, stripping them of the heroic presence that earlier generations of presidents and statesmen apparently enjoyed. "Many people still hope for the emergence of an old-style, dynamic 'great leader' but television is making it virtually impossible to find one," observes a recent article in *Psychology Today*. "There is no lack of potential leaders, but rather an overabundance of *information* about them. The great-leader image depends upon distance, mystery and careful management of public impressions," all of which occur naturally in "real life," but which TV uncontrollably distorts, the argument goes. By exposing too much of everyone, it is leveling a deathblow at old-time heroism.

8   The media have also reinforced an emphasis on the immediate, the here and now; children today seem to have far less of a sense of history as a result, and their choice of heroes reflects this. The current hot idol is preferred to the enduring, all-time historical greats who are more abstract and remote simply because they are from an earlier era and are not presented with glamour. Those adults who are making history *now* are also less highly regarded than those who gratify and entertain on an immediate scale.

9   In addition, the borderline between childhood and adulthood has become somewhat blurred, probably not only because of media frankness and the breakdown of the nuclear family, but also because children are simply more privy these days to adult anxieties, doubts, and concerns, whereas they were once shielded from much of these. The result is early maturity at the cost of the belief that adults are necessarily wise or special: this could lead to fewer adult heroes or at least more skepticism about heroism itself.

. . . And Why Do We Need Them?

10   The *absence* of heroes during childhood or later can be dangerous, Gerzon believes. A hero is, after all, an image of your own future, of what you admire in yourself or wish to become, a vision signifying hope, a striving toward excellence. But if you don't have such an image, it's easy to feel alienated or isolated from any sense of social value. "Some young people say, 'I don't have heroes. I just want to be myself.' This can be a healthy independence of spirit, or it can be a sign of cynicism and despair," Gerzon says. It's important to probe such statements further to find out what really underlies them.

11   "Also essential is for parents to share their own heroes with their children," Gerzon suggests. "Adults need to point out the people they admire most and explain why—this gives their children a point of reference when forming their own choices and deciding on 'worthy' images. Many parents are hesitant about doing this for fear of force-feeding their own views on their children or being criticized for sounding dated and corny," he notes. "But while parental cynicism is contagious and kids pick up on it very easily, if you can say, 'Here's someone or something I believe in, that gives my work meaning and direction,' this can serve as a valuable benchmark for a son or daughter. Even if the model chosen holds no magic for the child himself, he is at least encouraged by the example of an adult who has placed faith in someone and for whom that faith has been sustained."

Journal Entry

Giving yourself a time limit of three to four minutes, list media/celebrity figures who you think might be considered heroes by today's children and/or teenagers. Look over your list, adding the reasons why you think these figures might be perceived as heroes. Finally, write a short paragraph in which you try to define the qualities of today's media/celebrity hero figure.

Questions for Discussion

1. Paragraph 2 of this selection points out the differences between "heroes" and "celebrities." Use a dictionary to check the exact definitions of both terms. Then, in your own words, formulate your own definition for each term. How would you explain the differences between them?

2. The main point of paragraph 2—that children of all ages may feel "cheated and disillusioned" by celebrity heroes who quickly appear and are quickly replaced by newer celebrity heroes—provides the focus for the rest of the essay. What does Gerzon mean by the phrase "the sham of their immortal hero status"? Do you agree with his analysis? Why or why not?

3. Paragraph 4 discusses relative hero needs of boys and girls, focusing on boys' dependence on sports heroes. To what extent do you agree with Fortino's conclusions?

   Fortino devotes little space to girls' need for heroes. To what extent do you think girls need heroes? What kinds of heroes do girls choose?

4. In paragraph 5, Fortino points out that children and their parents often disagree on what makes a hero. Using information contained in the article and your own experiences and observations, explain why you think this disagreement occurs.

5. Paragraph 6 uses the phrase *in loco parentis*. After looking up the meaning of this Latin phrase, consider ways in which hero-figures might be said to stand *in loco parentis*. Would younger or older children be more likely to consider heroes in this role? Explain.

6. Early in paragraph 5, Fortino asks a *rhetorical question* (a question which doesn't expect an answer from the reader, but will be answered by the writer). Locate the question. What does this question suggest about today's heroes?

7. Paragraphs 5 through 9 suggest many reasons for the attitudes towards heroes which today's children hold. List the various opinions which these paragraphs give in answer to the rhetorical question in paragraph 5. Which answer(s) do you think are most convincing? Why?

8. Consider the definition of the hero which Fortino presents in paragraph 10. Would you consider this statement to be the thesis of the essay? Why or why not?

9. Look up the meanings of the following words and phrases and explain how they are appropriate in *context* (the situation in which they appear): "wellspring" (paragraph 1); "superseded" (paragraph 2); "constellation" (paragraph 3); "pass muster" (paragraph 5); "on the wane" (paragraph 6); "privy" (paragraph 7); "benchmark" (paragraph 11).

   How do these words influence the reader's attitude toward both the author of this selection and the expert opinions which she presents?

10. Although this essay is titled "Why Kids Need Heroes," its final paragraph discusses the importance of hero-figures for parents, and the further importance of sharing those heroes with children. Do you think that this paragraph is an effective ending for the essay? Why or why not?

THE HEROES WE KNOW

David and Barbara Bjorklund

About the Reading

This article by David and Barbara Bjorklund, both of whom work in the psychology department at Florida Atlantic University, first appeared in *Parents* magazine in September 1989. Its focus on unsung heroes, particularly those in our own families, responds to parents' concerns that today's children lack heroes to admire.

Before You Read

Many psychologists have pointed out that children's first heroes are their parents and, by extension, members of their families and communities. What do you remember about your earliest heroes? In thinking back, can you remember the reasons why you selected the childhood heroes you did?

As You Read

1. This essay begins with an *anecdote,* or brief story—the story of a family member whose real-life experiences not only teach the children of the family about history, but also offer important lessons about achievement, heroism, and role models. Notice how the second and third sections of the essay move from the specific example of a member of one family to focus on the essay's thesis.

2. This essay is written in the first person plural (the "we" voice). Watch how the authors' use of "we" changes at different points in the essay. In paragraph 1, for example, "we" refers to the authors. By paragraph 4, "we" refers to "we parents"; by the final paragraph of the essay, "we" refers to families.

1   We heard a good story recently from Aunt Ellen. While visiting her grandchildren in Chicago, Aunt Ellen was invited by her nine-year-old granddaughter to come to the girl's school to visit her third-grade class. Aunt Ellen asked why—was there a special program planned, or was it Grandparents' Day? "No," her granddaughter explained, "it's just that we are studying the Statue of Liberty, and I wanted the other kids to see what a real *immigrant* looks like!"

2   It's a good story on several levels: first, because Aunt Ellen is a stylish, suntanned lady who spends winters in Florida and summers traveling the four corners of the world—hardly the stereotypical image of an immigrant with tattered luggage, wearing native clothing. And it's also a good story because Aunt Ellen really *is* an immigrant. She came to this country as a young child with her parents and her sister, Gulli, sailing from Sweden to New York, past the Statue of Liberty. The family had relatives here to sponsor them, so they didn't have to go through immigration on Ellis Island, but her story of leaving her home and adjusting to a new culture is an exciting saga of Bjorklund family history, and of American history as well.

3   Aunt Ellen did go to her granddaughter's class and spent the afternoon telling the story of her trip to America to a group of spellbound third graders. They asked her questions and added accounts of their own grandparents' histories, and a good time was had by all.

4   In an age when we parents lament the lack of heroes for our children to admire, we would be wise to look to our own family tree. Not many of us had forefathers who sailed over on the *Mayflower* or whose names would appear in history books, but we all have our share of Aunt Ellens, who were participants in or witnesses to important chapters in history.

5   **Remembering family achievements.** The children in our family have two grandfathers who were World War II combat veterans, one who served in Europe and one in the Pacific. It is

interesting for us to hear our children ask them questions about the war and to hear the old stories that were too new to tell when we were children. Then there was Great-aunt May, who retired after teaching kindergarten for 45 years and spent the next several decades of her life developing new strains of amaryllis lilies, registering each one with the name of a child in our family. And in a younger generation there is Aunt Marcia, who was one of the first women to graduate from the U.S. Military Academy at West Point. Her experiences have made a good story for the girls in the family, and her success and determination have made it easier for them to follow in her footsteps if they, too, decide to pursue a military career.

6   **Passing on values.** Stories about heroes help make history interesting and real for school-age kids. They are good topics for imaginary play. They give kids someone to emulate when they grow up and something to talk about when they compare family backgrounds with their friends. When children's heroes are members of their family, it elevates their self-esteem and sense of family pride. When we tell our children about interesting family members, we spell out our values and our expectations for them. We make them feel that they are part of an important group, even though the family may be scattered across the country.

7   It's not necessary to become expert genealogists to find heroes in our family tree. Everyone has stories about where they were when big events occurred. Maybe we should ask some questions the next time the relatives get together. We could write down the stories or turn on a tape recorder while they answer. We could retell the stories to our children at bedtime. And maybe, at other times, we could just turn off the TV and talk.

———————————

Journal Entry

Tell about someone in your family who is a hero to you now, or was a hero to you when you were a child. Be sure to focus on the heroic qualities of the person when you explain why this family member has provided you with an example of a hero figure.

Questions for Discussion

1. In paragraph 2, the authors describe Aunt Ellen's immigration to the United States as a *saga*. Use your dictionary to look up the exact meaning of this term. How is this choice of words particularly appropriate to the Bjorklunds?

2. In paragraph 4, the authors use a well-known phrase, "family tree." This term is a *figure of speech*, a way of using words imaginatively to add beauty or vividness to what is being said or written. Provide your own definition for the term "family tree."

3. After reading this essay, list the reasons why the authors believe that heroes from our own families are important for children. Which would you consider the most important reasons? Why?

4. In the essay's final paragraph, the author says that "It's not necessary to become expert genealogists to find heroes in our family tree." Look up the word "genealogists" (you might need to first look at the *root word* "genealogy") in a dictionary. Then explain the difference the Bjorklunds make between being a genealogist and being a story-teller. Why do you think the authors make this distinction?

5. Do you agree that stories about family members always inspire younger members of the family with pride and serve as positive examples for their own lives? Can such family stories have other, less positive effects? Explain your opinion.

FROM "THE LITTLE ROCK CRISIS, 1957–1958"

Melba Pattillo Beals

About the Reading

Melba Pattillo Beals found herself thrust into international attention as a teenager in 1957, when, as one of the Little Rock Nine, she joined eight other African-American high school students between the ages of fourteen and sixteen in integrating Central High School in Little Rock, Arkansas. The court-ordered integration of the school, which followed the landmark Supreme Court case of *Brown v. The Board of Education*, attracted world-wide attention as mobs of rioters tried to prevent the nine students from entering their classrooms. Finally, President Eisenhower assumed command of the National Guard, and troops marched down the main street of Little Rock. On September 25, 1957, escorted by soldiers with drawn bayonets and protected by paratroopers and hovering helicopters, the Nine walked up the front steps and into Central High. Beals' account of her experiences appeared in *Voices of Freedom* edited by Henry Hampton and Steve Fayer. The book is an outgrowth of the *Eyes on the Prize* television history of the Civil Rights Movement.

Before You Read

While some people make conscious decisions to attempt heroic acts, as Melba Pattillo Beals says, others seem to become caught up in an "accident of fate." Of the many heroes of the American Civil Rights movement, the Little Rock Nine hold a special place not only because of their youth but because of the enormous impact of their contribution to the struggle for educational equality for all Americans. In making the legal decree of school integration in the South a physical reality, how did they change education in the United States?

As You Read

1. This first-person narrative is a transcription of an interview. Look for indications, such as the changes in verb tense and the informal structure of her memories, that Melba Pattillo Beals originally told her story orally. Notice especially the phrases such as "Oh no" (paragraph 1) and repetition of "and" which links together elements of her story.

2. Watch for the way in which Beals helps her listener/reader to feel the emotions which she felt at the time of her experience and which she relives as she recalls events. In paragraph 3, for example, she uses multiple words, such as "terrible, wrenching, awful" and "any stark terror or any fear" to describe her experiences.

---

1   I wanted to go to Central High School because they had more privileges. They had more equipment, they had five floors of opportunities. I understood education before I understood any-thing else. From the time I was two, my mother said, "You will go to college. Education is your key to survival," and I understood that. It was a kind of curiosity, not an overwhelming desire to go to this school and integrate this school and change history. Oh no, there was none of that. I just thought it'd be fun to go to this school I ride by every day. I want to know what's in there. I don't necessarily want to be with those people; I assumed that being with those people would be no different than being with people I was already with. My getting into Central High School was somewhat of an accident. I simply raised my hand one day when they said, "Who of you lives in the area of Central High School?" That was two years before, in 1955. And they said, Who had good grades? and I had excellent grades. It was an accident of fate.

2　In late August, I was sitting in Cincinnati, Ohio, with my mother on a couch, and Walter Cronkite came on television and said that Central High School was going to be integrated in Little Rock, Arkansas, that they were already beginning to have difficulty with the white Citizens' Council and the Ku Klux Klan, and that these were the children who were going, and he mispronounced my name. My mother said, "What did he say?" And that was it, my mother started making phone calls back home. Then we came back to Little Rock and I began to be involved in the preparation that the NAACP was making for us to go to Central High School. But before that I had no real consciousness that I was going to go. . . .

3　The first day I was able to enter Central High School, what I felt inside was terrible, wrenching, awful fear. On the car radio I could hear that there was a mob. I knew what a mob meant and I knew that the sounds that came from the crowd were very angry. So we entered the side of the building, very, very fast. Even as we entered there were people running after us, people tripping other people. Once we got into the school, it was very dark; it was like a deep, dark castle. And my eyesight had to adjust to the fact that there were people all around me. We were met by school officials and very quickly dispersed our separate ways. There has never been in my life any stark terror or any fear akin to that.

4　I'd only been in the school a couple of hours and by that time it was apparent that the mob was just overrunning the school. Policemen were throwing down their badges and the mob was getting past the wooden sawhorses because the police would no longer fight their own in order to protect us. So we were all called into the principal's office, and there was great fear that we would not get out of this building. We were trapped. And I thought, Okay, so I'm going to die here, in school. And I remember thinking back to what I'd been told, to understand the realities of where you are and pray. Even the adults, the school officials, were panicked, feeling like there was no protection. A couple of kids, the black kids, that were with me were crying, and someone made a suggestion that if they allowed the mob to hang one kid, they could then get the rest out. And a gentleman, who I believed to be the police chief, said, "Unh-uh, how are you going to choose? You're going to let them draw straws?" He said, "I'll get them out." And we were taken to the basement of this place. And we were put into two cars, grayish blue Fords. And the man instructed the drivers, he said, "Once you start driving, do not stop." And he told us to put our heads down. This guy revved up his engine and he came up out of the bowels of this building, and as he came up, I could just see hands reaching across this car, I could hear the yelling, I could see guns, and he was told not to stop. "If you hit somebody, you keep rolling, 'cause the kids are dead." And he did just that, and he didn't hit anybody, but he certainly was forceful and aggressive in the way he exited this driveway, because people tried to stop him and he didn't stop. He dropped me off at home. And I remember saying, "Thank you for the ride," and I should've said, "Thank you for my life."

Journal Entry

Tell about a time when, because of "an accident of fate," you, someone you know, or someone you know of, rose to an occasion and handled a situation in a manner which you would consider heroic.

Questions for Discussion

1. What were Melba Pattillo Beals' reasons for wanting to go to Central High School? Why do you think that she describes her involvement in school desegregation as "an accident of fate"?

2. Chart the chronology of events which leads to Beals' first day at Central High.

3. What effect does the second part of Beals' story have on the reader? Consider the events she reports, her use of descriptive adjectives, the verbs she uses to recount what she thought and felt at the time, and her use of quotes.

4. The *tone* (attitude) of paragraphs 3 and 4 is very matter-of-fact. Does the tone seem consistent with the information contained in these paragraphs? Why or why not?

5. What is the impact of the final sentence? How effective is it in ending the essay?

6. In your opinion, does Beals qualify as a hero? Why or why not?

HERO STREET, U.S.A.

John Culhane

About the Reading

John Culhane's article, which originally appeared in the May 1985 edition of *Reader's Digest*, explores the contributions in lives and heroism made by Mexican-American residents of a single street in the town of Silvis in northwestern Illinois. "Hero Street, U.S.A." not only describes the lives and deaths of Second Street residents who died in combat; it also chronicles the community's fight for recognition of Mexican-American veterans who had served and died for their country.

Before You Read

You may have heard of the film *Hero Street, U.S.A.*, which also explores the material which John Culhane writes about in this essay, or you may have heard or participated in discussions about the roles which different ethnic groups have played in American wars. What do you think "patriotism" means to most Americans—do you think that most Americans are willing to fight and, if necessary, die for this country?

As You Read

1. Notice that this article really falls into two quite distinct parts: part one, paragraphs 1 through 23, is written as a history and concerns the background of Second Street and the contributions which the residents of Second Street made to American war efforts. Part two, from paragraph 24 to paragraph 43, details the struggle to make Hero Street a reality and discusses the efforts of individuals, local industry and the community in making the dream of recognition for the Second Street heroes come true.

111

2. This essay raises a large number of issues: patriotism among ethnic and immigrant Americans, prejudice against ethnic groups that persists in spite of their demonstrated commitment to this country, the question of what some have called the "disproportionate" numbers of minority/ethnic Americans who have fought and died in American wars, and the powerful impact of one individual's vision. Watch how Culhane introduces these various issues, linking them together through stories about and descriptions of individual and community history.

---

1   In a sense, the fight for Hero Street, U.S.A. began with the revolution that ravaged Mexico from 1910 to 1917. In Mexico, in those days, you could be made to join either side, and you could end up fighting your own father or brother. So thousands of Mexicans fled to the United States.

2   A few came as far as northwestern Illinois, where the communities of Rock Island, Moline, East Moline and Silvis run into one another along the Mississippi. Some found work at the huge locomotive-repair shop being built by the Rock Island Railroad in the tiny town of Silvis (pop. 2500).

3   The railroad not only gave the Mexicans jobs; it let them live in boxcars in the yard. Elated, the Mexicans sent word back to relatives and friends that there was steady work for adults and uninterrupted schooling for children.

4   It was a hard life. A railroad laborer was paid just 35 cents an hour. When the Mexicans in their boxcars woke up in the wintertime, the children had to break ice in the washbowls before they could clean up for school. But the hardship was worth it. School meant a chance to learn English and to succeed in sports. And, in those days, success in sports was one of the few ways a Mexican-American could be accepted as an equal.

5   One American who wanted to see the Mexicans make it in the United States was the basketball coach at McKinley School in Silvis, Willard Gauley. On the basketball court and off, Coach Gauley showed the young seventh- and eighth-graders how to achieve their goals: by teamwork.

6   In 35 years, Gauley led little McKinley to 30 winning seasons against much larger schools, winning 313 games and losing 121. But, more than anything else, the coach gave the young Mexican-Americans opportunities to show what they were made of.

7   A one-eyed boy badly wanted to play basketball, but Coach Gauley was afraid the lad would injure his other eye. When the youngster kept begging, Gauley finally went to his mother and asked her, "Do you think it's worth the risk?" The mother said, "His whole heart is in it. Let him play." Gauley gave the boy a uniform, and he was good enough with one eye to make the team. That uniform meant so much to him that when his home burned down he had rushed into the burning building to rescue it. "That kind of spirit," Coach Gauley always said, "is why we win."

8   By 1928, the Mexicans who lived in boxcars had saved enough money to buy land that no one else wanted at the west end of town. Twenty-two families built their houses on either side of Second Street—little more than a muddy stretch between Honey Creek and Billy Goat Hill. The hill had that name because the children said it was so steep that only billy goats—and they themselves—could climb it.

9   And climb it they did, to play war games and to hunt rabbits with slingshots. The older boys, of course, had already given up the hill. They had jobs, and were getting married and having families of their own.

10   **"Greatest Street in the World."** Then the United States was attacked, and went to war, and so did the Mexican-Americans of Second Street.

11   Tony Pompa lied about his age to get into the Army Air Corps at 17. He loved airplanes, and was honored to be made a B-24 tail gunner in the 449th Bombardment Group. Over Aviano, Italy, on January 31, 1944, Tony's plane was hit. As he was trying to get out

of the burning aircraft, his chute opened, trapping him inside. Tony Pompa was the first from Second Street to die. He left a young, pregnant widow and a small son.

12   The Sandoval family alone sent six young men to defend their country: Frank, Joe, Tanilo ("Tony"), Emidio, Eddie and Santiago ("Yatch"). Their mother, Angelina Sandoval, said in Spanish— her English was never good—"They didn't complain about going. This was their country, and they were willing to die for it." Their V-mail letters home eventually filled a canvas bag.

13   While serving with Company C, 209th Engineer Combat Battalion, Frank was killed in combat on the Burma Road. Ten months later, on April 14, 1945, Frank's brother Joe, fighting with Company I, 41st Armored Infantry Regiment, was killed by German forces on the bank of the Elbe River. His body was never found.

14   Another Sandoval family, unrelated to the first, lived on Second Street. This family sent seven sons to war, including William. On October 6, 1944, William's unit—Company F, 2nd Battalion, 504th Parachute Infantry—attacked German-held woods near Nijmegen, Holland. Between the Americans and their objective stood a fence. William was going over it when he was shot to death.

15   Claro Soliz made a will when he went to war. To various members of his family he bequeathed his ring, his typewriter, and the bicycle that often couldn't be ridden along his unpaved street. "Second Street is really not much—just mud and ruts," he admitted in a letter home. "But, right now, to me it is the greatest street in the world." Staff Sgt. Claro Soliz, Company E, 120th Infantry Regiment, died on January 19, 1945, of wounds received during the Battle of the Bulge.

16   Peter Masias wanted to be a singer. Many people on Second Street still remember his sweet, clear baritone. In the war he served with Company C, 139th Engineer Battalion. Enemy bullets cut him down in Wesel, Germany, on March 4, 1945.

17   **Far, Far Away.** The Mexicans' sacrifice did not end with World War II. Five years later, when war broke out in Korea, Second Street continued to send its sons.

18   Two of the first Sandoval family's World War II veterans—Eddie and Yatch—went to Korea. Both came home. Five weeks later, Yatch was killed in a car crash.

19   Joe Gomez had served in World War II and done occupation duty in Germany afterward. Then he came home, joined the Reserves, got married and had a daughter. When the Korean War broke out, he was called up.

20   On May 17, 1951, Joe Gomez, Company K, 38th Infantry Regiment, charged alone up a hill into point-blank enemy gunfire, to clear the way to a vital position where American and United Nations forces were trapped and being slaughtered. Because of Joe's bravery, many lives were saved, but he lost his own to Communist Chinese bullets. His young widow held their baby daughter in her arms as she received Joe's Silver Star for gallantry.

21   Johnny Munos had married Mary Bessera only three months before he was called up, and he missed her terribly. By mid-July 1951, Johnny was serving in Company F, 38th Regimental Combat Team, 2nd Infantry, in the mountains of Korea, living in a bunker, eating "C" rations.

22   They used to say on Second Street that running up and down Billy Goat Hill was good practice for the battles they had to fight in war. On Monday, August 27, Johnny Munos was killed fighting his way to the top of a hill in Korea—far, far away from Silvis, Ill.

23   **Our Flag, Too.** After the war, despite their sacrifices, the people of Second Street still hadn't won acceptance by most white Americans in Silvis—as they discovered when they tried to join the local post of the Veterans of Foreign Wars. All were turned down, they later learned, because some members of the post were afraid they'd be outnumbered by so many Mexican-American veterans. "You guys should form your own post," one man said. So they did.

24   Meanwhile, Second Street itself had become a bitter reminder that the rest of the community still considered Mexican-Americans to be second-class citizens. Some of those who had come home in flag-draped coffins had had to be carried up the unpaved street by their military escort on foot, because the hearses had bogged down in the mud.

25   Even before they went to war these men had been heroes to Joe
Terronez, a younger kid who lived on Third Street. Now Joe grew
angry at the sight of his heroes being carried into Our Lady of
Guadalupe Catholic Church by men with muddy boots just because the town wouldn't pave the street.

26   Terronez decided to fight the American way—with votes. In
the late 1950s, he and a friend began paying for any Mexican-born
person's citizenship-application photographs, driving applicants
to the Rock Island courthouse and, after they were sworn in,
showing them how to register to vote. One year they helped
create 27 new voters.

27   In 1963 the Mexican-Americans of his ward in Silvis helped to
elect Joe Terronez to the city council. Soon he was making a
motion that Second Street be paved and renamed "Hero Street,
U.S.A.," and that Billy Goat Hill, where his heroes used to play,
be turned into a park in their memory.

28   An ugly controversy erupted. The council said it didn't have
the money. As for the name change, it was pointed out that Second
Street wasn't the only street in Silvis that had sent men to fight
and die.

29   True, conceded Terronez. But he bet that no other street in
America had sent so many men, or lost so many of them in combat.

30   "The most from one family to be killed in World War II were
the five Sullivan brothers, and there's a destroyer named after
them," he reminded the council. "But the eight guys from Second
Street who were killed were like brothers, because they were all
raised together. We want their street named after them."

31   Terronez's fight for Hero Street finally caught the attention of
the U.S. Department of Defense, which looked into the matter.
The department's director of military equal opportunity made it
official: 57 men from Second Street fought in both World War II
and Korea. As far as he could determine, this was the largest
number of servicemen of the same ethnic background to come
from any area of comparable size during those conflicts.

32   "When you are willing to fight—even die—for your country,
who can say, 'It's my flag more than yours'?" asks Joe Terronez.

"Those boys could have said, 'I'm going back to Mexico so I don't have to risk my life.' Instead, fifty-seven put their lives on the line for the United States, and eight of them died."

33   **Spirit of Silvis.** Finally, on Memorial Day, 1971, Second Street officially became Hero Street, U.S.A. A red-white-and-blue sign was unveiled at the corner of Second Street and First Avenue (the main street) to proclaim it, and the Los Amigos marching band swung into "America" from *West Side Story*.

34   U.S. Rep. Thomas Railsback of Moline told the crowd: "I am proud to represent this neighborhood whose families generously gave the best they had to this country. I question whether any group in this country has done more."

35   Railsback had been working to obtain a federal grant to make the Billy Goat Hill park possible. Finally, the Department of Housing and Urban Development agreed to pay half the $88,000 cost if the town would match the funds.

36   Volunteers swung into action. Local 1304 of the United Auto Workers collected money at factory gates all over the area. Other local Mexican-American communities raised money with fiestas. The John Deere and International Harvester companies contributed machinery, as did the city of Silvis.

37   Gradually, a third of Billy Goat Hill was cut away and a concrete monument shaped like an Aztec temple was fashioned into it. Where the heroes once dropped a rubber ball into a hoop nailed to a tree, there was a full basketball court. And where they once played in the mud, there was a playground with a jungle gym.

38   Hero Street Park was dedicated October 30, 1971, and Hero Street, U.S.A. was finally paved in 1975. Claro Soliz's family could at last ride their bicycles in all seasons.

39   Ironically, in the late 1950s, the Silvis V.F.W. post, which had blackballed the Mexican-American veterans, was forced to sell its building because it could no longer afford the mortgage payments. So the Mexican-American veterans asked the "Anglos" if they wanted to meet in their building, an abandoned church they had bought and converted themselves. Today, all of Silvis's Veterans of Foreign Wars meet there.

40   **Victory in Peace.** Last winter, already planning the 1985 V-E Day observance in Hero Street, U.S.A. Memorial Park, Joe Terronez climbed the snowy hill to the plaque that bears the names of the eight heroes from Second Street. As he climbed, he talked about his children and the children of other Mexican-Americans born in Silvis, kids who are now lawyers, chemists, nurses, teachers—working at better jobs than their grandfathers would have thought possible.

41   But of course Terronez was really talking about his dead heroes—Tony Pompa; Frank, Joe and William Sandoval; Claro Soliz; Peter Masias; Joe Gomez; Johnny Munos—because suddenly he said: "Coach Gauley, who died in January, used to say the problem was that most people wouldn't give us a chance to show what we're made of." He pointed to the names on the plaque. "*They* showed what we're made of."

42   What the citizens of Silvis will be celebrating on May 8, the 40th anniversary of the end of the war in Europe, is more than a victory in war. It is also a victory in peace: a victory over prejudice and a victory for democracy. Most of all, it is a victory for the principle that all men are created equal. That is the bedrock of the American way of life for which the men of Hero Street, U.S.A., like so many others, fought and died.

———————

Journal Entry

Until the Vietnam War, most Americans agreed that war veterans were clearly heroes, and also believed that they should be treated and remembered as such. The bitter opposition to the Vietnam War, however, divided public opinion about war veterans; that division has continued to influence American public opinion. Do you think that veterans are heroes? Explain the reasons for your opinion.

Questions for Discussion

1. This selection begins with the assertion that "In a sense, the fight for Hero Street, U.S.A. began with the revolution that ravaged Mexico from 1910 to 1917." What does this statement mean?

   In light of the remainder of the article, explain why the reason for fleeing Mexico to settle in Silvis might seem somewhat *ironic* (a result that is the opposite of what might be expected).

2. What is the significance of including in the article the history of how Mexicans immigrated to Silvis and their early experiences there? What point does Culhane want to make by establishing that life for the early settlers of Second Street was very difficult?

3. Why does Culhane devote so much space (paragraphs 5 to 7) to a discussion of Coach Gauley and the McKinley School basketball team? What is Gauley's importance to the making of Hero Street?

4. Look carefully at the *case histories* of the eight young men and their deaths which Culhane presents in paragraphs 11 through 22. Why does he choose to detail some aspect of the life of each individual? How does the reader respond to this series of mini-biographies?

5. How does the information in paragraphs 23 and 24 affect the reader? Consider the issues which these paragraphs raise—in what sense might these paragraphs be considered the *turning point* of the essay?

6. After reading about Joe Terronez (paragraphs 25 through 32 and paragraphs 40 and 41), how would you describe him? How would you explain his battle for Hero Street and Billy Goat Park? Why do you think he fought? What do you think he fought for?

7. Paragraph 31 concerns the official determination of the U.S. Department of Defense. Do you think that this official determination is important? If so, how?

Do you believe that the Sullivan family's loss of five sons in World War II (paragraph 30) and the eight Second Street deaths in World War II and Korea are comparable? How can you account for the fact that the Sullivans (who all served on the same ship and died together when the ship sank in battle) were honored by having a destroyer named after them and by a 1944 film which told their story (*The Fighting Sullivans*) while the men of Second Street were not formally honored until 1971?

8. Some pieces of writing have an *explicit* (clearly stated) thesis, while others have an *implicit* (suggested) thesis. What kind of thesis does "Hero Street, U.S.A." have? What is the thesis of this article?

9. What do you think the dedication of Hero Street Park and the naming and paving of Hero Street, U.S.A. mean to the Mexican American community of Silvis?

10. The phrases "Show what they were made of" and "show what we're made of," which appear in paragraphs 6 and 41, tie the two halves of the essay together. In your opinion, what were the young men of Second Street/Hero Street, U.S.A. "made of"?

A WOMAN'S FIGHT

Pretty Shield

About the Reading

This first-hand account of a Crow-Lacota battle was told through sign language and translation to Frank B. Linderman by Pretty Shield, a wise-woman of the Crow tribe; he published her biography in 1932. According to Paula Gunn Allen, who recently reprinted this story in her anthology *Spider Woman's Granddaughters*, Crow society has been well-known for "belittling the status of women." In Gunn Allen's opinion, "Pretty Shield makes it clear: the one who tells the stories rules the world."

Before You Read

In spite of the progress which women have made since the days of the Women's Liberation Movement, our culture still holds some strong views about behavior which is or is not appropriate for women. The image of fighting women—whether in the armed forces or on a personal level—is distasteful to a segment of the American population. What image does the title "A Woman's Fight" suggest to you? What kinds of images does American culture have about women's fights?

As You Read

1. From its beginning, Pretty Shield's story contains vocabulary ("lodge," "parfleches"), names ("Corn-woman," "Strikes-two") and forms of expression ("sent out as a wolf") which may seem foreign to the reader. Notice how these elements provide a sense of atmosphere and authenticity for the story.

2. Until almost the end of the story, it seems as though its hero will be Pretty Shield herself. Notice how the focus of the action shifts only in the final paragraphs to the real hero of the story. Pretty Shield's narrative therefore provides a sort of "surprise" ending for the reader, and effectively establishes both Strikes-two and the child Pretty Shield as main characters. The implication is that both share heroic traits.

———————

1   Once, when I was eight years old, we moved our village from The-mountain-lion's-lodge [Pompey's Pillar] to the place where the white man's town of Huntley now stands. There were not many of us in this band. Sixteen men were with us when the women began to set up their lodges, and one man named Covered-with-grass was sent out as a wolf. I could see him on the hill when my mother was setting up her lodge-poles. I was dragging the poles of my play-lodge to a nice place that I had selected when I saw Covered-with-grass, the wolf on the hill, signal, "The enemy is coming."

2   Instantly two men leaped upon the backs of horses, their war-horses, that were always kept tied near lodges, and rode out on the plains to drive the other horses into camp.

3   There was great excitement, much running about by the women, who left their lodges just as they happened to be when the signal came. Some of the lodges had but a few poles up. Others, whose owners were quicker, had their lodge-skins tied, hanging loosely from the skin-poles.

4   Men, watching the hills, stationed themselves, one between every two lodges. Mothers, piling packs and parfleches into breast-works, called their children; and horses whinnied. Then I saw the horses that had been out on the plains coming fast, their hoofs making a great noise and much dust. I must get out of the way.

5   Dragging my poles, a load beneath each arm, I ran between two lodges whose lodge-skins were flapping in the wind, my own little

lodge yet on my back. In came the horses, more than a hundred, sweeping into the camp between two lodges that were far apart, too far apart, I thought. And this thought gave me an idea. Why not close that wide gap between those two lodges? Why not set up my little lodge between the two big ones, and shut this wide place up?

6   While yet the horses were running around within the circle of the camp I dragged my poles to the spot, and quickly pitched my lodge there. I heard my mother calling me. I had to work very fast to shut up that wide place, believing that my little lodge would keep our horses from getting out, and the Lacota from getting in; but I did not finish pegging down my lodge-skin, not quite. Corn-woman found me. "Ho! Ho!" she cried out, "here is a brave little woman! She has shut the wide gap with her lodge. Ho! Ho!"

7   But just the same she picked me up in her arms and carried me to my mother, as though I were a baby. Corn-woman told this story every year until she died.

8   Now I shall have to tell you about the fighting, a little, because it was a woman's fight. A woman won it. The men never tell about it. They do not like to hear about it, but I am going to tell you what happened. I was there to see. And my eyes were good, too. [. . .]

9   Yes [. . .] a woman won that fight, and the men never tell about it. There was shooting by the time my play-lodge was pitched. A Lacota bullet struck one of its poles, and whined. Arrows were coming among the lodges, and bullets, when Corn-woman carried me to my mother, who made me lie down behind a pack. I saw what went on there.

10   Several horses were wounded and were screaming with their pain. One of them fell down near my mother's lodge that was not yet half pitched. Lying there behind that pack I did not cover my eyes. I was looking all the time, and listening to everything. I saw Strikes-two, a woman sixty years old, riding around the camp on a gray horse. She carried only her root-digger, and she was singing her medicine-song, as though Lacota bullets and arrows were not flying around her. I heard her say, "Now all of you sing, 'They are whipped. They are running away,' and keep singing these words until I come back."

11   When the men and even the women began to sing as Strikes-two told them, she rode out straight at the Lacota, waving her root-digger and singing that song. I *saw* her, I *heard* her, and my heart swelled, because she was a woman.

12   The Lacota, afraid of her medicine, turned and ran away. The fight was won, and by a woman.

Journal Entry

Tell about a time when you witnessed an act which you found heroic. First, write down who the person was, and both the circumstances in which the action took place and what the person did to earn your admiration. Then, explain what effect witnessing this act had on you.

Questions for Discussion

1. In paragraph 3, Pretty Shield describes Covered-with-grass as "the wolf on the hill"; his job is to signal the Crows when he sees the enemy approach. The English translation of "wolf" in this *context* (situation) would be "lookout." How would you describe the difference between the English "lookout" and the Crow "wolf"? Why do you think Linderman's English translation of Pretty Shield's story does not use the term "lookout"?

2. In the final sentence of paragraph 4, Pretty Shield's use of the past tense shifts, and she uses the present tense "must" rather than "had to." What is the effect of this tense shift on the reader?

3. Pretty Shield says the men never tell about the fight because a woman won it. Why do you think that the men "do not like to hear about it"? What does their attitude suggest about male-female relationships among the Crows?

it promptly went downhill. It looked as though it were being drawn in a bank.

8   But, oh, those early drawings! Superman running up the sides of dams, leaping over anything that stood in his way. (No one drew skyscrapers like Shuster. Impressionistic shafts, Superman poised over them, his leaping leg tucked under him, his landing leg tautly pointed earthward), cleaning and jerking two-ton get-away cars and pounding them into the sides of cliffs—and all this done lightly, unportentiously, still with that early Slam Bradley exuberance. What matter that the stories quickly lost interest; that once you've made a man super you've plotted him out of believable conflicts; that even super-villains, super-mad scientists and, yes, super-orientals were dull and lifeless next to the overwhelming image of that which Clark Kent became when he took off his clothes. So what if the stories were boring, the villains blah? This was the Superman Show—a touring road company backing up a great star. Everything was a stage wait until he came on. Then it was all worth-while.

9   Besides, for the alert reader there were other fields of interest. It seems that among Lois Lane, Clark Kent, and Superman there existed a schizoid and chaste ménage a trois. Clark Kent loved but felt abashed with Lois Lane; Superman saved Lois Lane when she was in trouble, found her a pest the rest of the time. Since Superman and Clark Kent were the same person this behavior demands explanation. It can't be that Kent wanted Lois to respect him for himself, since himself was Superman. Then, it appears, he wanted Lois to respect him for his fake self, to love him when he acted the coward, to be there when he pretended he needed her. She never was—so, of course, he loved her. A typical American romance. Superman never needed her, never needed anyone—in any event, Lois chased *him* —so, of course, he didn't love her. He had contempt for her. Another typical American romance.

10   Love is really the pursuit of a desired object, not pursuit by it. Once you've caught the object there is no longer any reason to love it, to have it hanging around. There must be other desirable objects out there, somewhere. So Clark Kent acted as the control for Superman. What Kent wanted was just that which Superman

didn't want to be bothered with. Kent wanted Lois, Superman didn't—thus marking the difference between a sissy and a man. A sissy wanted girls who scorned him, a man scorned girls who wanted him. Our cultural opposite of the man who didn't make out with women has never been the man who did—but rather the man who could if he wanted to, but still didn't. The ideal of masculine strength, whether Gary Cooper's, Li'l Abner's, or Superman's, was for one to be so virile and handsome, to be in such a position of strength, that he need never go near girls. Except to help them. And then get the hell out. Real rapport was not for women. It was for villains. That's why they got hit so hard.

Journal Entry

Think about your childhood images of super-heroes. Did you get your ideas about super-heroes from comic books, television, or some other source? Think back to a specific time in your childhood when super-hero figures were important to you and your friends. Write the name of either the super-hero who most influenced you or the one you best remember. Then, list all of the qualities that you can remember of this super-hero. Finally, in a short paragraph, tell why you think this super-hero figure captured your imagination or appealed to you.

Questions for Discussion

1. This essay opens with a quote from a 1939 issue of *Superman*. How does the quote prepare the reader for the essay which follows? Which of Superman's characteristics does the quote identify?

2. In paragraph 1, Feiffer uses the word *advent*. What does this word mean, and what does it suggest when it is applied to super-heroes?

   What is a "comeuppance"? What does Feiffer mean when he says in the first paragraph that the "advent of the super-hero was a bizarre comeuppance for the American dream"?

3. Feiffer makes extensive use of *allusions,* or references. Ask an older person or use a dictionary or specialized encyclopedia to check the meanings of the following allusions: Horatio Alger (paragraph 1), the Shadow, the Green Hornet, the Lone Ranger (paragraph 3), Alex Raymond, Dior, and Joe Shuster (paragraph 7), Gary Cooper and Li'l Abner (paragraph 10). Because these allusions are to many different types of people/characters, you may wish to pool information with your classmates, and/or get assistance from your instructor or a reference librarian.

4. In paragraph 3, Feiffer uses the phrase "fetishist folde-rol" in describing the Green Hornet and the word "accoutremental" in describing the Lone Ranger. After you look up the meanings of these terms, consider how they suggest Feiffer's *tone,* or attitude, towards these super-hero figures.

5. In paragraph 2, Feiffer uses the term "alter ego"; he uses the terms "hair shirt," "imprimatur," and "masochist" in paragraph 5. Each of these terms refers to a concept of religion or psychology. After looking up the exact meaning of each, consider why Feiffer decides on this *word choice.* What do these words *connote* (suggest) about his subject?

6. In paragraph 6, Feiffer says of Superman that "His fake identity was our real one." What does this *paradoxical* (seemingly contradictory) statement suggest about the relationship between Superman and fans of the super-hero character?

7. At the beginning of paragraph 7, Feiffer calls Superman a "parody." Look up the meaning of "parody," and then consider how both paragraphs 7 and 8 go on to praise Joe Schuster's drawing style. What effect does the initial criticism have on the reader's expectations? How does the reader respond to the praise which follows the initial criticism?

8. In paragraph 9, Feiffer describes the relationship between Superman, Lois Lane, and Clark Kent as a *"menage a trois."* After you have looked up the definition for this phrase, explain why Feiffer uses it to describe this situation.

9. The final paragraph of this essay begins with a definition of love. Do you think that this is an appropriate ending for an essay about Superman? Why or why not?

10. Do you believe, as Feiffer suggests in this essay, that Superman represents an ideal of masculine strength to Americans? To what segment of American society do you think Superman and other super-heroes appeal most strongly? How might you explain the appeal?

THE WESTERN: THE LEGEND AND THE CARDBOARD HERO

Peter Homans

About the Reading

The Western hero, considered by many to be the original and authentic American hero-figure, is the subject of Peter Homans' essay, which appeared in *Thinking and Writing* (1980) edited by Donald McQuade and Robert Atwan. Homans' special academic interest is exploring and analyzing cultural phenomena; in this piece, he blends psychology, culture and mythology in order to look closely at a kind of film that has always been particularly associated with American culture—the Western.

Before You Read

Generally recognized as the first "classic" American film, *The Great Train Robbery* was released in 1903 to audiences who flocked to see it and were astounded by its powerful images. *The Great Train Robbery* also had a tremendous impact on movie-makers. They quickly responded to the public appetite for Westerns by making hundreds of them, thereby also making the Western one of the most typical and well-loved *genres* (kinds) of American films. Think about Westerns you have seen—what would you consider to be the characteristics of Westerns? How would you describe the heroes of these movies?

As You Read

1. Homans begins his essay with the attention-getting device of explaining who "he" is. Notice the large numbers of *allusions* (references) in the early paragraphs, as Homans

establishes the seriousness of his subject by making connections between the figure of the Western hero and
mythology. In starting out his essay by defining the hero,
he also prepares the reader for the essay that follows and
which is concerned with the listing and defining of the
various elements of the Western movie.

2. The paragraph structure of this essay is worth noticing.
Watch especially for the short paragraphs in the early part
of the essay; these move the reader along quickly to the
next idea. In the second part of the essay, as Homans
develops ideas more complexly, his paragraphs become
longer and more theoretical.

———————

1   He is the Law West of Tombstone, he is The Virginian at High
Noon. He is Frontier Marshal, Knight of the Range, Rider of the
Purple Sage. He Has Gun, Will Travel, and his name is Matt
Dillon. Destry. Shane.

2   He is the hero of every Western that ever thundered out of the
movies or TV screen, this Galahad with a Colt .45 who stalks
injustice on the dusty streets of Dodge. Or Carson City. Or
Virginia City.

3   Once he accomplishes his mission, he vanishes into the mists,
as do all true heroes of all true legends. But where Hercules goes
to Olympus and King Arthur to Avalon, this galoot rides Old
Paint into the sunset.

4   With few variations, the movies have been telling this story for
more than half a century. There have, in fact, been Western
movies as long as there have been movies; the first American
narrative film was a Western, The Great Train Robbery, made in
1903. Without the Westerns, it would be hard to imagine television today. Far outstripping the rowdy little boys who were its
first enraptured audience, the Western has gone round the globe
to become the youngest of the world's mythologies.

5   For each of us, even the word "Western" brings to mind an ordered sequence of character, event and detail. There may, of course, be variations within the pattern—but the basic outline remains constant. Details often vary, especially between movie and television Westerns, because the latter are essentially continued stories. Nonetheless, from the endless number of Westerns we have all seen, a basic concept emerges:

6   The Western takes place in a desolate, abandoned land. The desert, as a place without life, is indispensable. The story would not be credible were it set in a jungle, a fertile lowland or an arctic wasteland. We are dealing with a form of existence deprived of vitality.

7   This desert effect is contradicted by the presence of a town. Among the slapped-together buildings with false fronts, lined awkwardly along a road forever thick with dust, only three stand out—the saloon, the bank and the marshal's office (the hero's dwelling).

8   The saloon is the most important building in the Western. It is the only place in the story where people can be seen together time after time. It thereby functions as a meetinghouse, social center, church. More important, it is the setting for the climax of the story, the gunfight. No matter where the fight ends, it starts in the saloon.

9   The bank is a hastily constructed, fragile affair. Its only protection consists of a sniveling, timid clerk, with a mustache and a green eyeshade, who is only too glad to hand over the loot. Has there ever been a Western in which a robber wondered whether he could pull off his robbery?

10   The marshal's office appears less regularly. Most noticeable is the absence of any evidence of domesticity. We rarely see a bed, a place for clothes or any indication that a person actually makes his home here. There is not even a mirror. The overall atmosphere is that of austerity, which, we are led to suspect, is in some way related to our hero's virtue, and not to his finances.

11   The town as a whole has no business or industry. People have money, but we rarely see them make it. Homelife is conspicuous by its absence. There are no families, children, dogs. The closest thing to a home is a hotel, and this is rarely separated from the saloon.

12   One of the most interesting people in the town is the "derelict professional." He was originally trained in one of the usual Eastern professions (law, medicine, letters, ministry), but since his arrival in the West, he has become corrupted by drink, gambling, sex or violence. The point is that the traditional mentors of society (counselor, healer, teacher, shepherd) cannot exist in an uncorrupted state under the pressure of Western life. Somewhat similar is the "nonviolent Easterner." He often appears as a well-dressed business man, or as a very recent graduate of Harvard. In the course of the plot's development, this character is either humiliated or killed. The East, we soon note, is incapable of action when action is most needed.

13   The "good girl" is another supporting type in the cast of characters. Pale and without appetite, she, too, is from the East and is classically represented as the new schoolmarm. The "bad girl" is alone in the world and usually works for her living in the saloon as a waitress or dancer. Both girls have their eye on the hero.

14   The bartender observes the action, but rarely becomes involved in it. "The boys," those bearded, grimy people who are always "just there" drinking and gambling in the saloon, function as an audience. No hero ever shot it out with his adversary without these people watching.

15   Then we come to the principals. We meet the hero in the opening phase of the action. He is, above all, a transcendent figure, originating beyond the town. He rides into the town from nowhere; even if he is the marshal, his identity is disassociated from the people he must save. We know nothing of any past activities, relationships, future plans or ambitions. There are no friends, relatives, family, mistresses—not even a dog or cat—and even with his horse, he has a strangely formal relationship.

16   At first, the hero is lax to the point of laziness. Take his hat, for example. It sits exactly where it was placed—no effort has been made to align it. With feet propped up on the porch rail, frame balanced on a chair or stool tilted back on its rear legs, hat pushed slightly over the eyes, hands clasped over the buckle of his gun belt, he is a study in contrived indolence. Now he has time on his hands, but he knows his time is coming, and so do we.

17   The hero indicates no desire for women. He appears somewhat bored with the whole business. He never blushes, or betrays any enthusiasm. His monosyllabic stammer and brevity of speech clearly indicate an intended indifference.

18   In the drinking scenes, we are likely to see the hero equipped with the traditional shot glass and bottle. We seldom see him pay for more than one drink. He gulps his drink, rarely enjoys it and is impatient to be off. In the gambling scenes, his poker face veils any inner feelings of greed, enthusiasm or apprehension. We note, however, that he always wins or refuses to play. Similarly, he is utterly unimpressed by and indifferent to money.

19   There are hundreds of variations of the villain, but each is unshaven, darkly clothed and from the West. Like the hero, he is from beyond the town. He is inclined to cheat at cards, get drunk, lust after women who do not return the compliment, rob banks and, finally, shoot people he does not care for, especially heroes.

20   The impact of this evil one on the town is electric, suddenly animating it with vitality and purpose. Indeed, it is evil, rather than good, that actually gives meaning to the lives of these people. Nevertheless, they all know (as we do) that they are themselves ultimately powerless to meet this evil. What is required is the hero—a transcendent power originating from beyond the town.

21   Notice what has happened to this power. Gone are the hero's indolence and lack of intention. Now, he is infused with vitality, direction and seriousness, in order to confront this ultimate threat. Once the radical shift has been accomplished, the hero (like the audience) is ready for the final conflict.

22   While the fight can take many forms (fistfight, fight with knives or whips, even a scowling match in which the hero successfully glares down the evil one), the classic and most popular form is the encounter with six-guns. It is a built-up and drawn-out affair, always allowing enough time for an audience to gather. The two men must adhere to an elaborate and well-defined casuistry as to who draws first, when it is proper to draw, etc. Although the hero's presence makes the fight possible—i.e., he insists on obstructing the evil one in some way; it is the latter who invariably attacks first. Were the hero ever to draw first, the story

would no longer be a Western. With the destruction of the evil one, the action phase is completed.

23   In the closing phase, the town and its hero return to their preaction ways. One more event must take place, however, before the story can conclude. The hero must renounce any further involvement with the town. Traditionally, the hero marries the heroine and settles down. The Western hero always refuses—at least on television. He cannot identify himself with the situation he has influenced. When this has been made clear, the story is over.

24   The Western is, as most people by this time are willing to acknowledge, a popular myth that sets forth certain meanings about what is good and bad, right and wrong. Evil, according to the myth, is the failure to resist temptation. Temptation consists of five activities: drinking, gambling, moneymaking, sex and violence. In the drinking scenes, the hero is offered not one drink, but a whole bottle. He has at his disposal the opportunity for unlimited indulgence and its consequent loss of self-control. Gambling is a situation over which one has rather limited control—one loses, but the hero does not lose. He wins, thereby remaining in control. Wealth is not seized, although it is available to him through the unguarded bank. And both good girl and bad girl seek out the hero, to no avail—he remains a hero.

25   We perceive in the evil one a terrible power, which he has acquired at a great price; he has forfeited the control and resistance that sustain and make the hero what he is. The villain is the embodiment of the failure to resist temptation; he is the failure of denial. This is the real meaning of evil in the myth of the Western, and it is this that makes the evil one truly evil. He threatens the hero's resistance; each taunt and baiting gesture is a lure to the forfeiture of control and leads to the one temptation that the hero cannot afford to resist: the temptation to destroy temptation.

26   But why must the hero wait to be attacked? Why must he refrain from drawing first? The circumstances are contrived in order to make the violent destruction of the evil one appear just and virtuous. This process whereby desire is at once indulged and veiled is the "inner dynamic." It is the key to the Western,

explaining not only the climax of the story, but everything else uniquely characteristic of it. What is required is that temptation be indulged while providing the appearance of having been resisted. Each of the minor temptation episodes—drink, cards, moneymaking and sex—takes its unique shape from this need and is a climaxless Western in itself.

27　　The derelict professional is derelict, and the nonviolent Easterner is weak, precisely because they have failed to resist temptation in the manner characteristic of the hero. Because these two types originate in the East, they have something in common with the good girl. Everything Eastern in the Western is weak, emotional, feminine. This covers family life, intellectual life, professional life. Only by becoming Westernized can the East be redeemed. The Western therefore is more a myth about the East than it is about the West: it is a secret and bitter parody of Eastern ways.

28　　In summary, then, the Western is a myth in which evil appears as a series of temptations to be resisted by the hero. When faced with the embodiment of these temptations, he destroys the threat. But the story is so structured that the responsibility for the act falls upon the adversary, permitting the hero to destroy while appearing to save.

29　　The Western bears a significant relationship to puritanism, in which it is the proper task of the will to rule and contain the spontaneous, vital aspects of life. Whenever vitality becomes too pressing, and the dominion of the will becomes threatened, the self must find some other mode of control. The puritan will seek a situation that allows him to express vitality while appearing to resist it. The Western provides just this opportunity, for the entire myth is shaped by the inner dynamic of apparent control and veiled expression. Indeed, in the gunfight, the hero's heightened gravity and dedicated exclusion of all other loyalties present a study in puritan virtue, while the evil one presents nothing more or less than the old New England Protestant devil—strangely costumed, to be sure—the traditional tempter whose horrid lures never allow the good puritan a moment's peace. In the gunfight, there are deliverance and redemption.

30   Here, then, is the real meaning of the Western: It is a puritan morality tale in which the savior-hero redeems the community from the temptations of the devil. Tall in the saddle, he rides straight from Plymouth Rock to a dusty frontier town, and though he be the fastest gun this side of Laramie, his Colt .45 is on the side of the angels.

Journal Entry

Think of Western movies which you have seen (or, if you haven't seen one in a while, watch a Western on television or rent or borrow a Western on video). Do you agree with Homans' opinion that the Western is a "morality tale" about good versus evil? What does the Western suggest to you about America's need for hero-figures?

Questions for Discussion

1. Paragraph 3 of this essay asserts that Western heroes are like "true heroes of all true legends." Look up the word "legend" and then consider what Homans means by *true* legends. How can a legend be "true"?

2. In the early paragraphs of this essay, Homans gives a number of alternative titles for the Western hero and the town he cleans up. What do all of these names suggest about Homans' perception of the Western hero? What assumptions do paragraphs 1 through 3 of this essay make about the reader's knowledge?

3. In paragraph 6, Homans compares the desert to other landscapes. Why does he conclude that the desert is the "indispensable" setting for the Western?

4. In paragraph 15, Homans describes the hero as "above all, a transcendent figure." After looking up the meaning of

transcendent, list all of the other qualities which Homans attributes to the Western hero.

Are there any contradictions in these qualities? Taken together, do they support the idea that the Western hero is "cardboard"?

5. What would you consider to be the *thesis* of this essay? Is it *explicit* (clearly stated) or *implicit* (suggested)? Where does he most clearly define the Western hero?

6. According to Homans, what are the important features of towns in Westerns? Does your viewing experience confirm Homans' opinion?

7. List the characters which Homans considers essential to Westerns. Explain the functions of these characters in terms of Homans' opinion of the meaning of the Western.

8. In paragraph 27, Homans asserts that "the Western . . . is more a myth about the East than it is about the West. . . ." Consider the support which Homans provides for this argument. How convincing do you find his point of view?

9. In paragraph 29, Homans compares the Western and puritanism. Is the comparison favorable to the Western? Why or why not?

10. How thoroughly does Homans convince you that the Western hero is a "savior-hero"? How else might you describe the function of the Western hero?

SUGGESTIONS FOR WRITING

Assignment 1

Write an essay in which you identify and discuss a hero or heroes in your own family, focusing on the heroic qualities of the person or persons you have chosen to write about.

Strategies for Prewriting and Planning: Before you begin this assignment, you might discuss it with your family members. Think about stories you have heard about people in your family. These might be people who have come to a new land to make a new life, people who have served in wars or other dangerous situations, people who have helped others in their communities, people who have triumphed educationally or professionally, people who have overcome a "handicap," or any other family members who have performed what you consider to be an heroic act. You might wish to interview this person if that is possible. If you have several family members who have done noteworthy things, you may wish to write an essay telling about the several heroes in your family. If, however, one family member stands out as a hero, you may wish to devote your entire essay to this person.

Assignment 2

Write an essay in which you analyze the qualities of your favorite super-hero. You could write about a super-hero you looked up to as a child and analyze why, at the time, you were drawn to that figure. Or you might discuss a super-hero who intrigues you now.

Strategies for Prewriting and Planning: Before you begin to write, select your super-hero. Then brainstorm all of the admirable qualities you can find in this figure. Then, go back and look at those qualities to find what significance they hold or held for you as an individual. For example, Superman often allows others to take credit for what he has done; perhaps you find this modesty to be an appealing characteristic. Once you have selected the qualities you will discuss, try to think of an example of the behavior of the super-hero that would illustrate that quality in action. Be sure to show in your essay not only the admirable qualities of your super-hero, but why you find these qualities particularly admirable.

Assignment 3

After reading "Hero Street U.S.A.," write an essay that describes a hero who you feel has been treated badly or whose act of heroism has gone unrewarded.

Strategies for Prewriting and Planning: After you have selected an individual to write about, devise a rationale for your choice. This rationale, which reflects why you felt the person was treated badly, or the fact that the person received no recognition, will serve as the basis for your thesis. As you organize your essay, concentrate first on the act which you feel qualifies this person as a hero. Then, describe the reaction or lack of reaction to this deed. Finally, analyze why your hero has not been treated as a hero.

Assignment 4

Write an essay in which you describe an individual who is a hero to a certain group, community or nation and explain why this person is considered a hero. This could be a well-known hero like Rosa Parks or Cesar Chavez, or you could write about a hero within a particular community who is little known outside that group.

Strategies for Prewriting and Planning: Depending on your knowledge about the figure you decide to write about, you may wish to do some research, either by interviewing others or by looking up information on this figure at a library. List either this person's accomplishments or heroic traits. As you begin writing, give your reader a description of the hero or an overview of the hero's significance. Then use details from your list to develop the body of your essay. Whenever you mention an abstract quality such as bravery or kindness, be sure to illustrate it by a concrete example of this quality at work.

Assignment 5

Write an essay about someone who has become a hero by virtue of media exposure. For example, you might focus on an athlete, an entertainer, a politician or a celebrity.

Strategies for Prewriting and Planning: To decide on a subject, you might list as many media stars as you can think of; you might look at newspapers, magazines or talk shows to get ideas. Once you have chosen your media star, try to determine just why it is that this person has become a star—because of talent, by chance, because of family background? Decide whether this person is a hero to you personally, or whether the media has created an heroic image where none exists. Choose one of these two approaches as the basis for your analysis of the stardom of this figure. Be sure to include in your essay only those details which reinforce the attitude you have chosen to take.

4

THE TRICKSTER

The figure of the "trickster" is found in mythology and folklore around the world. In some cultures, the trickster takes the form of an animal, such as a spider, rabbit, or coyote. In others, the trickster may be a god or an ordinary human being. Sometimes the trickster is a "shape shifter," a being which changes from one form to another or even from one sex to the other.

Regardless of shape, the trickster can be distinguished by certain characteristics. First and foremost, this figure is a player of tricks, usually malicious tricks, which sometimes backfire and often lead to humorous situations. The trickster is a composite of opposites, combining cunning with foolishness or stupidity, and acting at once as a creator and a destroyer. The trickster not only tricks others, but is tricked by others as well.

Trickster tales tend to exaggerate. Many are very violent, containing scenes of mutilation and murder which may disturb the modern reader. For the audiences who originally heard these stories, however, this violence not only mirrored a difficult and violent world, but served as a form of entertainment, perhaps even as a relief from stress, much as cartoons, horror movies, and shoot-'em-up Westerns provided entertainment to later audiences.

In its most ancient and primitive forms, the trickster figure, described by Karl Kerenyi as a "spirit of disorder," is usually driven by its appetites; the trickster is often strongly sexual. The trickster is sometimes credited with responsibility for natural phenomenon, such as the movement of the sun. In a number of animal tales, the trickster is responsible for originating the characteristics of other animals, such as causing the leopard to have spots or the bear to have a stubby tail. In more modern folk and fairy tales, we can identify the trickster in those figures who use cunning and ruses rather than bravery or goodness to get what they want—usually material rewards. The trickster figure is still very much with us today. In popular culture, for instance, the trickster appears from time to time as characters like Beetlejuice, Batman's arch-enemy the Joker, Bugs Bunny, or the Roadrunner.

PREREADING

Before reading any of the selections in this chapter, look up and copy down the definition of a folk tale, a fairy tale, and a myth. What, if any, common elements do these definitions include? How are they different?

POSTREADING

After reading the selections in this chapter, consider your exposure to trickster figures in stories, in movies, or on television. Why do you think so many cultures have trickster figures? What aspects of modern American culture do you think our trickster figures reflect?

JACK AND THE BEANSTALK

About the Reading

Jack, a young man who tricks an ogre (or in some versions a giant) out of his wealth and possessions, is one of the best-known of all English-language tricksters. The story of Jack and his adventures has been adapted to cartoons, such as the one which stars Mickey Mouse; it has also been published everywhere from Little Golden Books to scholarly collections of folklore. The version of the Old English folk tale "Jack and the Beanstalk" reprinted here has been adapted by Amy Ehrlich for *The Random House Book of Fairy Tales*.

Before You Read

Of the many issues raised in this story, one of the most obvious is the deception which Jack practices on the giant's wife; in spite of the kindness she shows him, he takes advantage of her good nature to enrich himself. The ideas of deception and taking advantage of others are central to the character of the trickster. How widespread do you think the practice of taking advantage of someone's kindness is? Why do you think people allow others to take advantage of them?

As You Read

1. Notice that this story really falls into three very distinct parts, according to Jack's changing motivations for climbing the beanstalk. He undertakes his first climb out of curiosity. Later, hunger motivates him to try his luck at gaining a new source of income. He undertakes his final climb because he now wants adventure and excitement. Each of these reasons is significant, as, taken together, they reveal a great deal not only about Jack, but also about human nature.

2. The main character of this story has the *generic* (common) name "Jack," which seems to suggest that he represents the common, ordinary man. Perhaps the most obvious quality of this character in the early part of the story is his innocent belief in what the stranger tells him about the beans. Later, however, Jack's experiences with the beanstalk appear to cause him to undergo a *metamorphosis* (change) during which he becomes less innocent. Look for the signals within the story which suggest that as Jack loses his innocence he metamorphoses into a very different person.

---

1   There was once a widow who had a son named Jack and a cow called Milky White. They were very poor and had only the milk from the cow, which they sometimes sold for food. But one morning Milky White gave no milk at all and they didn't know what to do.

2   "Do not worry, Mother," said Jack at last. "Today is market day. I shall take Milky White with me and sell her. She is a fine-looking cow and will fetch enough money to start us up in a trade."

3   So he took the cow's halter in his hand and set off for town. He hadn't gone far when he met a funny-looking old man along the road. "Good morning, Jack," he said.

4   "Good morning to you," said Jack, wondering how the man knew his name.

5   "Well, Jack, and where are you off to?"

6   "I'm going to market to sell our cow here."

7   "You seem the sort of lad who will get a good price," said the man. "I wonder if you know how many beans make five."

8   "Two in each hand and one in your mouth," said Jack, quick as a wink.

9   "Right you are," said the man. "And here they are, the very beans themselves." He took from his pocket a number of beans, unlike any Jack had ever seen before. "These are magical beans,

Jack. Plant them at night and by morning they'll grow right up to the sky."

10   "You don't say!" said Jack.

11   "I do indeed," the stranger told him. "And since you are such a clever lad, I'll happily swap them for your cow there."

12   "It's a deal," said Jack. And he handed over Milky White and pocketed the beans.

13   Back home Jack went. It wasn't even dusk when he came through the door.

14   "Home already?" his mother said. "I see you haven't got Milky White so you must have sold her. How much did she fetch? Five pounds?"

15   Jack smiled and shook his head.

16   "Ten?"

17   Jack shook his head again.

18   "Can it have been twenty pounds?" said his mother, clapping her hands with excitement.

19   "No, Mother," said Jack. "I got something better still." He opened his hand to show the beans. "Plant them at night and in the morning—"

20   "You dolt! You idiot!" his mother screamed. "You gave away my Milky White, the best milker in the district and prime beef besides, for a handful of beans? I'll teach you!" Then she threw the beans out the window, thrashed Jack soundly, and sent him to bed without his supper.

21   In the morning when Jack woke up, the room looked very strange. Shadows of leaves were on the walls and the sun did not shine through the window. Quickly he got dressed and went to look outside. There right next to the house grew a huge beanstalk that went up and up and up until it reached the sky. Jack couldn't see the top of it and then he knew that the man had spoken the truth.

22   He threw open his window and climbed right onto the beanstalk. It grew straight and true, just like a ladder leading up to the sky. Higher and higher Jack climbed until he came out upon a long, broad road. So he walked along and walked along until he

came to a great big tall house. On the doorstep there was a great big tall woman.

23   "Good morning, to you, ma'am," said Jack politely. "Could you kindly give me some breakfast? I've had nothing to eat from midday past and it was a long walk to get here."

24   "It's breakfast you want, is it?" said the great big tall woman. "It's breakfast you'll be if you don't move off from here. My man is an ogre and there's nothing he likes better than boys broiled on toast. You'd best be moving on, for he'll soon be coming."

25   "Oh, please, ma'am, give me something to eat," said Jack. "My stomach is so empty. I may as well be broiled as die of hunger."

26   Well, the ogre's wife was not a stingy woman, so she took Jack into her kitchen and gave him bread and cheese and a jug of milk. Jack wasn't half finished with it when—*thump! thump! thump!*— the house began to shake.

27   "Hurry, hurry!" the ogre's wife said. "It's my man. He's coming. You can jump in here." And she pushed Jack into the oven just as the ogre walked through the door.

28   He was a big one, to be sure. At his belt he had three calfs strung up by the heels, and he unhooked them and threw them on the table. "Here, wife, broil me a couple of these for breakfast. Ah! What's this I smell?" He looked all around him and said:

29   "Fee fi fo fum,
I smell the blood of an Englishman.
If he's alive or if he's dead,
I'll use his bones to grind my bread."

30   "Nonsense, dear, you must be dreaming," said his wife. "Here, go and wash up and by the time you come back, your breakfast will be ready."

31   Jack was just about to jump out of the oven and run away when the woman told him not to. "Wait until he has his nap," she said.

32   With a great deal of munching and licking of lips, the ogre ate the calfs. Then he went to a big chest and took from it two bags of gold. Down he sat and counted the gold until his head began to nod and his snores shook the house.

33   Jack crept out of the oven and grabbed one of the bags of gold. Off he ran as fast as his legs would carry him. When he reached

the beanstalk, he threw the bag of gold into his mother's garden and climbed down himself. Down and down and down he climbed until he was home. "See, Mother," he said, handing her the bag of gold. "The beans were magic and that's all there is to it."

34 Jack and his mother lived on the bag of gold for some time, but at last they came to the end of it. With hunger gnawing at his belly, Jack made up his mind to try his luck at the top of the beanstalk again.

35 On a fine morning he woke up early and got onto the beanstalk from his window. He climbed and he climbed and he climbed until he came out on the road again. Then he walked along and walked along until he saw the great big tall woman standing on her doorstep.

36 "Good morning, ma'am," said Jack, bold as you please. "Could you be so kind as to give me something to eat?"

37 "Go away, my boy," the big tall woman said, "or else my man will have you for breakfast." Then she drew back and looked Jack in the eye. "But aren't you the same lad who came here once before? Do you know, that very day my man missed one of his bags of gold."

38 "That's strange, ma'am," said Jack. "I daresay I could tell you something about it, but I'm so hungry I can't speak."

39 Well, the big tall woman was so curious that she took him into her kitchen and gave him some food. Scarcely had Jack begun to eat when—*thump! thump! thump!*—they heard the giant's footsteps.

40 "Quick! Into the oven with you!" said his wife.

41 In came the giant, sniffing the air and looking all around him. "Fee fi fo fum, I smell the blood of an Englishman," he said as he had the first time. His wife did not let on that Jack was there, but broiled three oxen for his breakfast.

42 Then the giant said, "Wife, bring me the hen that lays the golden eggs." When she did so, the ogre said, "Lay!" and the hen laid an egg of solid gold. Now it was time for his nap. Soon his head began to nod and his snores shook the house.

43 Jack crept out of the oven, caught hold of the golden hen, and was off as fast as his legs could carry him. But this time the

hen gave a cackle that woke the ogre. "Wife," he yelled, "what have you done with my hen?"

44 "Why do you ask, my dear?" she answered.

45 But that was all Jack heard, for he ran off to the beanstalk and climbed down faster than the first time. When he got home he showed his mother the wonderful hen. "Just another creature to feed," she said.

46 Then Jack said to the hen, "Lay!" and it laid an egg of solid gold.

47 Each day Jack told the hen to lay another egg and though she always did so, he still longed for adventure. At last he decided to climb the beanstalk once more. But this time Jack knew better than to go straight to the great big tall house, as the ogre's wife would surely betray him. Instead he waited behind a bush until he saw her come out with a pail of water. Then he dashed into the house and hid himself in the coal scuttle. He had been there for only a short time when he heard *thump! thump! thump!* and the ogre came in with his wife.

48 "Fee fi fo fum, I smell the blood of an Englishman!" cried the giant in a rage. "I smell him, wife! I smell him!"

49 "Do you, my dear?" she answered. "If it's that same lad who stole your bag of gold and the hen that laid the golden egg, he's sure to be in the oven." They both rushed there at once, but of course Jack wasn't there.

50 So the ogre sat down to breakfast, but every now and then he muttered, "Well, I could have sworn . . ." and he got up and searched the larder and the cupboards and looked behind the door. But he never thought of the coal scuttle.

51 After he had eaten, the ogre called out, "Wife, wife, bring me my golden harp." So she brought it and set it on the table before him. Then the ogre said, "Sing!" and the harp sang and went on singing until the ogre fell asleep.

52 As soon as the ogre's snores began to shake the house, Jack lifted the lid of the coal scuttle and crept on his hands and knees over to the table. Quickly he took the golden harp, then dashed toward the door. But the harp called out loudly, "Master! Master!" and the ogre woke in time to see Jack running off with his harp.

53   Jack ran as fast as he could and the ogre came rushing after. Closer and closer he came until Jack could feel his hot breath burning him. But Jack ran down the long broad road and swung himself onto the beanstalk. The giant hesitated, for he did not like to trust himself to such a spindly plant. But the harp called again, "Master! Master!" and the ogre followed Jack down.

54   The beanstalk trembled and swayed beneath the ogre's weight. Jack was sorely frightened, but he was almost home now and could see his mother standing in the garden. "Mother! Mother!" he called out. "Bring an axe! Bring an axe!"

55   She came rushing up with the axe in her hands. Then she saw the ogre's legs just coming through the clouds and stood stock-still with terror.

56   But Jack jumped down and got hold of the axe and swung it at the beanstalk with all his might. With two chops the beanstalk was cut in two. The giant held on for dear life, but it was no use; he was dead as soon as he hit the ground. Then Jack and his mother buried the giant and the beanstalk with him.

57   They became very rich from selling the golden eggs and making the golden harp play for the curious. Jack's mother's scolding tongue was still and all their days were happy.

Journal Entry

List in the order that they occur Jack's actions in the story.

Example: 1. Trades cow for beans

2. Climbs beanstalk

and so on.

Questions for Discussion

1. J. C. Cooper identifies one function of the trickster as a symbol of the underdog, often small in size or young in years, who overcomes his or her situation in life. In what ways does Jack fit this view of the trickster?

2. What aspects of the trickster that are identified in the introduction to this chapter can you identify in this story?

3. Jack changes as the story progresses. How would you describe him at the beginning of the tale? What character changes does he undergo as a result of his trips up the beanstalk?

4. Based on his actions in this story, do you think Jack is an admirable character? Why or why not?

5. In some versions, a fairy reveals to Jack that an ogre murdered Jack's father and stole all of the family's wealth; the fairy then commands Jack to recover the family's stolen items and to avenge his father's death. In these versions, the fairy is responsible for giving Jack the magic beans. Would inclusion of the fairy's information about the ogre's actions against Jack's father and family change your view of Jack? Explain.

6. How are women portrayed in the story? How are women treated? How do they act? How do they react to others?

7. This story, in some form or another, has been told or read to children for many years. What lessons about life, growing up, and so on, do you think it teaches children?

THE STORY OF
BALDER THE BEAUTIFUL

E. M. Wilmot-Buxton

About the Reading

Loki is the trickster figure of Norse (Scandinavian) mythology. As Norse mythology tends to be serious in tone, Loki is no light-hearted prank-player, but a jealous disrupter of the happiness of others. Ultimately, Loki is set upon by the other Norse gods, who drive him out of Asgard (the Norse version of Heaven) and arrange that he will be punished into eternity for his many evil deeds. In "The Story of Balder the Beautiful," Loki commits the most terrible of his crimes, the act which leads to his terrible punishment. This version of Loki's tale appears in volume three of *The Junior Classics* (1938), edited by E. M. Wilmot-Buxton.

Before You Read

Jealousy is an unpleasant emotion, although it is one which we have all experienced. This ancient story focuses on great jealousy—jealousy so great that it leads to murder. The story becomes even more terrible in that Hoder, because of his desire to fit in, becomes Loki's unwitting tool and kills his own brother. One of this story's major themes—someone who is so jealous that he exploits another person's weakness to achieve his own aims—appears throughout literature as well as in real life. Can you think of books or news stories which you have read, or films which you have seen, in which this theme appears?

As You Read

1. This story strongly contrasts Balder and Loki. Notice all of the positive qualities of Balder which the story emphasizes, and then look for its emphasis on the corresponding negative qualities which Loki possesses.

2. This story uses the literary device of *foreshadowing*, the suggestion of a future event toward which the story inevitably moves. Notice all of the information about the death of Balder which is presented as the story opens. In particular, watch how the story builds to its climax and then quickly tapers off.

---

1   Fair beyond all the sons of Odin was Balder the Beautiful, Balder of the snow-white brow and golden locks, and he was well beloved not only by the Asa folk, but also by the men of the earth below.

2   Balder had a twin brother named Hoder, who was born blind. Gloomy and silent was he, but none the less he loved his bright sun-brother best of all in heaven or earth.

3   The home of Balder was a palace with silver roof and pillars of gold, and nothing unclean or impure was allowed to come inside its doors.

4   Very wise in all magic charms was this radiant young god; and for all others save himself he could read the future; but "to keep his own life safe and see the sun" was not granted to him.

5   Now there came a time when Balder's bright face grew sad and downcast; and when his father Odin and his mother Frigga perceived this they implored him to tell them the cause of his grief. Then Balder told them that he had been troubled by strange dreams; and, since in those days men believed that dreams were sent as a warning of what was about to happen, he had gone heavily since these visions had come to him.

6   First he had dreamt that a dark cloud had arisen which came before the sun and shut out all brightness from the land.

7   The next night he dreamt that Asgard lay in darkness and that her bright flowers and radiant trees were withered and lifeless, and that the Asa folk, dull and withered also, were sorrowing as though from some great calamity.

8   The third night he dreamt yet again that Asgard was dark and lifeless and that from out of the gloom one sad voice cried:

9   "Woe! Woe! Woe! For Balder the Beautiful is dead—is dead!"

10   Odin listened to the recital of this story with heavy heart, and at its conclusion he mounted his coal-black horse and rode over many a hard and toilsome road till he came to the dark abode of Hela. And there he saw, to his surprise, that a great banquet was being prepared in the gloomy hall. Dishes of gold were set upon the table and all the couches were covered with the richest silken tapestry, as though some honored guest were expected. But a throne that stood at the head of the table was empty.

11   Very thoughtfully Odin rode on through those dim halls, till he came to one where dwelt an ancient prophetess whose voice no man had heard for many a long year.

12   Silent he stood before her until she asked in a voice that sounded as though it came from far away: "Who art thou, and from whence dost thou come to trouble my long rest?"

13   Now Odin was fearful that she would not answer him did he give his real name, so he told her that he was the son of Valtam, and asked anxiously for whom the grim goddess of death was preparing her banquet.

14   Then, to his great grief, the hollow voice of the prophetess replied that Balder was the expected guest, and he would shortly be sent thither, slain by the hand of Hoder, the blind god of darkness.

15   And learning thus of the fate of his two favorite sons, All-Father Odin went sadly back to Asgard.

16   Meantime Mother Frigga had not been idle. Filled with anxiety for her darling son, she decided to send her servants throughout the earth, bidding them exact a promise from all things—not only living creatures, but plants, stones, and metals, fire, water,

trees and diseases of all kinds—that they would do harm in no way to Balder the Beautiful.

17 Theirs was an easy task, for all things loved the bright Sun-god and readily agreed to give the pledge. Nothing was overlooked, save only the mistletoe growing upon the oak tree that shaded the entrance of Valhalla. It seemed so insignificant that no one thought it worth while to ask this plant to take the oath.

18 The servants returned to Frigga with all the vows and compacts that had been made; and the Mother of Gods and Men went back with heart at ease to her spinning wheel.

19 The Asa folk, too, were reassured, and, casting aside the burden of care that had fallen upon them, they resumed their favorite game upon the plains of Idavold, where they were wont to contend with one another in the throwing of golden disks.

20 And when it became known among them that nothing would hurt Balder the Beautiful they invented a new game.

21 Placing the young Sun-god in their midst they would throw stones at him, or thrust at him with their knives, or strike with their wooden staves; and the wood or the knife or the stone would glance off from Balder and leave him quite unhurt.

22 This new game delighted both Balder and the Asa folk, and so loud was their laughter that Loki, who was some distance away pursuing one of his schemes in the disguise of an old woman, shook with rage at the sound. For Loki was jealous of Balder and, as is usual with people who make themselves disliked, nothing gave him such displeasure as to see a group of the Asas on such happy terms with each other.

23 Presently in his wanderings Loki passed by the house of Fensalir, in the doorway of which sat Frigga, at her spinning wheel. She did not recognize Red Loki but greeted him kindly and asked:

24 "Old woman, dost thou know why the gods are so merry this evening?"

25 And Loki answered: "They are casting stones and throwing sharp knives and great clubs at Balder the Beautiful, who stands smiling in their midst daring them to hurt him."

26 Then Frigga smiled tranquilly and turned again to her wheel, saying: "Let them play on, for no harm will come to him whom all things in heaven and earth have sworn not to hurt."

27   "Art thou sure, good mother, that *all* things in heaven and earth have taken this vow?"

28   "Ay, indeed," replied Frigga, "all save a harmless little plant, the mistletoe, which grows on the oak by Valhalla, and this is far too small and weak to be feared."

29   And to this Loki replied in musing voice, nodding his head as he spoke: "Yea, thou art right, great Mother of Gods and Men."

30   But the wicked Asa had learnt what he desired to know. The instrument by which he might bring harm to Balder the Beautiful was now awaiting him, and he determined to use it to the dire sorrow of Asgard.

31   Hastening to the western gate of Valhalla, he pulled a clump of the mistletoe from the oak, and fashioned therefrom a little wand, or stick, and with this in his hand he returned to the plain of Idavold. He was far too cunning, however, to attempt to carry out his wicked design himself. His malicious heart was too well known to the Asa folk. But he soon found an innocent tool. Leaning against a tree and taking no part in the game was Hoder, the blind god, the twin brother of Balder, and to him he began:

32   "Hark to the Asas—how they laugh! Do you take no share in the game, good Hoder?"

33   "Not I," said Hoder gloomily, "for I am blind, and know not where to throw."

34   "I could show you that," said Loki, assuming a pleasant tone; "'tis no hard matter, Hoder, and methinks the Asas will call you proud and haughty if you take no share in the fun."

35   "But I have nothing to throw," said poor blind Hoder.

36   Then Loki said: "Here, at least, is a small shaft, 'twill serve your purpose," and leading innocent Hoder into the ring he cunningly guided his aim. Hoder, well pleased to be able to share in a game with his beloved brother, boldly sped the shaft, expecting to hear the usual shouts of laughter which greeted all such attempts. There fell instead dead silence on his ear, and immediately on this followed a wail of bitter agony. For Balder the Beautiful had fallen dead without a groan, his heart transfixed by the little dart of mistletoe.

———————

Journal Entry

One characteristic of Norse mythology is that the Norse gods are not all-powerful. For example, Balder, the sun-god, dreams of his own death but cannot prevent it. List some of the other Asa folk mentioned in this story (Frigga, Hoder, Odin, and Loki himself, for example) and explain how these gods prove themselves to be less than all-powerful.

Questions for Discussion

1. "The Story of Balder the Beautiful," like the Biblical story of Cain and Abel, concerns the death of one brother at the hands of the other. If you know the Biblical story, explain the major difference between the two stories. Are there any similarities?

2. Hoder is described as an "innocent tool" in Loki's scheme. His literal blindness is one reason why Loki can make use of Hoder. In what other important way is Hoder "blind"?

3. Loki deliberately plots the death of Balder because he is jealous. Why is he jealous of the sun-god?

4. Many of the occurrences in this story are not totally unexpected. The story contains information which hints at what will eventually happen. The hints, or predictors of what will follow, constitute a literary device called *foreshadowing*. What examples of foreshadowing can you identify in this story?

5. Although Frigga considers the mistletoe too insignificant to harm Balder, Loki is quick to take advantage of its importance as well as its power to do harm. As the stories of mythology were originally intended to teach human beings important truths, what are the lessons of "The Story of Balder the Beautiful"?

6. Although this story is primarily one in which Loki, as trickster, exercises his powers of destruction, is there any evidence of his powers of creation?

WINABIJOU LOOKS FOR THE WOLF

John Pete

About the Reading

Winabijou, also known as Nanabush or Manabozho or by a number of other names, is a trickster figure in the folklore of North American Indian tribes. In a classic Chippewa creation story, Winabijou is responsible for bringing on a huge flood, much like the flood in the Biblical story of Noah. The version which follows was collected in 1946 by Richard M. Dorson, to whom it was told in Ojibwa by John Pete and translated by George Cadotte, residents of the Watersmeet reservation in Michigan. This story appears in *Folktales Told Around the World* (1975), edited by Richard M. Dorson.

Before You Read

A creation story, as its name suggests, explains the creation of the world and its inhabitants. Every culture and/or religion has its own creation story to explain the origins of things. What creation story or stories are you familiar with? What sorts of elements might you expect a creation story to contain?

As You Read

1. The *plot*, or story line, of this selection turns on Winabijou's desire for revenge against the gods for the death of his brother, the Wolf. Watch carefully for ways in which this myth teaches its listeners not only about the creation of the world but also about concepts such as loyalty and revenge.

2. Like many trickster stories, this one is deeply *paradoxical* (contradictory); out of destruction comes creation. Watch for the *turning point* of the story, where there is less emphasis on revenge and more on explaining how the world came to be ready for habitation.

---

1   The Wolf was Winabijou's adopted brother, and killed meat for him, always moose. The other animals had to dry it, hang it up, and smoke it, and that displeased their friends the gods. So one day the gods thought they'd get him. They enticed him to take a trail across the river, he fell through a hole in the ice and was swimming near the entrance of their cave down below, and they grabbed ahold of him. They kept him captive quite a while, then killed him.

2   Next morning Winabijou started out to look for him. The trails of the previous hunts led home, but he finally struck one which led to the hole in the ice. Then he started to cry, and tears fell down his cheeks. Now he wanted revenge, so he wished that the Thunders (the good gods) would send the summer warmth right away, to bring the Serpents (the bad gods) up from their cave. In four days, the ice melted and the river began to flow.

3   Then he started searching the river for likely remains. He looked up and saw a kingfisher sitting on a sharp cliff, looking down at a pool of water. Every once in a while he'd see the fragments of the Wolf and sneak down and get them. Winabijou asked the kingfisher why he was looking so intently. Finally the kingfisher told him that he was eating the Wolf who had been killed by the gods in a cave close by, underneath the ground. Winabijou wanted to know if they ever came out of there to travel around. "Yes, they come out to bask in the sun in a clearing, but they are closely guarded by snakes and birds and turtles, so it is hard to surprise them." Winabijou said he would pay him for that information, and he gave him a necklace of shells which had belonged to the Wolf. That is why the kingfisher has a white band around his neck today.

4   But Winabijou was angry because the kingfisher had been eating part of his brother. So he asked him to come down and sit beside him, so he could ask some more questions. But Winabijou really wanted to twist his neck. When he grabbed at him the

kingfisher flew away, and Winabijou just caught a tuft of hair. So now the kingfisher's head has a tuft sticking up.

5   Next day Winabijou asked for good hot weather to bring the gods out. He was at the pool way ahead of daylight, and started making a bow and arrow and spears. He wanted the water boiling hot, and sure enough it started to steam. But the gods have many sentinels, and they showed up first—lizards, snakes, crocodiles. They stretched out on the grass: "We'll have a good sleep here." Winabijou turned himself into a charred stump, an old hemlock stump, quite high. Pretty soon the gods came up, in the shape of bears. One was a big brown bear, the other was a white one. The sentinels said to them, "Everything is prepared for you to bask here." Brown bear looked around—"I've never noticed that stump before." "Oh yes, that's been there." "Oh no, I'm going over to see." So he walked over there and clawed the charred stump from the top down, scraping the bark off. After the fourth time the bear walked off, saying "No, that's a stump." Winabijou was afraid he couldn't stand that clawing and would scream out. He kept his bow right against his body, so it wouldn't be seen. The sentinels kept arguing back and forth. "That's a stump." "No, it isn't a stump." Finally the big black boa constrictor walked over and wrapped himself around it three or four times, and started to tighten up. Winabijou didn't dare make a move, but he was just about choked up when the snake let go. The boa constrictor said, "That's a stump."

6   "Well, we're all going to have a sleep." But one little turtle wasn't satisfied, kept looking at the stump to see it move. Finally he went to sleep too. So Winabijou came over and shot the brown bear with the speared arrow, right under the forepaw, in the vitals. The bear went "Poh." Then he shot the white bear, saying "You're the ones that ate my brother up." All the animals jumped into the river, afraid, and dug for their cave. The bears went with them, the arrows still sticking in them; they weren't killed outright.

7   Winabijou goes off on his wanderings again. He put a reed around his head to disguise himself. An old toad-lady comes along, carrying a lot of basswood bark. She was inquisitive and accused

him, "You are Winabijou." "No, I'm not Winabijou," he said in a singsong voice. "Don't you know what would happen to us if I were Winabijou?" He was trying to trick her into answering, he wanted to find out all she knew. She began singing, "Winabijou shot the Ogema (the gods), I'm going to draw the spears out of their sides." He tried to find out more and asked her, "What are you going to do with all that basswood?" She said, "We're going to tie up the earth with it, and string it around the world like telephone wires. When Winabijou touches the strings, the gods will know where he is and ask for water, to flood him out."

8   She kept suspecting he was Winabijou, and turned to go. So he picked up part of a root, hit her on the head, and killed her. (The blow knocked her swelling down, so the toad is little today; he used to be big like the other animals.) Then he cut the inside out of her and put on her hide and clothes, and went on to the kings' place. They lived in a regular wigwam now, above ground, for the summer. The sentries saw him and thought he was the old toad, and told him the kings were in bad shape, and he should come along right away. Winabijou sang a song like the old woman, "I'm going to draw out the arrows." Then he said, "I'm going to do it different this time. Everybody get out, I'm going to do it all alone. It's getting serious now."

9   When he was alone with the kings he grabbed the arrows and pushed them further inside, tearing and twisting until he had killed them. "You are the ones who killed my brother!" he said as they lay there dying.

10   He noticed the Wolf's hide over the door so he took it along with him. When he came out they all knew right away who he was. The flood started. Winabijou kept running on higher land, but the water followed him. He saw a badger and asked him to dig a hole where they could hide, and promised to paint him up nice. (Like with lipstick. The badger has stripes across his face today, you know.) But in the hole the badger made a vile smell, so Winabijou got mad and killed him. Then he had to go on again.

11   Every time he got to a higher level the water rose some more. Finally he reached the summit of a hill where a big pine tree was standing. He asked it if he could find refuge there, by sitting on

the branch. The tree said, "That's what you get for all your wrongdoing. Now the gods are mad at us and we'll all perish." But he let Winabijou climb up the branches to the top. The water rose up to his mouth. He asked the pine tree, "Can't you stretch a little?" The tree stretched four times its own height. "That's all I can do for you." The water rose again till it came up to his mouth, and stayed there. Winabijou sat on a branch holding on to the treetop with his hands, just able to breathe above water. He had to evacuate, and an evil current floated his stuff back to him, so he had to keep blowing it away as it swirled around the tree. That was part of his punishment for his killing of the gods.

12   Now the water animals showed up. They had nowhere to go, because the land was all covered with water, and they were tired swimming around. So Winabijou asked the loon to dive down and bring him up some earth. The loon went down and stayed a long while; then his body came up feet first, drowned. Winabijou blew on him to revive him. Next to go down was the otter. He was gone quite a little while, and drowned too. Winabijou brought him to life by breathing on him. Next to go down was the muskrat. He was the longest of any. All he could do was grab with both paws and feet on the bottom, and was lucky enough to hang on to some earth. He floated up drowned, but still had the earth in his paws and feet. Winabijou blew on him too to bring him back. Then Winabijou took the earth, dried it out in the sun, and threw it out over the water. It turned out to be a little island.

13   All the water animals went there to make their home. In order to reward them he told them what they could eat—the muskrat could eat rushes, the loon could eat muck from the bottom, the otter could eat fish. Then he sent the fox around the island to see how big it was. The first day he came back early in the morning. The second day he came back a little later. After a week or so he didn't come back until late in the afternoon. On the tenth day he didn't come back at all. (That's why you often see a fox trotting alongside the shore today.) Then Winabijou knew the world was ready for living. He called to the gods above and below to come down and live on this earth. That's Christ and the Devil. He wanted them to be in trouble.

Journal Entry

Folklorist Paul Radin describes Winabijou as "both creator and destroyer." Draw a line down the middle of your paper. On the left side of the paper, list the details in this story which exemplify this trickster's creative side. On the right, list details which illustrate his destructive side.

Questions for Discussion

1. If you are familiar with the Biblical story of Noah or any other "flood stories," what similar elements do you find in the Winabijou tale? What are the differences?

2. In a number of cultures, trickster stories are used to explain natural phenomena, such as how the fox got its tail or why the sun rises in the east. What animal characteristics are explained in "Winabijou Looks for the Wolf"?

3. Is Winabijou supposed to be an admirable character or not? Explain your answer.

4. While the trickster tale cycles of the North American Indians are ancient, this version is a fairly modern retelling which includes elements not in the original. How can you tell that this is a fairly modern version? What non-Indian items are referenced?

5. What elements of the trickster that are identified in the introduction to this chapter can you identify in this story?

ANANSI BORROWS MONEY AND THE HAT-SHAKING DANCE

Harold Courlander

About the Reading

Anansi the spider is the West African trickster figure of the Ashanti people in Ghana. Anansi is also known in the Caribbean as Anancy, Nancy, Sis' Nancy, or Aunt Nancy. Anansi sometimes takes on human shape. In some African stories, Anansi assumes the shape of an old man; in the Antilles he becomes a young man. In addition to explaining how the spider's appearance and behavior came about, Anansi stories typically explain something that occurs in the world: characteristics of other animals or of plants, the relationship of the earth to the heavens, the peculiarities of human behavior and so on. Anansi does not always triumph in the tales, and often there is a moral to his defeat or embarrassment. The two very short tales included here, "Anansi Borrows Money" and "The Hat-Shaking Dance," are both folk tales from Africa collected by Harold Courlander in A *Treasury of African Folklore* (1975).

Before You Read

The desire to know why the world is as it is and why things happen as they do seems to be inborn in us. Both of these short Anansi stories respond to that need; both explain natural phenomena—why some aspect of nature is as it is—and they do so in an entertaining as well as an informative way. The quality by which Anansi can be easily identified, his characteristic desire to outsmart others, remains consistent whether the story explains why snakes turn belly-up when they die, or why spiders are bald. What natural mysteries fascinated you as a child or still fascinate you now? What kinds of explanations for natural phenomena did you like hearing or did you make up for yourself?

As You Read

1. Although many cultures have stories which explain natural phenomena, these Anansi stories are clearly African in origin. Notice the specific details contained in these stories which set them firmly in time and place, and which explain not only natural phenomena but also culturally accepted practices and attitudes.

2. Attributing human characteristics to nonhumans is called *anthropomorphism,* and it is not especially surprising that humans should attribute human thoughts and behaviors to animals. Watch for ways in which these stories express anthropomorphism in speech and in behavior.

Anansi Borrows Money

1   It happened once that Anansi needed money. He went to his neighbors for help, but because of his bad reputation, no one would lend him anything. He went to the leopard and the bush cow, but they refused him. He went to the guinea fowl, the turtle and the hawk, but they all refused him. Then he went to a distant village where Owoh, the snake, lived. Owoh lent him the money he needed, on condition that it would be returned by the end of twenty-one days.

2   But when twenty-one days had passed, Anansi had no money to repay the loan. He began to think of ways to get out of his predicament. He went to his garden and dug up a basket full of yams. He put the basket on his head and carried it to the house of Owoh, the snake.

3   He said to Owoh: "This is the day I was to repay the money you lent me. But there is a small complication. I won't have the money for two or three days yet, and I hope you will be kind enough to wait. In the meanwhile, I have brought some yams to share with you in gratitude for your help."

4   Anansi used many sweetened words, and the snake agreed to wait three more days for his money. Of the yams he had brought, Anansi gave half to the snake. Owoh shared his portion with his friends. Anansi kept his portion in the basket. Owoh treated Anansi with great hospitality and invited him to stay overnight in his house. So Anansi stayed.

5   But in the middle of the night Anansi arose from his sleeping mat quietly and went out. He took the yams he had saved for himself away from the house. He carried them into the bush and hid them in the ground. When he returned, he placed his empty basket in front of the house and went back to sleep.

6   In the morning he came out and said to Owoh, "Where are my yams?" But Owoh knew nothing about the yams. So Anansi took his empty basket and returned home. He went to the headman of the district to make a complaint that his yams had been stolen. The people of the district were very concerned. They said to each other, "What kind of a thief is it who would steal yams from someone who has been as generous as Anansi?"

7   The headman called for a trial to find the guilty person. The people of all the villages came. Anansi said to them: "There is only one test to prove innocence. I have a magic knife. I will draw it across the skin of each person. It will not cut those who are innocent of this crime. It will cut only those who are guilty."

8   Then each of the animals came forward for the test. When the guinea fowl came, Anansi drew his knife across the guinea fowl's skin, but he used the blunt edge instead of the sharp edge. He did the same with the turtle, the rabbit, and the other animals. No one was hurt. When the snake's turn came, he said, "Test me."

9   But Anansi refused, saying: "Oh, no. It is unthinkable that you who have been so good as to lend me money would steal my yams." But Owoh insisted, saying: "I also must have my turn. You were in my house when the yams were stolen. All the others have taken the test. I, too, must prove my innocence." Anansi protested that it was unnecessary, and Owoh protested that he must be cleared of any suspicion of guilt.

10   "Very well," Anansi said at last. "Since it is your wish, I will let you take the test."

11   So Anansi drew his knife across the skin of Owoh, but this time he used not the blunt edge but the sharpened edge, and he killed him. The people said, "He has failed the test; he must be guilty!"

12   As Owoh died, however, he rolled on his back, turning his belly to the sky, as if to say: "Oh, God, look at my belly and see whether I have eaten Anansi's yams!"

13   It is for this reason that whenever a snake is killed, he turns his belly to the sky, calling upon God to judge his innocence.

The Hat-Shaking Dance

1   If you look closely, you will see that Anansi has a bald head. It is said that in the old days he had hair, but that he lost it through vanity.

2   It happened that Anansi's mother-in-law died. When word came to Anansi's house, Aso, his wife, prepared to go at once to her own village for the funeral. But Anansi said to Aso, "You go ahead; I will follow."

3   When Aso had gone, Anansi said to himself: "When I go to my dead mother-in-law's house, I will have to show great grief over her death. I will have to refuse to eat. Therefore, I shall eat now." And so he sat in his own house and ate a huge meal. Then he put on his mourning clothes and went to Aso's village.

4   First there was the funeral. Afterwards there was a large feast. But Anansi refused to eat, out of respect for his wife's dead mother. He said: "What kind of man would I be to eat when I am mourning for my mother-in-law? I will eat only after the eighth day has passed."

5   Now this was not expected of him, because a person isn't required to starve himself simply because someone has died. But Anansi was the kind of person that when he ate, he ate twice as much as others, and when he danced, he danced more vigorously than others, and when he mourned, he had to mourn more loudly than anybody else. Whatever he did, he didn't want to be outdone by anyone else. And although he was very hungry, he couldn't bear to have people think he wasn't the greatest mourner at his own mother-in-law's funeral.

6 So he said, "Feed my friends, but as for me, I shall do without." So everyone ate—the porcupine, the rabbit, the snake, the guinea fowl and the others. All except Anansi.

7 On the second day after the funeral they said to him again, "Eat, there is no need to starve."

8 But Anansi replied: "Oh, no, not until the eighth day, when the mourning is over. What kind of person do you think I am?"

9 So the others ate. Anansi's stomach was empty, and he was unhappy.

10 On the third day they said again, "Eat, Anansi, there is no need to go hungry."

11 But Anansi was stubborn. He said, "How can I eat when my wife's mother has been buried only three days?" And so the others ate, while Anansi smelled the food hungrily and suffered.

12 On the fourth day, Anansi was alone where a pot of beans was cooking over the fire. He smelled the beans and looked in the pot. At last he couldn't stand it any longer. He took a large spoon and dipped up a large portion of the beans, thinking to take it to a quiet place and eat it without anyone's knowing. But just then the dog, the guinea fowl, the rabbit, and the others returned to the place where the food was cooking.

13 To hide the beans, Anansi quickly poured them in his hat and put it on his head. The other people came to the pot and ate, saying again, "Anansi, you must eat."

14 He said, "No, what kind of person would I be?"

15 But the hot beans were burning his head. He jiggled his hat back and forth with his hands. When he saw the others looking at him, he said: "Just at this very moment in my village the hat-shaking festival is taking place. I shake my hat in honor of the occasion."

16 The beans felt hotter than ever, and he jiggled his hat some more. He began to jump with pain. He said, "Like this in my village they are doing the hat-shaking dance."

17 He danced about, jiggling his hat because of the heat. He yearned to take off his hat, but he could not because his friends would see the beans. So he shouted: "They are shaking and jiggling the hats in my village, like this! It is a great festival! I must go!"

18 They said to him, "Anansi, eat something before you go."

19   But now Anansi was jumping and writhing with the heat of the beans on his head. He shouted: "Oh, no, they are shaking hats, they are wriggling hats and jumping like this! I must go to my village! They need me!"

20   He rushed out of the house, jumping and pushing his hat back and forth. His friends followed after him saying, "Eat before you go on your journey!"

21   But Anansi shouted, "What kind of person do you think I am, with my mother-in-law just buried?"

22   Even though they all followed right after him, he couldn't wait any longer, because the pain was too much, and he tore the hat from his head. When the dog saw, and the guinea fowl saw, and the rabbit saw, and all the others saw what was in the hat, and saw the hot beans sticking to Anansi's head, they stopped chasing him. They began to laugh and jeer.

23   Anansi was overcome with shame. He leaped into the tall grass, saying, "Hide me." And the grass hid him.

24   That is why Anansi is often found in the tall grass, where he was driven by shame. And you will see that his head is bald, for the hot beans he put in his hat burned off his hair.

25   All this happened because he tried to impress people at his mother-in-law's funeral.

Journal Entry

Draw a picture, devise a cartoon, or make a collage out of pictures cut from magazines to illustrate *one* of the Anansi stories.

Questions for Discussion

1. What aspects of human nature does Anansi exhibit? What is it that gets him into trouble in each of the stories?

2. What characteristics of the trickster that are described at the beginning of this chapter are present in these stories?

prickly pears with the thorns on, and I got stuck all over." And this and that and the other. . . . And that . . .

27 The rabbit said, "I'm here holding up this big rock," he said. "They're going to bring me my dinner here, a great big meal."

28 "No, I just don't believe you any more, rabbit. You're just a big liar."

29 "No, this is the truth," said the rabbit. "Why don't you take my place," he said, "and you'll see." So the coyote took his place and got stuck there holding up the rock.

30 After a while a fox went by, and the coyote said, "Dear little fox, help me hold up this rock."

31 "Who left you there?"

32 "Why, a rabbit."

33 "All right. You are there, you stay there." And, "Feet. . . ." The fox ran off and didn't help him.

34 He managed somehow to get out from under the rock, and he caught up with the rabbit. And the rabbit said, "No, dear little coyote, don't hurt me. Look. See this little stick? I'm a schoolmaster, and these are my pupils. Be sure not to disturb them if I'm not here," he said. "They're going to pay me with a lot of chickens and other food, plenty of it. How can I eat it all? And if I don't eat it, they'll kill me."

35 "Well, I am hungry indeed," said the coyote.

36 "All right, why don't you stay here. And after a long while, one or two hours, you whip them. You whip them two or three times and tell them, 'Study, study.'"

37 The coyote was there for a long time, and nobody brought him chickens or food or anything else, and he said, "It's too quiet in there. I don't hear any sound." He put his ear to the hole and struck three times with his little stick. So out come all the wasps, and you should have seen them go at him. He rolled about in the dirt, and the wasps just. . . . Till he went and jumped into a lake.

38 He went along, and he went along, and he went along, until he caught up with the rabbit again. And he said, "No, little rabbit, you've told me just too many lies. I won't believe you for anything."

39   "No, *hombre*, I swear this is the truth. A policeman just went by and said that anybody who relieves himself in the paths will be thrown in jail or killed."

40   "Oh, little rabbit! I just relieved myself right in the middle of the path."

41   "Well, go clean up." So the coyote went back, but no policemen or anybody came.

42   And then the rabbit got inside a cave, and the coyote came. From a distance he smelled him in the cave, and he went and knocked. But the rabbit kept quiet. Then he said, "Hello there, cave of mine." Nothing. Again, "Hello there, cave of mine. That's strange; when I call, my cave always answers." And he called again. And it answered. So he said, "What the devil! The rabbit's in there." And the coyote ran away.

43   He went away, and then the rabbit said, "What can I do to get rid of this coyote?" He went into a canebrake, and he cleared a spot very well, burned and cleared it all around, and the coyote found him there. The coyote said, "Now I got you, rabbit. This time you won't get away for anything at all." He said, "I'm going to eat you this time. What are you doing there?" He was always asking questions.

44   "I'm waiting for a wedding party. There's going to be a lot to eat, meat and plenty of everything. They'll have a lot of things."

45   "You're not lying to me, rabbit?"

46   "Of course not. When you hear the popping of the fireworks, you shut your eyes and dance and shout." That's because he meant to set fire to the cane all around, and it would pop.

47   "All right, but you'd better not be lying to me. I won't let you off again." Well, so the rabbit went off, but to set fire all around. The cane was thick, and it began to burn. And the coyote yelled and yelled and sang and sang, with his eyes shut. Then all of a sudden he felt the heat. Well, like it or not, he had to run through the fire. And he got out of it, anyway.

48   The rabbit was by the edge of a lake, looking at the moon on the water. The coyote came and said that now he had him and all that, and just look, it had been a bunch of lies, there was a big fire, and I don't know what.

49   "No, dear little coyote; it was the truth. I just don't know what happened. Some accident, perhaps."

50   "And now, what are you doing there?" the coyote said.

51   He said, "You know what I'm doing? I'm looking at that beautiful cheese in there. But I'm so little. If I go in after it, I'll drown."

52   "Is it a cheese?" the coyote said.

53   "Yes, it is," he said, "of course."

54   So the coyote jumped in the lake. And the coyote said, "I can't get to it."

55   "Dive deeper."

56   "I can't get to it."

57   "Dive deeper."

58   "I can't get to it."

59   "You'd better come out so I can tie a stone to you. Then, you can go all the way to the bottom, and you will get to it."

60   So the coyote died there. The rabbit tied a stone to him, and he went all the way down to the bottom. But he drowned and never came out again.

61   And *colorín* [1] so red, the story is finished.

Journal Entry

The story ends with the episode in which the rabbit drowns the coyote. Write an alternative ending in which the coyote tricks the rabbit and gets revenge instead.

Questions for Discussion

1. In what ways does the rabbit reflect the traits of the trickster listed in the introduction to this chapter?

---

[1] Shiny red seeds that were used by Mexican water carriers to count the number of trips they made delivering water to each house. A seed was left with the housewife for each trip. Its use as a counter may be related to the use of *colorín* to signal the formal ending to the story.

2. The rabbit is not the first character to introduce trickery in this story. What is the first trick played? Why does it work so well?

3. Compare the rabbit in this story to the other animal tale tricksters in this chapter, Winabijou and Anansi. How are they similar? How is the rabbit different from the others?

4. Is the rabbit an admirable character? Why or why not?

5. As "About the Reading" indicates, this story was an oral tale which was copied down as told by the storyteller. What clues are there in the selection that reflect this fact? Do you think the story might be "improved" with a little editing? If so, what would you change? If not, explain why.

SI' DJEHA CHEATS THE ROBBERS

Inea Bushnaq

About the Reading

The figure of Si' Djeha is well-known in North African folklore as a mischief maker. Often harsh and cruel in his mischief, Si' Djeha usually begins as a dupe of others but then exacts a cunning revenge on his enemies. Like many of these stories, "Si' Djeha Cheats the Robbers" relates a chain of events rather than focusing on one single episode. This version, which is from Algeria, was translated by Inea Bushnaq and included in her collection of *Arab Folktales*.

Before You Read

Many cultures expect people to take action if a wrong is done to them, to their families, or to members of their group, and many pieces of literature reflect this code of behavior. As in many trickster tales, in this story revenge is a motivating force in the story's action. Think about a time when the desire for revenge affected you. Perhaps you wanted to get revenge for something that happened to you, or perhaps you observed a person who just wouldn't let a matter drop even though the desire to get back at someone only made the original problem worse. Why do you think people so strongly feel the need to revenge a wrong?

As You Read

1. Pay careful attention to the qualities of this story which mark it as belonging to a written rather than an oral tradition. Watch for clues to its literary characteristics: adjectives such as "hollow-sided," word choice such as "tethering," and the contrast between the *tone* (mood and style) of the dialogue spoken by the characters and the *omniscient* (detached from the action but all-seeing and all-knowing) voice of the narrator.

2. Although this story turns on an ever-escalating desire for revenge on the parts of both the main character and the four robbers, it also gives the reader insight into the habits and beliefs associated with Arab culture. Notice how the story teaches or reminds its reader of culturally acceptable lessons about hospitality, revenge, good manners, greed, and the appropriate role and behavior of women.

---

1 One day Si' Djeha was riding the fine white mule his father had left him when he died. As he rode, he happened to meet four men, robbers by profession, leading a hollow-sided little donkey to market.

2 "Si' Djeha!" they called. "You are mad to risk your life on that mule! What if you should fall? You would break your head dropping from that height. Look, we have a neatly built little donkey here, a safer animal by far."

3 "What you say is true, by Allah," said Si' Djeha.

4 "Ha! But what will you give us for the exchange?"

5 "Do I owe you anything?"

6 "Si' Djeha, have some shame," said the robbers, "here we are saving your life, and you begrudge us fair payment."

7 "What you say is right," said Si' Djeha. "Tell me what I should give you."

8 "What does the amount matter among generous men? But since you are dear to us, we will content ourselves with one hundred silver pieces." So Si' Djeha dismounted, paid the money, and rode the puny little donkey home.

9 When she saw him tethering the donkey in the yard, Si' Djeha's mother shouted to him, "Where is your father's mule, child?" "I was afraid that if I fell off its back, I might get killed and leave you with no one to look after you. So I exchanged it and one hundred pieces of silver for this donkey."

10 "May Allah forgive you your foolishness," sighed his mother. "If you don't show a little more sense, we shall surely be ruined."

11   When the next market day came round, Si' Djeha decided to take his donkey to town. But before he went, he glued a few gold coins under the donkey's tail. As he entered the *suq* he met the four robbers again. "Greetings, O my benefactors, may Allah increase your fortunes!" he hailed them. "I praise God and thank Him every hour for causing me to make your acquaintance." "Why, O Si' Djeha?" asked the robbers. "Because of your donkey, of course! The thorny cactus is sweet inside, but who would have guessed that an ordinary donkey, no different from any other except for his lankness, drops nothing but gold coin!" "A thing not to be believed!" said the robbers, and they walked alongside Si' Djeha to the stable where he had tied the donkey. There they saw for themselves the gold pieces on the animal's flanks, and they bit their fingers in remorse.

12   They began to blame each other and quarrel in whispers. Then they cried, "May Allah reward you with nothing but good, Si' Djeha, if only you will let us have our donkey back! Take your mule and the hundred pieces of silver." But Si' Djeha refused. The men begged him again and offered him more silver. At last when they promised to return the mule with two hundred pieces of silver, Si' Djeha consented. "Be sure to feed him well, and spread rugs beneath him to catch the gold," he said as they led the donkey away.

13   The first of the robbers to have the use of the donkey ran home, took his sickle down, and cut a whole field of grass. Bringing the fodder into the stable, he covered the floor with matting and locked the donkey in for safety. All night long the donkey feasted, and in the morning the robber found his carpets full of dung. He was ashamed to seem a fool, so he said nothing to the second robber except, "Enjoy your fortune, brother!" The second robber and the third suffered as the first robber had, and they too remained silent. When the fourth robber turned on them angrily and accused them, "You have taken the gold and left me nothing but the dung!" they realized that they had all been tricked and swore to take their revenge.

14   Now Si' Djeha was expecting to hear from the four men. He bought two roosters and a hen and asked his mother to fry them

in butter and steam a dish of couscous to go with them. When the meal was ready, he put it in a covered bowl and buried it in the earthen floor of his house. "Four men will come to visit me," he told his mother, and he gave her careful instructions what to do when they came.

15   Sure enough, before midday the four robbers came marching up to Si' Djeha's door. "Welcome, O my benefactors!" said Si' Djeha on his doorstep. "You should have sent word that you were intending to honor me thus. Then I might have had time to prepare for you as you deserve. But never mind. I have my Hoe of Hospitality, and it will save me from disgrace." The men were curious to know what he meant, and forgetting what they had come for, followed him into the house.

16   When the guests had been seated for a while, Si' Djeha called, "Mother, I have visitors today; bring me my Hoe of Hospitality." And his mother came in and handed him an old garden hoe as if there were nothing odd about his request. With the robbers watching him attentively, Si' Djeha began to dig at the earthen floor. In the glancing of an eye he uncovered the dish of chicken and couscous. "Come favor us with your company!" he invited his guests, and the fragrance of warm chicken broth filled the room.

17   "Whenever I am surprised by company," explained Si' Djeha after they had eaten, "I never need worry about being unprepared and ill-provided as long as I have this Hoe of Hospitality. Whether my cupboard is full or empty, I know that this tool will enable me to entertain as a good host should. You yourselves saw that the food it brings me is the best." The robbers agreed that, praise be to Allah, they had indeed eaten well. Then one of them uttered the thought that was in all their minds. "Si' Djeha, how much would you sell this useful hoe for?" "It is not for sale," said Si' Djeha shortly. But although he tried to turn the conversation to other things, the robbers kept returning to the hoe. And eventually Si' Djeha parted with it for one hundred silver pieces.

18   "My wife's brother is coming to eat with me tomorrow," said one of the robbers on the way home. "Let me have my turn first." But next day, though he dug until he plowed up the whole floor of his house, he found no covered dish and no warm meal.

On top of that, he was despised by his brother-in-law for being a miserly host.

19   The other three robbers were as disappointed in their expectations of the hoe. When the last of them threatened to take his partners to court for eating all the food and leaving him nothing, they showed him their ruined houses to prove that they too had been duped. "This time we must not let Si' Djeha escape us," they vowed.

20   But this time too, Si' Djeha was ready for them. "I think I shall go and weed the sesame," he said to his wife early in the morning. "If my four friends should come to see me again, send them out to the east field—that's where I shall be working. And as soon as they go, run to the butcher's shop, buy some spring lamb, and help my mother prepare a banquet for our noon meal." Then he picked up his tools and left the house. In the yard there was a sack holding two hares that Si' Djeha had trapped. Before leaving, he took one of them and carried it inside his robe, resting on his belt.

21   Very soon afterwards, the four robbers knocked on the door, talked to Si' Djeha's wife and followed him to his field. "Ho! Si' Djeha!" they called as soon as they could see him. "Come here, we have some things to discuss with you." "He who doesn't work doesn't eat," Si' Djeha shouted back to them. "I cannot stop, brothers." "Our errand is pressing; take a rest," they said when they drew near. "Very well," said Si' Djeha, "but let me send word to my wife to prepare some food for us—it will soon be time to eat." The robbers looked around in astonishment. "Whom do you mean to send?" they asked. "I have a messenger right here," said Si' Djeha, pulling the hare out of his bosom. And as they looked on in disbelief, he set it on the ground, saying, "Go find your mistress and tell her to cook a dish of tender lamb's meat, since we have guests this noon." In a flash the animal disappeared into the thornbushes at the edge of the field.

22   "Do you expect a hare to carry a message?" the robbers asked, laughing. "My father trained him," replied Si' Djeha, "and I am so used to him that I couldn't do without him, especially when I am out here in the fields." And he led the doubting guests to his house, where they found everything hospitably prepared down to the

ewer and bowl for them to wash their hands in rose water. "That hare is certainly a good servant," murmured the robbers. "That he is," said Si' Djeha bringing the second hare in from the yard and patting its neck. "He's a good worker and cheap to feed." "Would you consider selling him?" asked the robbers. "How can I do without him?" said Si' Djeha. "I have neither son nor daughter to send on errands." "Name your price," urged the robbers. And in the end Si' Djeha let them buy the hare for one hundred silver pieces.

23   "This time," said one of the robbers as they set out on the road home, "this time let us not basely suspect each other. Let me send the hare to my house with a message for my wife to cook supper for all four of us, so that we can all try our new messenger at the same time." "That's the best plan," said the others as they watched the hare leaping across the fields before them.

24   But when they came to the first robber's house toward evening, they found that his wife had not even lit her cooking fires. "What is the meaning of this neglect?" the first robber asked his bewildered wife. "Didn't I send instructions with our new messenger for you to have a meal ready when we arrived?" "What messenger?" said the wife. At this the robbers turned on their heels, cursing, and retraced their steps to Si' Djeha's house with murder in their hearts.

25   When they reached Si' Djeha's doorway, a sight met their eyes that left them rooted where they stood, their mouths dry with horror. Si' Djeha was shouting angrily at his wife with a knife raised in his hand. While they watched, the woman fell to the ground with blood on her dress. Forgetting their own troubles, the robbers could only gasp and ask him why he had done this evil deed. "How else can a man control the sour temper of his wife? All I asked for was a glass of water, but she refused me!" Then to their amazement, Si' Djeha touched his wife's wound with the knife and she raised herself up. Standing meekly before him, she asked her husband what he wished. "Brew coffee for our guests," he said, frowning. As soon as she left the room, the robbers questioned Si' Djeha. "What is this miracle that we have witnessed?" "Have you never heard of the knife that kills and brings back to life?" "Never!" said the four men together. "I would

not part with it for half the kingdom," declared Si' Djeha. "Every man married to a quarrelsome wife should have one!"

26   The robbers soon saw proof of the virtues of this singular tool. Wearing a fresh gown, her eyes modestly on the ground like a bride of one month, Si' Djeha's wife carried in a tray of coffee flavored with cardamom. Before they finished drinking the coffee, the robbers had succeeded in buying the knife off Si' Djeha for one hundred pieces of silver.

27   Each in turn used it in his home and discovered just how magical it was. All four robbers were soon tried for murder and never bothered Si' Djeha again.

Journal Entry

Make a chart of "Si' Djeha Cheats the Robbers" listing who tricked, who was tricked, the nature of the trick and the result.* The chart might look like:

Name of Story	Who Tricked?	Who Was Tricked?	Trick	Result

*From *Fairy Tales, Fables, Legends, and Myths: Using Folk Literature in Your Classroom* by Bette Bosma (New York: Teachers College Press, 1987).

Questions for Discussion

1. Trickster tales are often humorous. What humorous elements do you find in this story?

2. What trickster elements listed at the beginning of this chapter do you find in this story?

3. What similarities can you find between this story and "Jack and the Beanstalk," which is also included in this chapter? In what ways is the character of Si' Djeha different from the character of Jack?

4. This story hinges on two motivating forces. One is the desire for revenge. What is the other? What is the root of the communication problem among the robbers?

5. How would you describe the role and importance of women as portrayed in this story?

6. In your opinion, is Si' Djeha an admirable character? Consider especially his last trick and its outcome.

SUGGESTIONS FOR WRITING

Assignment 1

Assume that you have been asked to explain the trickster figure to someone who is not familiar with it. Using information from this chapter, write an essay which defines and illustrates the qualities of the trickster. Be sure to use specific examples taken from the readings.

Strategies for Prewriting and Planning: Drawing on the trickster stories you have read in this chapter, think about the qualities which these figures have in common and list these qualities. Look over your list and select what you consider to be the most important qualities of a trickster. Then find examples from the stories in this chapter which illustrate each of these qualities. For instance, if you decide that playing mean tricks is an important quality of a trickster, you might use the example of Loki's evil deed. Finally try to formulate a one-sentence definition of a trickster; this definition will be your thesis.

Assignment 2

After reading the two Anansi stories in this chapter, write an Anansi story of your own which explains some natural or social phenomenon. You may also wish to include a moral.

Strategies for Prewriting and Planning: There are many things about our world which we take for granted. Some natural phenomena, for example, include the movement of the sun, the migration of birds and animals, and the seasons of the year. Social phenomena might include celebration of birthdays, marriage ceremonies, or sending flowers when someone is ill. Decide on one phenomenon of your choice, either natural or social, which you have observed, and explain it through your Anansi story. Use the stories in this chapter as models. Be sure to end by explaining the lesson of the tale.

Assignment 3

Write an essay arguing that a particular figure in popular culture or folk literature is a trickster. Be sure to give the reasons you think the figure fits the description of the trickster and give specific examples of the figure's behavior to show the reader what you mean.

Strategies for Prewriting and Planning: Drawing on the description of the trickster that appears in the introduction to this chapter, identify a figure in comics, cartoons, movies, advertisements or storybooks that you think qualifies as a trickster figure. List the qualities of the figure and note how these qualities conform to the definition of trickster. Be sure to use specific actions by this figure to illustrate these qualities. For example, in "Jack and the Beanstalk," Jack foolishly trades the family cow for magic beans, yet he turns out to have made a smart move in the end, thus combining the qualities of stupidity and cunning.

Assignment 4

Write an essay contrasting two trickster figures taken either from this chapter or from your own reading or viewing, or from stories you have heard. Show how the two figures you have selected represent different trickster qualities yet are, nevertheless, both tricksters.

Strategies for Prewriting and Planning: Choose two trickster figures that are significantly different. For example, one trickster might be malicious; the other might be merely bumbling and stupid. Or one might be an animal while the other is a human being. First, decide why each character is a trickster. Then make a list of all of the differences between the two figures. Before you begin to write your essay, make sure there are enough differences to develop your essay. In your introduction, tell why both figures are tricksters. In the body of your essay, focus on the differences. Choose *one* of the following methods to organize your essay: (1) subject by subject method—discuss first one figure and then the other; (2) point-by-point method— devote one paragraph to each difference which you have identified. Do *not* combine methods! Be sure to use specific examples to illustrate the differences you discuss.

Assignment 5

Write an essay in which you argue that a particular trickster story should or should not be read to children. Be sure to give reasons why you think as you do.

Strategies for Prewriting and Planning: Reread several trickster stories in this chapter and choose one which you feel is clearly appropriate or inappropriate for a young audience. Look over the story carefully and record the reasons that you feel that this story is a good example of what children should or should not hear. Some issues which you find objectionable, for example, might be violence or deceit. Or you might think such stories are suitable for children if, for example, you believe that these stories teach valuable lessons about life or that they reflect the "real world." These reasons will provide the major points of your essay. Be sure to use specific information from the story to back up these reasons. For example, if you argue that "Jack in the Beanstalk" is too violent for children, you might then include the examples of theft and murder that appear in the story to support your argument.

5

ADVERTISING

Every day we are bombarded by advertisements on billboards, in magazines and newspapers, on television and radio. Even movie theaters are starting to show ads before a feature film, and video rentals now advertise products as well as upcoming films. Despite our constant exposure to ads, however, few of us give much thought to them or to the advertisers responsible for them.

The selections in this chapter examine advertising from several different perspectives, raising a number of issues of which we, as consumers, should be aware. One issue concerns advertising copy, the language used in advertisements to convince us that one product is superior to another when, in fact, it may not be. Another issue is the influence of advertising on American values. The changing ethnic make-up of this country as well as the growing affluence of ethnic consumers has raised the issue of ads directed at specific ethnic markets and changed the look of advertisements in general. Finally, the need for sensitivity towards the "new consumers," a term which includes not only ethnics but also senior citizens and other groups, has also become an issue facing the advertising industry of the 1990s.

PREREADING

Before you begin reading the selections in this chapter, think of an advertisement that sticks in your mind. What is the ad selling? Is the ad targeted toward a specific group of people? If so, which group? Where have you been exposed to the ad—on television, radio, or some other media? What is it about the ad that makes you remember it?

POSTREADING

In what ways have reading the selections in this chapter and applying the strategies for ad analysis made you think differently about advertising and advertisements? Do you look more closely at ads, or have you questioned why you buy certain products? Has your buying behavior changed as a result of your new knowledge?

ADVERTISING CLAIMS

Jeffrey Schrank

About the Reading

Jeffrey Schrank, author of *Snap, Crackle, and Popular Taste: The Illusion of Free Choice in America* (1977), specializes in the fields of communications and popular culture. "Advertising Claims," which is adapted from *Deception Detection* (1975), details ten "common and easy to identify" advertising techniques. Schrank considers these techniques essential to the creation of the "necessary illusion of [product] superiority."

Before You Read

Today we are confronted by so many ads that we often take their presence for granted and give them little thought; we rarely take the time to read the ad copy. Take a few minutes before you read this piece to look through a magazine and carefully study the wording used in several ads. What claims do the advertisers make for their products?

As You Read

1. Before he begins pointing out linguistic tricks used by advertisers to get consumers to believe one item is better than another, Schrank notes that advertisers spend the most money trying to sell products that are essentially the same, parity products. Notice what products fall into this category.

2. Watch the many "samples" that Schrank gives to illustrate the ten techniques that advertisers use in wording their claims to mislead consumers. Consider which techniques, if any, have fooled you in the past.

---

1   Students, and many teachers, are notorious believers in their own immunity to advertising. These naive inhabitants of consumerland believe that advertising is childish, dumb, a bunch of lies, and influences only the vast hordes of the less sophisticated. Their own purchases, they think, are made purely on the basis of value and desire, with advertising playing only a minor supporting role. They know about Vance Packard and his "hidden persuaders" and the adman's psychosell and bag of persuasive magic. They are not impressed.

2   Advertisers know better. Although few people admit to being greatly influenced by ads, surveys and sales figures show that a well-designed advertising campaign has dramatic effects. A logical conclusion is that advertising works below the level of conscious awareness and it works even on those who claim immunity to its message. Ads are designed to have an effect while being laughed at, belittled, and all but ignored.

3   A person unaware of advertising's claim on him is precisely the one most vulnerable to the adman's attack. Advertisers delight in an audience that believes ads to be harmless nonsense, for such an audience is rendered defenseless by its belief that there is no attack taking place. The purpose of classroom study of advertising is to raise the level of awareness about the persuasive techniques used in ads. One way to do this is to analyze ads in microscopic detail. Ads can be studied to detect their psychological hooks, how they are used to gauge values and hidden desires of the common man. They can be studied for their use of symbols, color, and imagery. But perhaps the simplest and most direct way to study ads is through an analysis of the language of the advertising claim.

4   The "claim" is the verbal or print part of an ad that makes some claim of superiority for the product being advertised. After studying claims, students should be able to recognize those that are misleading and accept as useful information those that are true. A few of these claims are downright lies, some are honest statements

about a truly superior product, but most fit into the category of neither bold lies nor helpful consumer information. They balance on the narrow line between truth and falsehood by a careful choice of words.

5   The reason so many ad claims fall into this category of pseudoinformation is that they are applied to parity products, those in which all or most of the brands available are nearly identical. Since no one superior product exists, advertising is used to create the illusion of superiority. The largest advertising budgets are devoted to parity products such as gasoline, cigarettes, beer and soft drinks, soaps, and various headache and cold remedies.

6   The first rule of parity claims involves the Alice-in-Wonderland use of the words "better" and "best." In parity claims, "better" means "best" but "best" only means "equal to." If all the brands are identical, they must all be equally good, the legal minds have decided. So "best" means that the product is as good as the other superior products in its category. When Bing Crosby declared Minute Maid Orange Juice "the best there is," he meant it was as good as the other orange juices you can buy.

7   The word "better," however, as grammarians will be pleased to hear, is legally as well as logically comparative and therefore becomes a clear claim to superiority. Bing could not have said that Minute Maid is "better than any other orange juice." "Better" is a claim to superiority. The only time "better" can be used is when a product does indeed have superiority over other products in its category or when the "better" is used to compare the product with something other than competing brands. An orange juice could therefore claim to be "better than a vitamin pill," or even that it was "the better breakfast drink."

8   The second rule of advertising-claim analysis is simply that if any product is truly superior, the ad will say so very clearly and will offer some kind of convincing evidence of the superiority. If an ad hedges the least about a product's advantage over the competition, you can strongly suspect it is not superior—maybe equal to but not better. You will never hear a gasoline company say, "We will give you four miles per gallon more in your car than any other brand." They would love to make such a claim, but it would

not be true. Gasoline is a parity product, and, in spite of some very clever and deceptive ads of a few years ago, no one has yet claimed one brand of gasoline better than—and therefore superior to—any other brand.

9   To create the necessary illusion of superiority, advertisers usually resort to one or more of the following ten basic techniques. Each is common and easy to identify.

1 The Weasel Claim

10   A weasel word is a modifier that practically negates the claim that follows. The expression "weasel word" is aptly named after the egg-eating habits of weasels. A weasel will suck out the inside of an egg, leaving it to appear intact to the casual observer. Upon closer examination, the egg is discovered to be hollow. Words or claims that appear substantial upon first glance but disintegrate into hollow meaninglessness on analysis are weasels. Commonly used weasel words include "helps" (the champion weasel), "like" (used in a comparative sense), "virtual" or "virtually," "acts" or "works," "can be," "up to," "as much as," "refreshes," "comforts," "tackles," "fights," "comes on," "the feel of," "the look of," "looks like," "fortified," "enriched," and "strengthened."

Samples of Weasel Claims

"*Helps Control* dandruff *symptoms* with *regular use*"
The weasels include "helps control," and possibly even "symptoms," and "regular use." The claim is not "stops dandruff."

"Leaves dishes *virtually* spotless"
We have seen so many ad claims that we have learned to tune out weasels. You are supposed to think "spotless," rather than "virtually" spotless.

"Only half the price of *many* color sets"
"Many" is the weasel. The claim is supposed to give the impression that the set is inexpensive.

"Tests confirm one mouthwash *best* against mouth odor."

"Hot Nestle's cocoa is the very *best.*"
  Remember the "best" and "better" routine.

"Listerine *fights* bad breath."
  "Fights," not "stops."

"Lots of things have changed, but Hershey's *goodness* hasn't."
  The claim does not say that Hershey's chocolate hasn't changed.

"Bacos, the crispy garnish that *tastes* just *like* its name."

2 The Unfinished Claim

11   The unfinished claim is one in which the ad claims the product is better, or has more of something but does not finish the comparison.

Samples of Unfinished Claims

"Magnavox gives you more."
  More what?

"Anacin: Twice as much of the pain reliever doctors recommend most"
  This claim fits in a number of categories; as an unfinished claim it does not say twice as much of what pain reliever.

"Supergloss does it with more color, more shine, more sizzle, more!"

"Coffee-mate gives coffee more body, more flavor."
  Also note that "body" and "flavor" are weasels.

"You can be sure if it's Westinghouse."
  Sure of what?

"Scott makes it better for you."
  Makes what better? How is it better?

"Ford LTD—700 percent quieter"
  When the Federal Trade Commission asked Ford to substantiate this claim Ford revealed that they meant the inside of the Ford was 700 percent quieter than the outside.

3 The "We're Different and Unique" Claim

12   This kind of claim states simply that there is nothing else quite like the product advertised. For example, if Schlitz were to add pink food coloring to their beer, they could say, "There's nothing like new pink Schlitz." The uniqueness claim is supposed to be interpreted by readers as a claim to superiority.

Samples of "We're Different and Unique" Claims

"There's no other mascara like it."

"Only Doral has this unique filter system."

"Cougar is like nobody else's car."

"Either way, liquid or spray, there's nothing else like it."

"If it doesn't say Goodyear, it can't be Polyglas."
  "Polyglas" is a trade name copyrighted by Goodyear. Goodrich or Firestone could make a tire exactly identical to the Goodyear one and yet couldn't call it "Polyglas"—a name for fiberglass belts.

"Only Zenith has Chromacolor."
  Same as the "Polyglas" gambit. Admiral has Solarcolor and RCA has Accucolor.

4 The "Water Is Wet" Claim

13   "Water is wet" claims say something about the product that is true for any brand in that product category (e.g., "Schrank's water is really wet"). The claim is usually a statement of fact, but not a real advantage over the competition.

Samples of "Water Is Wet" Claims

"Mobil: the Detergent Gasoline"
  Any gasoline acts as a cleaning agent.

"Great Lash greatly increases the diameter of every lash."

"Rheingold: the natural beer"
  Made from grains and water as are other beers.

"SKIN smells differently on everyone."
As do many perfumes.

5 The "So What" Claim

14   This is the kind of claim to which the careful reader will react by saying, "So what?" A claim is made that is true but gives no real advantage to the product. This is similar to the "water is wet" claim except that it claims an advantage that is not shared by most of the other brands in the product category.

Samples of "So What" Claims

"Geritol has more than twice the iron of ordinary supplements."
But is it twice as beneficial to the body?

"Campbell's gives you tasty pieces of chicken and not one but two chicken stocks."
Does the presence of two stocks improve the taste?

"Strong enough for a man but made for a woman"
This deodorant claim says only that the product is aimed at the female market.

6 The Vague Claim

15   The vague claim is simply not clear. This category often overlaps with others. The key to the vague claim is the use of words that are colorful but meaningless, as well as the use of subjective and emotional opinions that defy verification. Most contain weasels.

Samples of Vague Claims

"Lips have never looked so luscious."
Can you imagine trying to either prove or disprove such a claim?

"Lipsavers are fun—they taste good, smell good, and feel good."

"Its deep rich lather makes hair feel new again."

"For skin like peaches and cream"

"The end of meatloaf boredom"

"Take a bite and you'll think you're eating on the Champs Elysées."

"Winston tastes good like a cigarette should."

"The perfect little portable for all-around viewing with all the features of higher-priced sets"

"Fleischmann's makes sensible eating delicious."

7 The Endorsement or Testimonial

16   A celebrity or authority appears in an ad to lend his or her stellar qualities to the product. Sometimes the people will actually claim to use the product, but very often they don't. There are agencies surviving on providing products with testimonials.

Samples of Endorsements or Testimonials

"Joan Fontaine throws a shot-in-the-dark party and her friends learn a thing or two."

"Darling, have you discovered Masterpiece? The most exciting men I know are smoking it." (Eva Gabor)

"Vega is the best-handling car ever made in the U.S."
       This claim was challenged by the FTC, but GM answered that the claim is a direct quote from *Road and Track* magazine.

8 The Scientific or Statistical Claim

17   This kind of ad uses some sort of scientific proof or experiment, very specific numbers, or an impressive-sounding mystery ingredient.

Samples of Scientific or Statistical Claims

"Wonder Bread helps build strong bodies twelve ways."
       Even the weasel "helps" did not prevent the FTC from demanding this ad be withdrawn. But note that the use of the

number "twelve" makes the claim far more believable than if it were taken out.

"Easy-Off has 33 percent more cleaning power than another popular brand."

"Another popular brand" often translates as some other kind of oven cleaner sold somewhere. Also, the claim does not say Easy-Off works 33 percent better.

"Special Morning—33 percent more nutrition"
Also an unfinished claim.

"Certs contains a sparkling drop of Retsyn."

"ESSO with HTA"

"Sinarest: created by a research scientist who actually gets sinus headaches"

9 The "Compliment the Consumer" Claim

18   This kind of claim butters up the consumer by some form of flattery.

Samples of "Compliment the Consumer" Claims

"If you do what is right for you, no matter what others do, then RC Cola is right for you."

"We think a cigar smoker is someone special."

"You pride yourself on your good home cooking. . . ."

"The lady has taste."

"You've come a long way, baby."

10 The Rhetorical Question

19   This technique demands a response from the audience. A question is asked and the viewer or listener is supposed to answer in such a way as to affirm the product's goodness.

Samples of Rhetorical Questions

"Plymouth—isn't that the kind of car America wants?"

"Shouldn't your family be drinking Hawaiian Punch?"

"What do you want most from coffee? That's what you get most from Hills."

"Touch of Sweden: could your hands use a small miracle?"

20   Teaching someone how to build a log cabin or how to make yogurt is more exciting (or at least "different") than teaching the complexities of processed food deceptions, or the ins and outs of misleading ads from banks and savings and loan associations. But for 205 million Americans learning to stalk wild asparagus is far less important than learning to stalk honest value for hard-earned money in the neon neatness of the grocery store.

Journal Entry

Find a magazine ad which you think illustrates one of the claims discussed in the essay. Put this ad in your journal, and, on the facing page, tell what claim is being illustrated and explain how the claim functions in the ad.

Questions for Discussion

1. In the opening paragraph, Schrank identifies the people he expects to read his essay. Who are they?

2. Vance Packard, who is referred to in paragraph 1, wrote a 1957 bestseller called *The Hidden Persuaders*. In this book, Packard revealed the psychological techniques used by advertisers to sell their products to unsuspecting consumers. Keeping this information in mind, what do you think Schrank means by the term *psychosell* in the same paragraph?

3. In paragraph 3, Schrank gives several methods for analyzing advertisements. What are they? Which one will he discuss?

4. Why, according to Schrank, are ads effective even on people who claim to be immune to them?

5. In this essay, Schrank uses a number of *compound words*: words like *headline* or *newspaper* which are composed of two words that ordinarily stand alone. See how many of these words you can find in paragraphs 1 to 5.

6. In paragraph 5, Schrank refers to "parity products." What are parity products? Why do you think advertisers need to resort to tricky wording to get consumers to buy one brand of these products instead of another?

7. Sometimes Schrank "coins" words; that is, he devises new terms when no existing terms give exactly the meaning he wants to convey. One term which Schrank coins is *pseudoinformation* (paragraph 5). Look up the prefix *pseudo-* in the dictionary. What does it mean? What does the word *pseudoinformation* mean, and why do you think Schrank needed such a term to describe the claims applied to parity products?

8. Lewis Carroll's novel *Alice's Adventures in Wonderland* (1865) is about a little girl who falls down a rabbit hole and finds herself in a strange country where things happen with a fantastic illogicality. In paragraph 6, Schrank uses the hyphenated term "Alice-in-Wonderland" to describe the use of the words "better" and "best." Why is Schrank's reference to the novel appropriate?

9. Before he begins his discussion of individual advertising techniques, Schrank identifies two rules of advertising claim analysis. What are they?

10. The first technique that is discussed is "The Weasel Claim." What is the origin of the expression "weasel word"?

11. Each of the techniques identified in the essay is followed by numerous examples. Why do you think Schrank provides so many examples? What do the examples contribute to your understanding of the techniques he explains?

12. The conclusion of this essay is quite short—only two sentences. What strategy does Schrank use to close his essay?

13. The final sentence contains a *pun*, a play on words. What word does Schrank use here that has two possible meanings? What picture do you get of the consumer in the grocery store?

ADS, VIOLENCE AND VALUES

About the Reading

This editorial appeared in the April 2, 1990, issue of *Advertising Age,* a publication written for the advertising industry. The piece urges a reassessment of the messages advertisers are sending, especially to young audiences.

Before You Read

We have often heard that Americans have lost the values that made this country great: beliefs in working hard for what we want, saving for a better future, living within our means, being thankful for what we have, and so on. What values do you think we stress today? What connection might these values have with the appeals we see everyday in advertisements?

As You Read

1. This piece, as the head note tells you, is an editorial. Remember that an editorial gives an opinion. The editor is giving his opinion about what role advertisers should play in encouraging a return to some of the old-time values. Consider the appropriateness of letting this group set our values.

2. Watch how the editor traces his argument about the breakdown of American values and his defense of advertisers. Consider how convincingly he makes the point that advertisers are not to blame for this breakdown.

1   The recent slaying of one inner-city teen by another—to obtain the victim's pair of Nike Air Jordan tennis shoes—is frightening. But to hold superstar/endorser Michael Jordan or Nike responsible, as some commentators are doing, is ludicrous. Many factors, sociological and some perhaps psychological, led to the killing. But whatever supposedly uncontrollable desire might have been created by Nike's advertising and Mr. Jordan's endorsement belongs far, far down the list.

2   Absent any endorsements or ads, certain apparel would still be "in" with teens, and some youngsters would still break the law—even kill—to acquire those things. Recall that a few years ago, youngsters were killing each other for a particular brand of eyeglasses—an unadvertised eyeglass—that had become a fad item among them.

3   But this senseless violence over advertised shoes, jackets and unadvertised baubles requires a reassessment by all levels of society. For those who work in advertising, ask yourselves what your role should be in this age of instant gratification. Advertising people complain about companies that pander to Wall Street's cry for ever-greater short-term earnings but neglect long-range marketing and R&D investment. Yet so much of our advertising says, in effect, "You deserve it. Now." If Wall Street got that message, why do we wonder that young people got it, too?

4   Until recent decades, our appeals to "get it today" were routinely countered by an "Old World" society in which the Puritan ethic, in many manifestations, was still at work. Mothers, fathers, grandparents tried to teach their children about patience and prudence, the golden rule and the rewards for hard work. But the world has changed. For many reasons, all too many mothers and fathers aren't teaching those lessons, or watching their kids closely enough. Schools? Government? They're forbidden to teach morality. Family life and values are crumbling. What used to be a somewhat even battle between the exaggerations and lure of advertising and the prudence of authority figures at home has become dangerously one-sided.

5   In the face of this imbalance, this absence of a more widespread counterpressure, shouldn't more advertisers accept a greater

responsibility to soften their hedonistic appeals, especially to younger audiences? While advertising isn't responsible for the breakdown, and some advertisers are already dealing with old traditions in their campaigns, we believe it is time for all who create and approve advertising to at least keep this now-uneven playing field in mind. This is a time to help "the other side" by building into selling messages at least some encouragement for those values of prudence and self-denial that we so long sought to overcome.

6   Perhaps advertising can help bring basic values back into fashion.

7   If not us, who?

Journal Entry

According to this piece, a lot of advertisements give the message "You deserve it. Now." In your journal, describe an ad or paste a copy of an ad which has this message.

Questions for Discussion

1. Every writer must consider the audience who will be reading what he or she has written. To whom is this piece directed?

2. The article asserts that "to hold . . . Michael Jordan or Nike responsible" for teen violence is "ludicrous." What does *ludicrous* mean?

3. In your own words, restate the main point of paragraph 2 in a short sentence.

4. In paragraph 3, the essay refers to "this age of instant gratification." What is "instant gratification"? What does it mean to say that we live in an "age of instant gratification"?

5. Words have two kinds of meaning: denotative and connotative. The *denotation* of a term is its literal, non-emotional

meaning. *Connotations* of a term include emotional associations that the word might have. Thus *corpse* and *deceased* might both denote a dead body, but the first term has harsher or more negative connotations. We would hardly refer to our dead grandmother as "the corpse" though we might call her "the deceased." What is the denotative meaning of the verb *pander* (paragraph 3)? Does this term have a positive or negative connotation?

6. Paragraph 4 refers to old time values. What is "the Puritan ethic"? What is the golden rule?

7. Paragraph 4 says that schools and government are "forbidden to teach morality." Why might we not want these two entities to teach morality?

8. Do you agree that "Family life and values are crumbling"? Give specific examples to support your answer.

9. Paragraph 5 uses the word "hedonistic." Look up the word *hedonism*. What Greek word is it derived from? What does the Greek word mean? What does *hedonism* mean? What is a "hedonistic appeal"?

10. The essay urges advertisers to "help bring basic values back into fashion (paragraph 6). Why would advertisers want to bring back these values? Why wouldn't they want to keep promoting the "buy it now—I gotta have it" mentality?

11. What is frightening about the last sentence?

IT'S A SMALL WORLD AFTER ALL

Sophfronia Scott

About the Reading

In this article, which appeared in the September 25, 1989, issue of *Time* magazine, Sophfronia Scott explores the growing trend in the fashion and advertising industries away from blonde-haired and blue-eyed models. The new models, says Scott, represent diverse ethnic and racial groups.

Before You Read

In the past, advertisers tended to use for their ad campaigns models who fit a certain stereotype, usually that of the white, often blonde (especially in the case of female models), Anglo-featured individual. This stereotypical model is seen less and less in ads today. Why do you think this individual is being replaced by more ethnic-looking models?

As You Read

1. Notice how Scott opens her article by painting a picture using words. Consider how her description, which has an effect similar to showing the reader a photograph, is particularly suited to her subject matter.
2. Scott develops her piece by giving numerous examples. Pay close attention to the way she uses quotations from ad and modeling agency executives and descriptions of specific advertising campaigns to illustrate her point about the changing image of models in advertisements.

---

1   The model gazes serenely at the magazine reader from the country-club cool of a Ralph Lauren ad. Dressed impeccably in a tweed jacket, silk scarf and elegant suede gloves, she projects all the dreamy remoteness that is typical of Lauren models, with one notable difference: she is black.

2   It was a long time coming, but an ethnic rainbow is finally sweeping across the fashion and advertising industries—and brightening them considerably. The blond, blue-eyed ideal is out, diversity is in, and the concept of beauty is growing as wide as the world. The new cast of faces is appearing not only in ads aimed at specific ethnic groups but in mainstream advertising as well. Revlon's Most Unforgettable Woman of 1989, chosen in a search across the U.S., is Mary Xinh Nguyen, a 20-year-old Vietnamese American from California. Such companies as Du Pont, Citi-Bank and Delta Air Lines have populated current ads with a rich variety of blacks, Asians and Hispanics.

3   While many consumers still live in segregated neighborhoods, integrated ads have become the height of hipness. Reason: they have a sophisticated, global-village look.

4   "Advertisers don't want to insult people's intelligence. They are reflecting how the world is," says James Patterson, chief executive of the ad agency J. Walter Thompson USA. If an ad features nothing but a herd of Caucasians, it can appear dated and stiff. The inclusion of a lone minority-group member has a similar effect. Says Ron Anderson, vice chairman of the Bozell ad agency: "Ten or 15 years ago, there was a sense of tokenism. Some advertisers would throw a black or Hispanic into an ad because they were sensitive to minorities. Now we use blacks and Hispanics to sell a product."

5   From supermodel Suzy Parker in the 1950s to Christie Brinkley in the early 1980s, fair-skinned models used to dominate advertising. Most ad experts trace the change to Europe, where couturiers, notably Givenchy, began employing black women as runway models. The French fashion magazine *Elle* helped pioneer the polyethnic look in its editorial pages, then exported the philosophy to America when it launched a U.S. edition four years ago. (Catherine Alain-Bernard, fashion and beauty editor

of the French *Elle*, says her magazine still gets a few letters from people complaining about black models and "giving jobs to immigrants.")

6   One of the first advertisers to embrace the rainbow look was Benetton, the Italian knitwear maker, which launched its "United Colors of Benetton" campaign in 1984. The ads picture handsome youths of diverse nationalities often standing arm in arm. The purpose of such ads is not just to appeal to ethnic customers who might identify with people in the ads but also to pitch an alluring sentiment of brotherhood. Esprit, a San Francisco-based sportswear company, went one step further by putting its employees in ads. Says Esprit spokeswoman Lisa DeNeff: "We sat up and said, 'Hey, why not us?' We had a lot of great-looking folks here. Many were ethnically different."

7   All over the globe, advertising is becoming more multiracial. Many ads in Japan, which often used to depict blonds because they represented the Western good life, are populated by blacks, Asians and Latins. "Japanese consumers now want to see somebody unique and somebody they can easily empathize with," says Hidehiko Sekizawa, senior research director for Hakuhodo, Japan's second largest ad agency. In France the two hottest commercials of the summer, for Schweppes and Orangina, featured Brazilian music and casts of brown-eyed, mixed-race beauties.

8   Modeling agencies are finding ways to meet the demand for fresher faces by scouting all over the world and staging more contests. "If you see a beauty, you don't worry about her color. The perfectly proportioned features are no longer so important," says Ann Veltri, a vice president at Elite Model Management.

9   Since consumers want to see real people rather than idols, advertisers expect the ethnic look to be around for years to come. "We don't want a colorless, odorless soup," says Guy Taboulay, the executive creative director in Paris for B.S.B., a U.S.-owned ad agency. "We want to see national identities and character. Tomorrow's culture will be made up of different cultures. That will be its strength."

Journal Entry

According to the article, consumers want to see "real people rather than idols" in advertisements. Assume that you are going to be featured in a magazine ad. What product would the ad be for? Describe the ad. How would you be dressed? What would you be doing?

Questions for Discussion

1. What image does the author use to introduce the article?

2. The author's thesis sentence appears in paragraph 2. Underline the sentence and label it.

3. Who is Mary Xinh Nguyen and for what is she known?

4. Repeating the sound of a consonant is called *alliteration*. In the first paragraph, the consonant "c" is repeated when a Ralph Lauren ad is described as "country-club cool." See if you can find and underline an example of alliteration in paragraph 3.

5. In paragraph 4, an advertising executive is quoted as saying, "Ten or 15 years ago, there was a sense of tokenism. . . ." One meaning of token is "a small part representing the whole." Reread the entire quote in paragraph 4 and, without looking in the dictionary, see if you can explain what "tokenism" is.

6. In paragraph 5, the article refers to "couturiers." What is a "couturier"?

7. What is the "rainbow look"? What two advertisers are described as using this look?

8. According to the article, the ads in the "United Colors of Benetton" campaign have two purposes. What are they?

9. Many English words are formed by adding a *prefix* to another word. For example, the prefix "bi-" means "two," so when "bi-" is added to the word "cycle," the new word "bicycle" refers to a *two*-wheeled cycle.

Poly- and multi- are prefixes meaning "many;" what is meant by "the polyethnic look" in paragraph 5 and "multiracial" advertising in paragraph 7?

10. The last paragraph of the article says that "consumers want to see real people rather than idols." Are these new "ethnic models" more real than the models of the past? Why or why not?

11. The title of this article is not original; it is the title of a song. If you are familiar with the song, explain the song's message. Why do you think the author chose to use the song title as the title of her article?

JEST PLAIN OFFENSIVE

Ira Teinowitz

About the Reading

The article which follows originally appeared in the July 17, 1989, issue of *Advertising Age*, a publication aimed at advertisers. In the piece, Ira Teinowitz describes negative consumer response to ads which are perceived to be discriminatory.

Before You Read

Today, more than ever before, the public has become sensitive to remarks which are perceived to be racist, sexist, and so on. Public figures, from comedians to politicians, have suffered adverse publicity as a result of discriminatory comments. Think about instances of these types of remarks with which you are familiar. Why do you think the targets of the remarks react so strongly? Do you think they are justified in their reactions?

As You Read

1. Teinowitz uses specific examples which describe offensive ads. Notice how this technique is particularly effective in making sure the reader gets the point even if he or she is not familiar with all of the commercials mentioned.

2. In his discussion of the response to consumer outcry from advertisers, the author cites a number of ad people by name and quotes their exact words. Consider how these devices add authority to his article.

1   The TV commercial was intended as a harmless jest, but Adolph Coors Co. now finds itself accused of an ethnic slur and the target of a consumer boycott.

2   In the spot, comedian Tom Arcuragi—spokesman for Coors Extra Gold beer—offered this humorous tip on how to speed your order in a crowded bar: He walked to the jukebox, selected a polka and the bar emptied.

3   "Coors slanders Polka industry," said leaflets soon making the rounds, accompanied by charges Coors was anti-Polish.

4   Coors pulled the network and spot TV commercial, created by GSD&M, Austin, Texas, and learned a bitter lesson of marketing today: Consumers are reading negative implications into advertising and reacting angrily.

5   "There is greater sensitivity by individuals and groups," said Sidney Levy, chairman of the marketing department at Northwestern University's Kellogg Graduate School of Management. "There is a notion that you don't just accept implied slurs, whether ageism, racism or sexism. Part of being modern is that you protest."

6   Coors, now considering pro-polka advertising, is far from alone in having to deal with this phenomenon; advertisers large and small are feeling the wrath. For example:

■ American Home Products Corp. changed a Black Flag commercial from Partners & Shevack, New York, last month when veterans objected to the use of "Taps" to signify the bugs' deaths.

■ Chevrolet heard plenty when its "improbable spokesman" TV campaign on the West Coast used a quote from Mao Tse-tung. "We were called dope-smoking commies," said Vic Olesen, president of Vic Olesen & Partners, Culver City, Calif., which created the campaign.

■ Continental Airlines heard from Asian groups over its TV campaign showing a samurai warrior slashing high airfares. Chinese for Affirmative Action called the campaign from the Houston office of N W Ayer "racist," and Continental pulled the spots in Seattle and Spokane, Wash., after a threatened boycott.

■ Kellogg Co. has kept its "Nuttin' honey" campaign for Nut & Honey Crunch cereal despite demands from gay activist groups that one commercial be scrapped. The spot from Leo Burnett

USA, Chicago, had cowboys drawing their guns on a cook who uttered the words, and these groups claimed that promoted violence against gays.

■ In a celebrated reaction, Pepsi-Cola USA spent $5 million to hire Madonna as a celebrity endorser and then pulled her commercial after running it just once. Days after the spot from BBDO Worldwide, New York, ran, the singer's "Like a Prayer" video was released, sparking complaints about how Madonna was portraying religion.

7   There's widespread disagreement among marketers and agencies about how to react to these complaints.

8   A few advertisers have taken steps to ensure errors aren't repeated.

9   Miller Brewing Co. already had an extensive review process for commercials and most print ads. Now the company has added other types of advertising to the review after having to dump hundreds of thousands of copies of "The Beachin' Times," a college newspaper supplement that raised the ire of college groups amid accusations of blatant sexism.

10   Pepsi, too, says it will be more careful. The soft-drink marketer's deal with Madonna gave it no review rights of the music video to which the commercial was tied.

11   "It would be safe to say that we will be more cautious in the future," said a Pepsi spokesman.

12   Other companies are taking advantage of new technologies in testing creative work, including one developed by Richard Wirthlin, former President Reagan's pollster, to look at political messages.

13   Jim Granger, a researcher with the Wirthlin Group, McLean, Va., said the researcher's Speech Pulse Technology is now being used by marketers to look at commercials.

14   Mr. Granger said testing includes second-by-second tracking of a consumer panel's response to a spot, followed by focus-group interviews that pinpoint aspects with particularly negative or positive impacts.

15   Others question the desirability of responding to groups that voice anger at ads.

16 Many of the complaints are inspired by competitors while others come from groups whose future finances depend upon getting a commercial off the air, said Larry Charles, senior VP, Hill & Knowlton, New York.

17 "Don't ever kid yourself that the people who lodged the protest against Coors did it for the good of Poland," he said. "They did it to get funding for their organization."

18 Other advertisers say it's almost impossible to determine what will be seen as demeaning.

19 Before airing the samurai spot, Continental ran it past several Japanese-American consultants who said it wouldn't be insulting.

20 "We learned that you can't always trust consultants," said James O'Donnell, Continental senior VP-marketing.

21 "The problem is that there are so many sensitivities that it's a question of walking through a mine field," he said. "The real lesson learned is that before you get into anything with any ethnic or social overtones, you have to be sure that the return is worth the risks."

22 Other agency executives questioned the ability to do good advertising without upsetting somebody.

23 "Consider the day lost that you don't offend somebody over something," said Jim Ramsey, senior VP-executive creative director at McCann-Erickson Worldwide, Troy, Mich., agency for General Motors Corp.'s Buick and GMC truck divisions.

24 "I think a lot of people make a full-time job out of being offended," he said. "With our society as litigious as it is, I think there are a lot of people out there waiting to descend on somebody who makes an unwitting remark or interpreting some double meaning into a headline or visual that may not have been intended."

25 Christine Coyle has been through the mine field time and again. The creative director of Dick Orkin's Radio Ranch, a Los Angeles radio advertising shop known for its use of humor, said, "Advertisers have to realize there's always somebody that can complain about something. People don't usually complain if something's bland. If something's beige, they're not going to notice it.

26   "The unfortunate part of it is Coors is never going to hear from the hundreds of thousands of people who loved the spot and who went out and bought Coors beer."

27   Leo Shapiro, chairman of Leo Shapiro & Associates, a marketing consulting and research company, said ad agencies have to take more chances with their ads if they want to appeal to 1980s people.

28   "Betty Crocker was no sex object," he said. "Agencies at one point played it safe, avoiding ads that would probably offend. Now we have a new generation of consumers, and agencies have to evoke emotional responses to reach them."

29   Yet, at least one group says advertising can do better.

30   The Chicago-based Coalition Against Marketing/Media Prejudice, active in the Kellogg's battle, suggested agencies can reach people without offending any of them.

31   "It just seems to me that agencies and companies with bright creatives can create campaigns that promote people and groups—whether ethnic or cultural—in positive ways," said Linda Henderson, a spokeswoman. "It's so trite to say, 'Aren't we better than these folks'—whether they are gays, blacks or people who like doing the polka."

32   As for Coors and the polka spot that broke March 25, it's not over yet. Jimmy Sturr, a Grammy-winning polka player, said that what the group that distributed the fliers is "waiting for is some action to reverse [the effect of] that ad."

33   He added that the boycott won't be withdrawn until Coors favorably portrays polka in the commercial getting as much airtime as the one canceled.

34   In declaring that Coors never intended to knock anyone, Pat Edson, a Coors communications manager, noted that Mr. Arcuragi, the comedian in the commercial, played in a polka band for six years.

Journal Entry

Find a magazine ad which, in your opinion, might be offensive to a particular group. For example, a cosmetics ad might offend feminists because it encourages women to believe they need to enhance themselves in order to be attractive. Or, cigarette ads might be offensive to families of lung cancer victims. Paste or tape your ad in your journal. Then identify the group you think might be offended and explain why.

Questions for Discussion

1. The article opens with an example of a TV commercial that a particular group found offensive. Obviously the advertisers thought their ad was funny. Why did they think it might be humorous? Why did the group find it offensive?

2. The article's thesis is in paragraph 4. Find it, underline it and label it.

3. A *suffix* is added to the end of a word in order to change its meaning or form a new word. For example, *-ish* is a suffix which means "somewhat." When *-ish* is added to "thirty" to make the new word "thirtyish," the new word means about or near thirty.

   The suffix *-ism* means "a theory," often a derogatory or negative theory. In paragraph 5, the article refers to *ageism, racism,* and *sexism.* How would you define each of these "-isms"?

4. Writers often refer to names, titles, places, events, movies, and so on, that they assume their readers will recognize. Writers use these references to give added meaning to their work. Such a reference is called an *allusion.* Consider the following allusions given in the selection:

   A. In the Black Flag bug spray commercial, advertisers used the music "Taps." Describe this piece of music and explain why veterans found it offensive.

   B. The Chevrolet ad used a quote from Mao Tse-tung. Who was he and why were the advertisers called "commies"?

C. What is a samurai warrior and why do you think Continental Airlines used this figure in its ad? Why do you think the Chinese were offended by this ad? Why was Continental surprised by the negative reaction?

5. The word *slur* is used several times in the article. What is a slur? What is an "ethnic slur" (paragraph 1)? What is an "implied slur" (paragraph 5)?

6. Explain why gay activist groups feel that the Nut & Honey ad promotes violence against gays.

7. If you have seen the Madonna video "Like a Prayer," explain why Pepsi executives might be upset that they used the song of that title in their ads.

8. What are advertisers doing to avoid consumer complaints in the future?

9. Paragraph 15 states that some advertisers "question the desirability of responding to groups that voice anger at ads." Why do they think responding to all consumer complaints is a bad idea?

10. In paragraph 27, a marketing executive says that ad agencies must take greater chances if their ads are going to appeal to today's audience. How is today's audience different from audiences in the past, and why does he say ad agencies have to take greater risks to appeal to today's audience?

11. How does the conclusion of this article tie in with the introduction? What effect does this connection have?

12. The use of language or situations which are the opposite of what you might expect is called *irony*. What is ironic about the final paragraph of this essay?

13. Look at the article's title. We would expect it to read "*Just* plain offensive." Why do you think the author chose to use the word *jest* instead of *just*? What is a "jest"? What is the connection between this word choice and the rest of the essay?

FAST TIMES ON AVENIDA MADISON

Pete Engardio, Walecia Konrad, Ronald Grover, Jo Ellen Davis, and Lois Therrien

About the Reading

The following article appeared in the June 6, 1988, issue of *Business Week*. The piece is credited to five different authors, each working in a different U.S. city: Pete Engardio in Miami, with Walecia Konrad in New York, Ronald Grover in Los Angeles, Jo Ellen Davis in Houston, and Lois Therrien in Chicago. "Fast Times" focuses on the advertising industry's pursuit of the Hispanic consumer.

Before You Read

Especially in certain areas of the United States, Hispanics have become an increasingly visible portion of the population. Spanish-language cable television channels are offered in a number of cities; many major newspapers are available in Spanish-language editions; even the phone company advertises the Spanish Yellow Pages. Are you aware of Hispanic influences in your city? If so, what are they? If not, are there other ethnic groups with their own papers, TV channels, and so on?

As You Read

1. Notice the title of this article. In only five words it manages (1) to make an association with a film, *Fast Times at Ridgemont High;* (2) to suggest, with the use of the Spanish word for "Avenue," that the piece has something to do with Hispanics; and (3) to evoke the image of the advertising industry with the reference to Madison Avenue, the New York City street where a number of large advertising firms are located. Keep in mind the appropriateness of this title as you read.

2. Consider the article's mention of specific products which are advertised both in the traditional English-speaking market and the Spanish-speaking market as well. Notice how this device helps the reader, who previously may have been unaware of the influence of Spanish-speaking consumers, to see just how powerful an economic force the Hispanic consumer market is today.

---

1   Quick: What's the top-rated game show in Miami and Los Angeles on Saturday night? *Wheel of Fortune? Jeopardy?* ¡No! It's *Sabado Gigante*, a raucous Spanish-language extravaganza that is becoming as much of a family ritual for Hispanics as the *Ed Sullivan Show* used to be for Middle America. Every Saturday night, Don Francisco, the show's exuberantly grinning host, spends 3½ hours leading the studio audience and a battery of Latin stars in boisterous games, sizzling salsa numbers, and zany skits.

2   The show is a marketer's dream: It's hard to tell where the ads leave off and the show begins. Brands such as Coca-Cola and Coors are openly pitched during the program, their names repeated dozens of times. The studio audience of 300, flown in from around the country at the program's expense, claps and sings in unison to jingles for Kinney shoes, Ultra Pampers Plus, and Tide detergent. Each week, an audience estimated at anywhere from 4 million to 8 million Hispanics tunes in. Ad time is selling briskly, and among the new sponsors this year alone are McDonald's, Hershey Foods, and Maybelline.

3   The show is just one part of the headlong rush for the Hispanic market. Multinationals such as Colgate-Palmolive Co. and Coca-Cola Co. have been selling in Spanish for decades, but now almost every consumer-products company is joining in. According to *Hispanic Business Magazine*, marketers spent $490 million advertising to Hispanics in 1987—a 23% jump from 1986 and double the level of five years ago. Industry experts expect that number to grow as much as 25% annually for at least five years, at a time when overall

ad spending is rising just 8% a year. Crows Henry G. Silverman, chief executive of Telemundo Group Inc., a Spanish-language TV network: "What you are seeing is still the tip of the iceberg."

4   **LATIN BEAT.** There's already plenty to see. Switch on one of the Spanish UHF TV stations found in almost every major U.S. city these days, and you can watch all the icons of ad culture bopping to a Latin beat. You'll find Campbell Soup cans dancing to *La Bamba*, Latin jocks saying they drink Miller Lite because it's *más sabrosa* and *no llena*, and Madge the Manicurist pitching Palmolive to her *clientela*. Even Frank Perdue and Ronald McDonald are learning Spanish to sell their *pollo* and *hamburguesas*.

5   Hollywood studios, still awed by the success of the film *La Bamba*, which has grossed $54.2 million and whose soundtrack topped the pop charts, are producing more films with Latin themes and/or dual soundtracks: Note *The Milagro Beanfield War*, *Salsa*, and *Stand and Deliver*. Pop singers from Linda Ronstadt to Sting, Madonna, and Michael Jackson are performing in Spanish.

6   Sheer numbers account for much of the corporate and political ardor. The U.S. Census Bureau counts 18.9 million Hispanics, now 7.5% of the population. Include undocumented aliens and part-time residents, and the ranks swell to 25 million. "No consumer marketer can afford to let this market go," notes J. Walter Thompson Co. Chief Executive Burton J. Manning. "It's not just a matter of growing. It's a matter of surviving."

7   Not everyone is sold on the need for Hispanic marketing. Toymakers, for example, make no special efforts to attract Hispanic kids, claiming that most are bilingual and watch network cartoons. And few big financial houses and computer companies sell in Spanish. They figure that if customers don't know English, they probably aren't earning enough to buy their products. "I can't think of anything Merrill Lynch provides that has any relevance to 90% of Hispanics in this country," says Fairfield College Sociology Dept. Chairman Arthur L. Anderson.

8   But in such cluttered and competitive arenas as beer, soft drinks, and soap, where total sales usually increase only at the meager rate of overall population growth, Hispanics offer new possibilities for growth. The Hispanic population is expanding at four times the

national rate. With a high birthrate and massive inflows of immigrants, it has swollen by 4.3 million since 1980, or 29.4%. And with no letup in sight for the economic deterioration and population explosion of Latin America, immigration is likely to continue. Hispanics will surpass blacks as the biggest minority in a few decades. "If you can grow with that market, you have a tremendous opportunity in the long term," says Neil M. Comber, Procter & Gamble Co.'s target-marketing manager.

9   **BLAST FROM THE PAST.** But beyond their sheer number, Hispanics offer the prospect of new marketing leverage. More and more consumer-goods companies are scratching for business among customers who perceive brands as commodities and TV ads as tiresome background noise. But as the exuberant commercialism of *Sabado Gigante* shows, the Spanish-speaking audience is less jaded. Some Hispanics are just beginning to enjoy affluence, and many recent immigrants are experiencing American consumer culture for the first time.

10   For companies, these brand-conscious, brand-loyal Hispanics are a blast from a happier past. It's almost as if the last 20 years of erosion of marketing's ability to reach, captivate, and motivate consumers had never happened. Using promotions offering prizes such as a free trip to Puerto Rico, for example, Colgate has boosted sales of Palmolive dishwashing liquid in Miami by 50%, according to one estimate. The detergent's general market share nationwide is about 17%, but among Hispanics it's 35%.

11   The results of a $20,000, two-minute pitch on *Sabado Gigante* can be similarly impressive. Sales of Reese's Peanut Butter Cups are said to have nearly tripled in Miami after Hershey Foods had Don Francisco talk them up on the show. When P&G launched a $10,000 Tide sweepstakes on *Sabado Gigante* last year, there were 200,000 entries. Some 52,000 cereal box tops flooded in—some by Federal Express—three weeks after Ralston-Purina Co. made a similar offer. Says Joe del Cueto, the program's sales manager: "These people haven't been Ralph Naderized."

12   And despite the belief that Hispanics, particularly new immigrants, can't afford to spend freely, their consumption in many categories is higher than average. Hispanics make up 54% of the

population in San Antonio, for example, but account for 65% of total sales of sugared colas, according to ad agency Sosa & Associates. They spend 26% more in the grocery store each week and 36% more at fast-food restaurants than other San Antonio consumers. And as cigarette smoking declines in the general population, tobacco companies are stepping up marketing to Hispanics and blacks.

13   **OUT OF** *EL BARRIO.* Similarly, many brewers recognize that Latins drink more beer than Anglos, among whom beer consumption is flat or declining. Anheuser-Busch Cos. first tapped the market five years ago, using ads and local promotions to enthrone Budweiser as *El Rey de Cervezas.* Miller, Stroh, and Heileman have since jumped in. The top spender is Adolph Coors Co.: To improve its image among minorities and organized labor, the company launched an ad blitz, hired more Hispanics, and contributed to Latino charities.

14   The market is looking still more attractive as many Hispanics escape inner-city poverty. In the past decade, Hispanic family income has grown 10% annually, to an average of $22,900. While that's about a third lower than the general population's, Latinos are better off than many think. In Miami, the average Hispanic family earns $27,500, about on a par with its neighbors. Collectively, Hispanics have about $130 billion in buying power. "Now people are coming in, getting jobs, and making decent bucks in Spanish," says Richard W. Tobin, president of Strategy Research Corp. They're spending those bucks, too: Hispanics bought 7% of all new U.S. cars sold last year and 7.6% of the imports.

15   While Hispanics are virtually absent from vast stretches of Middle America, they are so concentrated elsewhere that they represent a seismic change in the demographics of some key areas. In California, Hispanics will outnumber Anglos within 12 years— that is, they will no longer be a minority in the largest state in the nation. They make up 23% of the population of South-western states and 21% of the Pacific states. Florida's Dade County is nearly half Hispanic, as is at least one-quarter of Los Angeles, New York, and Houston.

16   **FLY NAKED.** So marketers who want to remain in some of the biggest U.S. cities will have to learn Spanish. "This is scary to many companies," says New York-based marketing consultant Gilbert Sabater. "The choice becomes: Do I fight to stay in the market, or do I get out?" Kentucky Fried Chicken noted that the areas around its Southern California outlets were growing more Hispanic. It targeted the market with promotions and family-oriented commercials—and soon found that sales in those neighborhoods were 15% to 20% higher than in the general market.

17   Even financial institutions are getting in on the action. Metropolitan Life Insurance Co. advertises heavily in Spanish and has raised its Hispanic sales staff from 20 to 250 since 1984. As a result, the company has become the best-known insurer among Hispanics, although it is only No. 4 among the general population.

18   Hispanics pose a special challenge to marketers because they aren't disappearing into the melting pot as fast as earlier immigrant groups. Because of their numbers, local concentration, and frequent contact with their homelands, Latinos are clinging to their language and culture. Although the average Hispanic has lived in the U.S. for nearly 13 years, about half aren't fluent in English. As debates rage across the nation over the need for bilingual government services, corporations are facing up to the reality: The Spanish-speaking population will be a vast, important segment of the country for decades.

19   At first, most companies simply translated their general market ads into Spanish—often with embarrassing results. Braniff Inc. promoted its plush seats with an ad campaign that urged customers to "fly in leather." When it translated the slogan into Spanish, the company inadvertently wound up telling passengers to "fly naked." Eastern Air Lines Inc. translated its "We Earn Our Wings Daily" message in a way that implied that its passengers often ended up dead.

20   Besides the linguistic perils, there's a cultural minefield to cross. For example, 7Up's "Caffeine—Never Had It, Never Will" pitch backfired among Hispanics. Many Latins are enamored of coffee with the approximate octane of rocket fuel, so

they don't fret about caffeine. Pacific Bell wanted to run Spanish ads urging customers to call their overseas relatives on weekends to save up to 50%. Its Hispanic agency, Los Angeles-based Bermudez Associates, refused. The reason: Latinos don't like to think of themselves as cheapskates—especially when it comes to family. "If I waited until the rates went down to call home, that would be an insult," explains agency Chief Executive Eduardo Bermudez.

21   To avoid such blunders, more major advertisers are hiring agencies and marketing directors who specialize in Hispanics. As a result, ad campaigns are becoming increasingly sophisticated. Simple dubbing is out. Now advertisers are introducing entire campaigns for Hispanics. One spot from PepsiCo Inc. shows an 8-year-old Hispanic drumming on a Pepsi can and being transformed into a teenage rock star performing before a sellout crowd. It's the first Spanish-speaking ad to win a Clio.

22   **"STILL FOREIGNERS."** These newer ads reflect a subtler understanding of Hispanic concerns. "Hispanics are really still foreigners," says Roger S. Sennott, general manager of the San Diego consulting firm Market Development Inc. "They should be treated in a way that makes them feel more comfortable." American Telephone & Telegraph Co. spots depict Hispanics longing for their relatives and then picking up the phone. The slogan: "This close—only with AT&T." AT&T's market share among Hispanics is 12% higher than among the general population.

23   Marketers are increasingly aware of the role family life plays in Hispanic culture. An Eastman Kodak Co. ad shows an entire family, from grandparents down to kids, helping a girl prepare for her first big dance. Using the slogan *"De familia a familia"*—"From family to family"—Ford Motor Co. pushes its family vehicles such as the four-door Tempo and the Escort Wagon.

24   Some companies are also tinkering with their ads to reflect the distinctions among such groups as Puerto Ricans, Cubans, and Mexicans. Anheuser-Busch and Campbell Soup Co. change the voice-overs or background music depending on whether the spots will be shown in predominantly Puerto Rican New York, Cuban Miami, or Mexican California.

25   Campbell, which began courting Latinos 15 years ago by putting Spanish labels on its cans, even improvises with its recipes. Last year it rolled out a 50-product Casera line of soups, beans, and sauces for Hispanics to challenge Goya Foods Inc.'s market dominance. For Puerto Ricans and Dominicans on the East Coast, Campbell adds the condiment sofrito. The company plans to make the line spicier in the Southwest to appeal to Mexican tastes.

26   All this activity hasn't escaped Madison Avenue's notice. In December, WPP Group Inc., the giant ad-agency holding company, bought Mendoza, Dillon & Asociados, the largest Hispanic ad firm. Foote Cone & Belding, Saatchi & Saatchi, and Grey Advertising have all bought small Hispanic firms. "More and more clients are asking about Hispanic marketing and want to get some experience in it," says Arthur R. Klein, president of Young & Rubicam New York, which started a Spanish unit in 1975.

27   There's a boom in Hispanic media, too. The number of Spanish radio stations nationwide has jumped from 67 to 182 in 12 years. Advertisers spent $220 million last year on Spanish TV, up 56% from 1986. "The days of double-digit growth are gone for general-market stations," says José C. Cancela, general manager of KWEX TV in San Antonio. "But for us it's just beginning."

28   **GRASS ROOTS.** The concentration of Hispanics in well-defined communities dovetails with the growing interest among many companies in regional and local marketing. P&G, for example, has a bilingual sales and distribution force catering just to New York's 7,000 bodegas, which account for half of the groceries sold to the city's 2.4 million Hispanics.

29   Latino events such as Los Angeles' Cinco de Mayo celebration, New York's Puerto Rico Day Parade, and Miami's Calle Ocho Festival also offer opportunities for local promotions. "You have to be involved in the grass roots," explains Herney Nisimblat, Hispanic marketing director for Colgate.

30   Still, it will take years before the Hispanic market gets its fair share of ad and promotion dollars. Because surveying Hispanics is tricky, especially among recent immigrants, marketing managers lack data to convince top executives that their ads are working. But for an increasing number of companies, the only important numbers are those showing the market's huge potential.

31   A series of as-yet-unaired spots prepared for E. & J. Gallo Winery's Bartles & Jaymes wine coolers makes that point. "I'll make you a deal," says Frank in the first spot. "If you buy Bartles & Jaymes wine coolers, I'll learn Spanish." The next spots show him struggling to learn the tongue. By the fifth ad, he's speaking in complete sentences, albeit with an Anglo twang. Despite the occasional mispronunciation, Spanish lessons are paying off for a lot of companies, too.

———————

Journal Entry

If one is available in your area, watch 15 to 30 minutes of a television show in a language other than English. Record in your journal the products which were advertised on the show. Are they "mainstream" products or products with which most English-speaking Americans would be unfamiliar? What strategies are being used to sell these products?

Questions for Discussion

1. Why do you think the authors chose to open this piece with a reference to *Sabado Gigante*, a Spanish-language TV show? What is it about the show that makes it a fitting lead-in for the different ideas which will be presented in the rest of the piece?

2. In the last sentence of paragraph 9, instead of writing that Henry Silverman, chief executive of a Spanish-speaking television network, *explains*, "What you are seeing is still the tip of the iceberg," the authors begin the sentence with the verb "crows": "Crows Henry G. Silverman . . . ." How does the use of the word *crows* give a different meaning to the quote which follows? What other words might have been used (says, notes, etc.) and how would they have changed your interpretation of his words?

3. Paragraph 5 mentions a number of films "with Latin themes and . . . soundtracks" and pop singers who have recorded songs in Spanish. How many of these examples are you familiar with?

4. In paragraph 6, the expression "corporate and political ardor" appears. What does *ardor* mean? With what is it usually associated? What does it mean in the context of "*corporate* and *political* ardor?

5. In paragraph 18, the article mentions that Hispanics are a "special challenge to marketers because they aren't disappearing into the melting pot as fast as other immigrant groups." What is the "melting pot," and why aren't Hispanics disappearing into it as fast as other groups?

6. What problems arose when companies attempted merely to translate their English ads into Spanish rather than developing new ads geared toward Hispanics?

7. What advertising strategies are companies now developing in order to cater to Hispanic consumers?

8. Why, according to the article, will it "take years before the Hispanic market gets its fair share of ad and promotion dollars"?

9. This article uses a number of statistics as specific examples. Go through the piece and locate these statistics. How does the use of statistics contribute to the article?

10. How effective is the title for this piece? What connotations (associations) does "Fast Times" have? Why do you think the authors used *Avenida* instead of "Avenue"? What is the significance of Madison Avenue?

11. As the headnote explains, this piece was written by five different authors in five different cities. Why do you think all of these contributors were needed for one article? What is the significance of the particular cities in which they work?

A LONG WAY FROM "AUNT JEMIMA"

About the Reading

This article by Marcus Mabry appeared in the August 14, 1989, issue of *Newsweek*. Mabry discusses the growing trend in advertising toward "segmentation," the targeting of ads at specific segments or parts of the population. In particular, this article focuses on the rising number of advertisements directed at black consumers.

Before You Read

Increasingly, companies are targeting their advertising campaigns at specific groups of consumers—ethnic groups, groups of a particular age, groups with a particular interest, and so on. Why do you think this segmented approach is becoming so popular in the United States?

As You Read

1. Notice that Mabry distinguishes between advertisers who have removed offensive stereotypes from their campaigns or incorporated elements from black culture in their advertisements and others who are designing ads targeted specifically at the black consumer. Consider why both approaches might be advisable.

2. The title of this article draws on a familiar pancake-selling persona, Aunt Jemima. Mabry points out that Aunt Jemima was based on the stereotype of a black "mammy," a stereotype reinforced by the use of the title of "Aunt" in her name. Consider how the reference to Jemima in the title sets the overall tone of the essay.

1   Yo homes! Yo homes! Yo homes!" The black man in the over-size glasses and flipped-back bicycle cap presses his face up to the TV camera. "This is Mars Blackmon chillin for Air Jordan." The hip-hoppin' music picks up in the background, and basketball star Michael Jordan starts skyin'. "These sneakers be housin' across the country and every homeboy be bum-rushin' to get some," says Spike Lee, playing the character he created in his film "She's Gotta Have It." The bass kicks in as the shots of Jordan slammin' and jammin' come quicker, interspersed with frames of Mars showing the Air Jordans. "And I ain't frontin'," he says. (Read: "No joke.")

2   The scene has the look and feel of a rap video. In fact, it's a Nike ad. The athletic-wear giant is one of a growing number of companies that have begun to use ads made not only with, but by, blacks. The reason isn't hard to figure out: blacks have become a powerful consumer force. They spent more than $200 billion last year on goods and services and will probably spend twice that much by the year 2000, according to estimates based on Census Bureau data. Surveys show that blacks buy 16 percent of the orange juice, 32 percent of the malt liquor and 36 percent of the hair-conditioning products sold in America. To reach them— particularly affluent young "Buppies" (black urban professionals)—marketers are striving for ads with an "authentic" feel for black music, language and lifestyles. But the trend has also heightened competition for the new ad business, with black-owned agencies insisting they are better equipped than white-run firms to reach the black market.

3   At the very least, companies have moved to rid their ads of obvious stereotypes. Quaker Oats, which had already softened the original mammylike "Aunt Jemima" logo it used on the famous pancake mix, recently changed the image again to look like a modern homemaker. Under threat of a consumer boycott, Colgate-Palmolive dropped the name and black-face logo of a toothpaste called "Darkie" that it sold in Asia. Other companies are just using more blacks in their ads, even if the situations often seem indistinguishable from ones in which whites might appear.

4   Still other firms are going further and running ads that might be called distinctively "black." One is McDonald's, a company with

a long record of trying to reach the black market with both advertising and community spending. It hired a black-owned firm, Burrell Advertising, to create its current "breakfast club" campaign—a series of ads that show Buppies talking in a way that captures the pace of black conversation without resorting to "jive talk." The strategy has apparently paid off. "McDonald's is the leader in the black community according to market share by a lot," says Emil Teri, vice president for special marketing. (Teri declines to cite specific numbers.) "Of course telling any consumer that we welcome them and they're invited, we'll get a better response."

5   Advertisers are also finding that using elements of black pop culture can help reach a wider audience as well. Nike spokeswoman Liz Dolan insists that Spike Lee's Air Jordan ads are not aimed exclusively at blacks. In giving Lee creative control over the "Mike and Spike" series, Nike was betting the young black director's sensibility would strike a chord with blacks and whites alike. As Frank Mingo, CEO of The Mingo Group, a black ad firm, puts it: "What appeals to young blacks often appeals to young whites. [Blacks] set the trends in the market of the '80s." . . .

6   **Collecting data:** Until recently, companies that wanted ads aimed directly at blacks usually turned to a handful of black-run ad agencies. But as the "niche marketing" has increased, white-run agencies are bidding for more of the work. BBDO New York has established a research group to collect data about special markets and has made ads featuring blacks for Polaroid and Apple Computer. The Earle Palmer Brown Companies produced a controversial ad for Roy Rogers that shows a sassy black restaurant manager scolding the TV viewer ("I can't stand you eatin' as much as a leg anywhere but Roy's . . .").

7   The heads of several black-owned agencies cite that ad in particular as evidence that white-run firms can still be clumsy at portraying blacks. Mingo complains about the depiction of black women "bobbin' and diddlin' and shakin' their heads." (Roy Rogers says the woman in the ad is simply supposed to be a manager who's proud of her product.) Mingo cites an ad that one agency proposed but later killed that would have had a black sports star saying, "Feets don't fail me now." Caroline Jones, head of Caroline Jones Advertising, recalls a rice company that naively used the

image of an 1880s riverboat in a campaign aimed at black and Hispanic customers. The black execs stress the importance of distinguishing between black consumers and of recognizing "nuances" and "subtleties."

8   Black and white marketing experts do agree on one thing: the trend toward "segmentation" is here to stay. Ken Smikle, publisher of Target Market News, a trade magazine, estimates that as much as $700 million a year is already being spent on ads aimed at black consumers, and he predicts those numbers will keep growing. "We're changing from the melting-pot theory to a kind of salad bowl," says Gary Berman, president of Market Segment Research, a firm that specializes in niche advertising. As that happens, advertisers will grow even more sophisticated in their use of black influences, making images like the old Aunt Jemima ads just an embarrassing memory.

Journal Entry

Imagine that you are an advertiser. Pick a product to advertise and choose two different groups of potential buyers to target. Write a short paragraph telling what selling point you would use to get each group to buy your product. For example, if your product were breakfast cereal, you might use fiber content as a selling point to a target group of senior citizens concerned with their health. In contrast, you might stress the low number of calories in the product as a selling point to young adults who are concerned with appearance.

Questions for Discussion

1. This article begins with a very catchy introduction describing a Nike ad. In giving the dialogue of the ad and in his own descriptive details, Mabry uses black *dialect*. The term *dialect* refers to an identifiable pattern of speech other than what might be considered Standard English

(the kind of English you would use in writing for school). What words or phrases in paragraph 1 can you identify as being characteristic of black dialect?

2. Why, according to Mabry, are companies making more ads with and by blacks?

3. Mabry uses the term "Buppies" to describe black urban professionals. This term is obviously an adaptation of the more familiar term "Yuppie," which refers to young urban professionals. Why do you think he uses "Buppie"? What connotations (associations with emotions, images, etc.) does the word "Yuppie" have that Mabry might want to draw on?

4. In paragraphs 3, 4, and 5, Mabry discusses three different responses to the increasingly influential black consumer market. What are they?

5. Paragraph 4 discusses a McDonald's ad campaign that pictures blacks without "resorting to 'jive talk.'" What is jive talk, and why would this particular ad series want to avoid it?

6. Mabry notes that white-run ad agencies are now competing with black-run agencies for business directed at black consumers. What problems have arisen when white ad agencies have attempted to portray blacks or sell to specifically ethnic markets?

7. What point is being made by the example of the Roy Rogers restaurant ad? How does Rogers see the ad? What objection does The Mingo Group have to the ad?

8. The last paragraph quotes a marketing executive as saying, "We're changing from the melting-pot theory to a kind of salad bowl." Who are "we"? What is the "melting-pot theory"? What does he mean by this statement? Do you agree or disagree?

9. How does the mention of Aunt Jemima in the last sentence of the piece serve to tie the different elements of the article together and give the reader a sense of closure?

TAPPING INTO A
BLOSSOMING ASIAN MARKET

John Schwartz, Dorothy Wang, and
Nancy Matsumoto

About the Reading

This selection, written by John Schwartz and Dorothy Wang in New York with Nancy Matsumoto in Los Angeles, appeared in the September 7, 1987, issue of *Newsweek*. The article explores advertising strategies being used to sell products to Asian-Americans.

Before You Read

Ethnic groups in the United States are assuming greater and greater buying power, so, naturally, advertisers want to access these segments of the population. However, advertisers are finding that ad campaigns designed to sell products to the "American public" are often offensive to or ineffective with certain ethnic groups. Can you think of reasons that some ads you are familiar with might be ineffective with or offensive to a particular ethnic group?

As You Read

1. Notice how this article explains a number of Asian values, beliefs, and outlooks to help the reader understand why a particular strategy appeals to Asian-Americans. The color red, for instance, is described as a Chinese symbol of good luck. Consider how this information helps the authors to make their point.

2. Keep in mind as you read that "Asian-American" is a very general term, which is used to refer to people with a

238

number of different cultural heritages: Korean, Vietnamese, Chinese, Japanese, and others. Consider how this diversity complicates the task of advertisers.

————————

1   When Cecily Go Chua was growing up in the Philippines, she had chauffeurs to drive her. But last week she took the subway to get to Tung-Shing House, a Chinese restaurant in Queens, N.Y. The restaurant's cashier, Becky Yu, wanted to buy more than $100,000 worth of life insurance from Chua, who is a sales agent for Metropolitan Life Insurance Co. Closing the deal, Chua stressed that Met Life was a venerable 119 years old—a standard pitch to Chinese-Americans, who tend to be conservative. It probably worked better than Snoopy, the "Peanuts" character used in the insurer's mainstream ads. Says Ruben Lopez, Met Life's marketing director for special projects: "The Chinese aren't going to buy insurance from a dog."

2   But Asian-Americans *will* buy—especially from people or companies that speak their language and understand their culture. Following up their success in selling to Hispanics, a number of firms have bet that America's burgeoning Asian population of 5 million-plus will be the next hot ethnic market. Exploding old stereotypes—Asian-Americans "do not have bound feet [or] shop in little fish markets," says Rosemary Fincher, station manager for Los Angeles's KSCI-TV—companies have discovered a highly educated, brand-loyal and surprisingly well-heeled group. (The Asian-Americans' $23,600 median family income exceeds the $19,000 U.S. average.) "Man for man and dollar for dollar, [Asians are] the finest quality market around," Lopez says.

3   Met Life had early clues about the Asian market: the company's top U.S. sales offices in 1984 and 1985 had been in Asian neighborhoods of Houston and Los Angeles. The company targeted Chinese and Koreans, hiring L3 Advertising, a fledgling agency in New York's Chinatown, to produce unique ads geared

to Asian values. Market research showed Asian parents' top priority was their children's security and education, so one ad showed a baby in a man's arms. It read: "You protect your baby. Who protects you?" The company credits the ads, along with a drive to recruit more Asian staff, with increasing its Asian-American premiums by 22 percent in 1986.

4   Consumer goods can also profit from translation. Remy Martin's ads linked its cognac to special occasions when liquor tends to flow in the Chinese community, from New Year's banquets to celebrations such as, say, getting a child into Harvard. Remy reports that the $400,000 ad campaign doubled its sales to Chinese-Americans—at the expense of Johnnie Walker Red Label, which had been the favorite. (Red symbolizes good fortune to the Chinese.) Remy "knocked Johnnie Walker Red off the banquet tables," says Yvette Debow of the American Management Association (AMA), which will publish a report on Hispanic and Asian marketing next month.

5   The biggest beneficiaries of the growth in Asian marketing have been Asian-oriented media: San Francisco TV station KTSF is a mini-United Nations whose programming includes shows in languages from Philipino to Vietnamese. In the first half of 1987, its sales of advertising time showed a 161 percent increase over the same period in 1986. The commercials, mostly in English with subtitles, included national accounts like Safeway and McDonald's.

6   **Separate pitches:** Selling to the Asian market isn't without its difficulties. Playboy magazine ran a newspaper ad with a typical linguistic goof—heralding the Chinese Year of the Rabbit by wishing the world a "Year New Happy." Blindly imitating tactics used in other ethnic markets is apt to fail, according to Jane Fitzgibbon, senior vice president at Ogilvy & Mather. For example, toll-free telephone-sales centers, a boon to Met Life's Hispanic marketing effort, proved a dud with Asians—possibly because they prefer the face-to-face approach on such sensitive matters. The various Asian subcultures are also divided by language and cultural differences. A recent ad campaign for New

York Life Insurance Co. made separate, class-conscious pitches: Korean versions showed hardworking shop owners, while the Chinese ads featured a more subtle image of a solitary junk on the ocean.

7   Trying to get around the linguistic obstacles—and to ferret out latent Yuppies—several publishers have launched slick English-language publications geared to Asian-Americans. Rice, a monthly magazine, hopes its title will establish the gastronomic common ground of Asian cultures—even though chief executive Douglas F. Wong admits that "30 to 40 percent of the people I've spoken to say they hate the name." Still, two Los Angeles investors recently bought 50 percent of Wong's enterprise, injecting much-needed capital. The publishers of AsiAm, a clunkier product that dabbles in titillating cheese-and-beefcake photos, ran some of the magazine's first national ads for free; a year later they are waiting to see if advertisers will pull out their checkbooks. Critics of the magazines see them as marketing vehicles without a real audience; some doubt enough advertiser support will emerge. Jerry Jann, who pulled the plug on his 13-year-old Jade Magazine, says that ad agencies believe "if [Asians] are that affluent, then we'll get them in Los Angeles Magazine" or other upscale Anglo publications.

8   The Asian market seems destined to grow. The 1997 transfer of Hong Kong to Chinese control means America may welcome an increasing influx of well-heeled Chinese. As immigrants bring their families over, migration triggers mass consumerism—multiplying market clout for any advertiser with a toehold. The AMA's Debow says companies that don't jump into the Asian-American market early "are going to realize that they've missed an opportunity." Because, after all, opportunity doesn't knock for long.

Journal Entry

Suppose you are an advertiser who has been hired by a detergent manufacturer to sell its product to an Asian-American audience. What elements would you want to include in your ad campaign to make the product attractive to this particular group?

Questions for Discussion

1. Paragraph 1 contrasts an approach used by a Metropolitan Life Insurance saleswoman to sell insurance to a Chinese-American with the approach used in the company's mainstream ad. What cartoon character is used in the mainstream ad? Why do you think the mainstream approach is inappropriate for the Chinese-American customer?

2. Paragraph 2 mentions that Asian-Americans do not fit "old stereotypes." What is a *stereotype*? Explain the stereotypes associated with Asian-Americans that are mentioned in the paragraph.

3. Paragraph 2 describes Asian-Americans as a "highly educated, brand-loyal and surprisingly well-heeled group." When two words are used together to form one adjective (a word describing something or someone), they are often joined by a *hyphen* (-). Notice the two hyphenated terms, *brand-loyal* and *well-heeled*. What do these terms mean?

4. What specific examples of ad campaigns aimed at Asian-Americans does the article give? Why have some failed and others succeeded?

5. In paragraph 5, the Asian-oriented media are described as the "biggest beneficiaries" of "the growth in Asian marketing." The term *media* is one people use frequently. What exactly is meant by *the media*? *Media* is a plural term; what is the singular form of the word?

6. Paragraph 7 refers to ferreting out "latent Yuppies." What does the verb *ferret* mean? The term *latent?* The term *Yuppie?* Explain the phrase "ferret out latent Yuppies."

7. Why do some advertisers feel it is unnecessary to put ads directed at Asian-Americans in specifically Asian-American publications?

8. Paragraph 7 uses the phrases "cheese-and-beefcake" and "pulled the plug." Find the sentences using these phrases and explain what they mean.

9. What political event is referred to in the last paragraph? According to the article, what effect is this event expected to have on America?

10. A *cliche* is an old, worn-out figure of speech. Cliches include such phrases as "old as the hills," "dead as a doornail," and "the hands of time." What is the cliche in the last sentence and how effective is its use in ending this essay?

GOING FOR THE GOLD

Melinda Beck

About the Reading

The following article by Melinda Beck appeared in the
April 23, 1990, issue of *Newsweek*. Beck discusses the push by
advertisers in this country to sell to seniors and outlines the
difficulties and considerations inherent in this endeavor.

Before You Read

Senior citizens, long a forgotten group in our youth-
conscious society, are making themselves heard more and
more. Many of us think of older people as living on fixed
incomes or on their social security benefits. Think about the
older Americans you know. Why do you think advertisers
would be concerned about getting the business of this segment
of society?

As You Read

1. Beck points out how a number of campaigns geared toward
   seniors have failed because they tend to reinforce stereotypes of older people. As you read, consider the stereotypes
   that have been reflected in ads and whether or not you
   would be offended by them.
2. After explaining the problems with senior-targeted advertising, Beck presents a number of strategies that advertisers
   are finding effective in selling to this group. Notice how she
   illustrates each of these strategies by outlining senior concerns, by describing successful ads and by showing how
   different advertisers had to learn their lessons the hard
   way—by offending their intended consumers.

1   It seemed like a good idea at the time. Awash in research showing that people over 40 are particularly health-conscious, and no doubt eying their vast numbers as well, Kellogg's changed the name of its Bran Flakes cereal to 40 + Bran Flakes last year. Six months later it dropped the 40 + tag. Celeste Clark, a Kellogg's vice president, says consumers were confusing the name with a competitor's 40% Bran Flakes. But outside marketing experts sensed a bigger problem. Says Frankie Cadwell of Cadwell Davis Partners, a New York ad agency: "People didn't want to start every day with a cereal that reminded them they're over 40."

2   The audience is undeniably tempting. The 63 million Americans over 50 control half the nation's discretionary income and 77 percent of its financial assets. That's even before the baby-boom generation begins turning 50 in 1996. Nevertheless, advertisers have been remarkably slow to reach out to mature consumers—and some of those who try have made costly errors. Part of the problem may be the average age of ad-agency copywriters—thirtysomething. Then there's the persistent myth that seniors won't spend their money or change brands. "There seems to be a feeling at ad agencies that when you turn 50, you fall off the conveyor belt of life," says Treesa Drury of the American Association of Retired Persons (AARP).

3   But going for the golden agers can be tricky. The terrain is fraught with contradictions. Stressing age in ads can be a turnoff; so can leaving older people out of the picture. In a major study two years ago, Grey Advertising determined that there are 22 million active, affluent people age 50 to 64—it called them "Master-Consumers"—but found them particularly underrepresented in ads. "They told us they saw their children and they saw their parents, but they didn't see themselves," says executive vice president Barbara Feigin. Many people over 65 resent the images of themselves they do see. Gerald Hotchkiss, associate publisher of Ad Week and former publisher of the magazine New Choices for the Best Years, says he loved the AT&T spot in which the

elderly black woman's son calls "just to say I love you, Ma." Then he heard that some older people hated it. "They said, 'What do you think we do—just sit around waiting for someone to call?'"

4   Hard feelings can hurt sales. George Moschis, director of the Center for Mature Consumer Studies at Georgia State University, says his surveys indicate that one third of people over 55 have deliberately *not* bought products because they didn't like the way age was stereotyped in ads. With billions of dollars—even whole consumer markets—at stake, here are some lessons advertisers are learning as they try to reach beyond their years:

5   • **Don't Separate Them.** Like Kellogg's, other companies have tried to tailor products specifically for older consumers, only to find they don't like to be targeted. H. J. Heinz bombed with baby-food-like purées called Senior Foods in the 1950s; so did Gerber's jars of adult gourmet foods called Singles in the early '70s. Part of Gerber's problem was the name, says director of investor relations Leonard Griehs: "Nobody wanted to be reminded that they eat by themselves." Marketing experts say mature consumers resent feeling separated. "If the message you're giving the older person is, 'You are less able, so here's a product that will fill your need,' that'll turn him off," says James Thompson, AARP's manager of consumer affairs.

6   • **Subtract 15 years.** It should go without saying that when older people are shown in ads, they should look as active and attractive as possible. Grey Advertising's campaign for Post's Bran Flakes with Lena Horne, 72, gets high marks from mature-market consultants. So does a Jockey for Her ad featuring a grandmother/banker still svelte in her 60s. "Women, particularly, need women they can identify with who look *damn good,*" says Cadwell. Her agency, which represents Modern Maturity, has designed a series of ads instructing advertisers how to appeal to older consumers. One hint: cast models 15 years younger than the target audience. Studies repeatedly show that older people think of themselves as 15 years younger than they are.

7   • **Don't Mention Age.** Some products that appeal to the elderly can be marketed effectively with no age reference at all. Ads for Campbell's Special Request reduced-salt soups, for example,

stress only how good the soups taste. "Older people are smart—they'll find the product," says AARP's Thompson. "If you talk about age, you'll alienate the older person and lock out the younger person," says Jerry Gerber of LifeSpan Communications, a consulting group specializing in mature markets.

8   • **Span Generations.** Some of the best ads for older consumers are intergenerational. "Nobody has ever used grandchildren enough," says Ad Week's Hotchkiss. Art Carney's gentle sparring with his grandson speaks well for Coke and for grandfathers; Wilford Brimley warms elderly hearts with his wise admonitions to a youngster about Quaker Oats. David Ward, senior vice president at Ogilvy & Mather Worldwide, says, "The two things that older people worry about most are: will I be lonely, and will I be dependent?" Thus the best ads show mature people looking independent, yet related to everyone else.

9   • **Watch That Punch Line.** Sadly, some advertisers still use older people as the butt of jokes in ads designed for mass appeal—what Ward calls "the Wendy's syndrome." The fast-food chain's famed "Where's the beef?" ads became a social phenomenon in the mid-'80s, generating record sales and awards. But some older consumers had a beef with the image of aging that Clara Peller presented. Wendy's spokesman Denny Lynch insists that most viewers applauded Peller as a consumer advocate who stood up for her rights. That's more than can be said for Denny's Corlick Sisters, a dotty duo featured in more than 30 TV spots for the restaurant chain since 1988. The running gag is that one sister always mispronounces the name as "Lenny's"—an unfortunate way to build name recognition. "Most consumers take it in the way it's intended, as a way to make you smile," says Sue Henderson, a Denny's vice president. But critics contend that if Denny's intent is sheer comedy, younger actresses could have made the point instead.

10   Pepsi also steers close to the what's-so-funny line with "Shady Acres," a TV spot showing residents of a nursing home rocking to rap music as they drink Pepsi, while fraternity brothers play bingo and nod off over Coke. Pepsi-Cola spokesman Tod MacKenzie insists the aim is to "parody" outmoded stereotypes of the elderly. But the irony may be lost on some viewers. "We're

so terrified of getting old—baby boomers especially—that one thing that helps us think young is to make fun of older people," says Ward. One test of an ad's sensitivity is to substitute a racial or ethnic stereotype, and see if the joke still works.

11   • **Laugh With Them, Not at Them.** Humor *does* have a place—if it's done with taste and sincerity. One of Nike's best-loved "Just Do It" ads featured 80-year-old Walt Stack, who runs 17 miles a day. ("People ask me how I keep my teeth from chattering in the wintertime," says his voice-over. "I leave them in my locker.") "It's funny without putting anyone down for being old," says Nike spokeswoman Liz Dolan. Marketing consultants also frequently remind advertisers to remember romance when they feature older people. "Unfortunately, they often have silly smirks on their faces—as if they were caught doing something naughty," says Lee Cassidy of the Mature Market Institute, a nonprofit group.

12   • **Don't Generalize.** Advertisers should never forget that the over-50 population is extremely diverse. "Among people 65 to 70, there are people in wheelchairs and people who run marathons, people in poverty and people who are millionaires," says Mark Zitter of The Zitter Group, a California consulting firm. To capitalize on those differences, some ad executives now think in terms of "psychographics"—identifying markets by stage of life rather than by age. LifeSpan Communications has identified more than 100 "watershed events" such as retirement or the birth of a grandchild. "These are emotional situations that create advertising opportunities," says Gerber, a senior partner. Nevertheless, most ad-agency media buyers still think first of targeting standard age groups: 18 to 34, 35 to 49 and 50 and older. Within ad agencies, Ward says, "media buying is not changing as fast as the creative people are changing."

13   What needs changing most of all is the image makers have of aging. Whistler's Mother may have represented older women in the 1800s, but today's grandmothers are more likely to be sitting on the city council than in a rocking chair. "The people now approaching their 50s are Mick Jagger and Paul McCartney," says Feigin. "These people are the forerunners of the baby boom.

Marketers can't afford to ignore them much longer." Advertisers who don't learn to reach older consumers effectively will find themselves out of touch—and perhaps out of business—in the years ahead. As the population ages, and takes its spending power with it, *that's* where the beef will be.

––––––––––––

Journal Entry

Keeping in mind Beck's list of lessons that advertisers selling to older Americans have learned, come up with a list of three or four lessons for selling to a group into which you fit. First you will need to identify your group; you need not identify yourself on the basis of age, but might also consider interests (sports, hobbies), ethnicity, and so on. Be sure to explain the reason for each item on the list.

Questions for Discussion

1. Beck opens her article with a brief story about a failed marketing strategy aimed at seniors. What product does she mention and what was the problem with the selling strategy? Why do you think she chose this particular story to lead in to her piece?

2. In paragraph 2, the article presents some impressive figures about the buying power of seniors. What do these statistics add to the article?

3. In paragraph 3, Beck mentions that "going for the golden agers can be tricky." What does she mean?

4. In paragraph 5, Beck quotes AARP's manager of consumer affairs. What does AARP stand for?

5. In paragraph 6, the article advises advertisers to use models 15 years younger than the target audience. What reason is given for this practice?

6. Paragraph 8 mentions the two greatest fears of old people. What are they? Do you think, given what you have observed in our society, that these fears are justified?

7. In paragraph 9, the article mentions what one advertising executive refers to as "the Wendy syndrome." What is the Wendy's syndrome and where did it get its name?

8. In paragraph 10, Beck proposes a test of an ad's sensitivity. What is this test? How might this test be applied in other situations besides just in advertising?

9. Paragraph 12 contains the word "psychographics." Use a dictionary to look up both parts of this word, *psycho-* and *graphics*. What is the literal meaning of this term? How does Beck define the term?

10. Paragraph 13 contains several *allusions*. An allusion is a reference to a historical figure, famous person, work of art, Biblical event or figure, and so on. Identify the following: Whistler's Mother, Mick Jagger and Paul McCartney. What do these allusions add to Beck's point?

11. Consider the title of this article. With what do we traditionally associate the phrase "Going for the Gold"? In the context of this article, what is *gold* referring to? In what sense is someone "going for" something?

STUDY SHEET FOR AD ANALYSIS

This study sheet provides you with a number of strategies for analyzing the content of advertisements. Choose one magazine advertisement and apply these strategies, either as a group project or as an individual effort. This experience will give you practice in looking more critically at the ads you see everyday.

1. In what publication did the ad appear?

2. What method or methods are used to capture the consumer's attention so that he or she will read or look closely at the ad?

3. What target group is the ad designed to reach? How do you know?

4. What is the ad's purpose? Is it trying to sell a product, an idea, or an image of a company?

5. What nonlanguage components make up the ad?

   A. If the ad features a scene, what seems to be going on in the picture? Does the picture portray the product being used? Is the picture trying to get the consumer to feel a certain way?

   B. If the ad features a picture of an individual, what kind of person is pictured? What assumptions might you make about the person's income, interests, personality, age, profession, education, values, and so on?

   C. What has been done to make the product itself look important or interesting?

   D. Does the ad use visual symbols? If so, does their association with the product seem appropriate? For example, in the Murphy Oil Soap household cleaner ad, a group of older women is pictured cleaning the pews in a church. The church suggests the idea of God, which is then associated with cleaning to further suggest that "cleanliness is next to Godliness."

   E. Is the use of color important to the ad? Does it draw your attention to the product or some important aspect of the ad? Does the color suggest anything? For example, the color red might suggest excitement, while the color white might suggest purity.

6. Consider the language of the ad:

   A. What claims, if any, are made for the product? Are any of these claims questionable, such as the ones identified in Schrank's essay?

   B. What is the tone of the language? Is it serious and factual sounding, emotional, or humorous? Who seems to be speaking? For example, an ad for a cold remedy might take the voice of a knowledgeable, concerned physician. *To whom* is the ad speaking? An ad which uses the word *you*, for example, may seem to be talking in friendly manner directly to the reader.

C. Does the ad use metaphors, puns or rhyme?

D. Is the company's logo or slogan featured in the ad? What effect does its inclusion have on the viewer?

7. What is the ad's message? Is the ad's message stated explicitly or is it merely implied?

8. What social values does the ad reflect?

9. What is the major selling strategy of the ad?

10. Are there any other distinctive features of the ad?

11. How effective is the ad? Why?

SUGGESTIONS FOR WRITING

Assignment 1

Write an essay in which you analyze the effectiveness of an advertisement from a magazine. In your analysis, you will need to discuss both the language and nonlanguage elements in the ad and how they contribute to the ad's overall effectiveness. In your introduction, be sure to identify the ad and name the publication (for example, the Tide ad which appears in the November 1991 issue of *Good Housekeeping* . . .).

Strategies for Prewriting and Planning: In selecting an ad for this assignment, look for one which contains the following: an effective attention-getting device, a picture or drawing which shows more than just the product itself (such as someone using the product or the product within a scene), and at least a paragraph of written copy. After you have selected the ad, answer the questions on the Study Sheet for Ad Analysis which appears in this chapter. Use your completed study sheet to help you as you

6

TELEVISION

Ever since its inception, the medium of television has intrigued sociologists, thrilled advertisers, mesmerized viewers, and concerned societal watchdogs. And, in the last decade, this medium has even spawned a brand new medium—music television (MTV)—which is now also intriguing sociologists, thrilling advertisers, mesmerizing viewers, and causing concern among societal watchdogs. Critics charge that television promotes violence and reinforces racial and gender stereotypes. Others feel that television is merely a reflection of the values and concerns of the viewing audience. The effects of television viewing on children and on family life are hotly debated. The selections and discussion questions in this chapter all address some aspect of the television debate, from the use of cartoons as marketing tools to the portrayal of minorities on television.

PREREADING

Before you begin reading the selections in this chapter, record your attitudes toward television. Are you an enthusiastic viewer? Do you watch whatever is on or only selected programs? What kinds of shows do you like best? What is your favorite show and why?

POSTREADING

After you have read the selections in this chapter, reread your "Prereading" results. Have any of your attitudes changed? Did the pieces in this chapter cause you to question any of your viewing habits or the content of the shows you watch? Did the authors included here bring up concerns or ideas you were unaware of before?

FROM "THE COSBY SHOW AND THE CHANGING IMAGE OF THE BLACK FAMILY ON TELEVISION"

Melbourne S. Cummings

About the Reading

Melbourne S. Cummings is an Associate Professor in the Department of Communication Arts and Sciences at Howard University in Washington, D.C. The piece which follows is taken from a longer article in the *Journal of Popular Culture* which takes a look at the portrayal of blacks on television from the early days of television to today. In this excerpt, Cummings applauds *The Cosby Show* for helping to change the stereotypical portrayal of blacks on television.

Before You Read

Family programs—that is, programs about families and programs for family viewing—have always been a regular part of television programming. Many people have pointed out, though, that until recently most television families have been white families, and that apparently there has been very little interest in portraying minority families on network television. The success of *The Cosby Show*, however, not only placed a black family at the top of the television ratings, but has presented an image of middle-class black family life to Americans of all ethnic groups. Try to remember images of black television family in pre-Cosby days. If you have watched *The Cosby Show*, consider why Americans have found it so appealing. If you have never seen the program, try to think about other images of the black family which you have seen on television.

As You Read

1. Cummings' essay presents a forceful argument for the power of programming such as *The Cosby Show* to change the image of the black family. Watch how Cummings defines the show's blackness in paragraph 3 and then goes on to give examples of the symbols associated with black culture.

2. Notice how the major point of the first part of the article—the power of *The Cosby Show*—shifts in the second part of the article to a more general argument against the negative portrayal of black people on television. In this selection, the reader must follow both arguments and realize that Cummings' article has a dual focus.

---

1   . . . The ultimate black family television production to date is *The Cosby Show*. It has all the elements necessary for a successful production. It has excellent script writers, high priced and respected sponsors, a superb production crew—several members of which are black, seasoned directors, and a well educated, highly trained, experienced, attractive, "all-American" black cast, hand-picked by the star of the show, Bill Cosby.

2   *The Cosby Show* is about a black upper middle class family. The husband is a medical doctor; the wife is a practicing attorney; their five children are bright, witty and full of mischief. The family did not just appear from nowhere—it has historical roots. The audience is told where the family came from: grandparents are a part of the show—on a continuing basis; we are introduced to family friends and teachers, and occasionally, to the parents' co-workers. The children are not perfect: they fight; they take things without first asking permission; they make bad grades in school, sometimes; they pretend to study; the son keeps an atrociously dirty room; they abuse privileges; and they talk back, with various results, to their parents, but they love and respect each other—and their love is effusive.

3　The series is black not because it deals with racial issues or prejudice, or because there are poor people on the shows, or because it espouses a particular political point of view. It does none of these things. The series is unmistakably black because of the *Symbols* associated with it. The main character, Cliff Huxtable, wears sweat shirts from black colleges and universities; black paintings fill his home; famous black people appear on the shows; and black teachers, among others, who represent strong role-models are introduced.

4　On Dr. Martin Luther King's National Birthday Celebration, there was not a lesson on the Civil Rights Movement, but in the final scene of the show, and after a particularly angry fight scene between two of the daughters, everyone, including a youthful visitor, silently watched the television set as it displayed the 1964 March on Washington and King's extraordinary Speech. Moreover, during the height of the Free South Africa demonstrations around the United States, an Anti-Apartheid poster was prominently displayed in the Huxtable residence.

5　Dr. Alvin Poussaint, the noted psychiatrist, has pointed out that it is unnecessary and racist to always place all the burdens and problems of the black race on the shoulders of black people and black television shows. It sets these shows up for certain death and predictable negative criticism.[1]

6　Naturally, *The Cosby Show*, as one of the top ranking continuing series on television today, has its critics. Mostly these critics discuss aspects of the same topic: it is not black enough; it is not relevant enough; and it is not true to the life of the black family. The debates and discussions will continue for as long as there are more than one lifestyle which characterizes *the* black family.

7　Marketability has always been the central concern for any television show. If the shows disturb the innate sensibility of the viewing audience, they will not be viewed. And if no one watches, production companies and television stations lose money.

8　Shows like *The Jeffersons* appealed to the public, for it was a top rated show for years. For blacks, it showed an upwardly mobile couple going from 'rags to riches'. Though George Jefferson was a loud-mouthed buffoon, at least he did not shuffle; he *strutted*. He did not scratch his head and bow in deference to white folks; he showed that blacks found them as distasteful as they found blacks. To whites, there was the ease of observing blacks in a setting that said if they behaved and worked hard, they could live like whites. The show catered to whites' stereotypical image of black people. On a whole, it said that black people were different; they are separate and distinct from other Americans; that no matter what the political, social, and economic situation, they just are not regular human beings.

9   At a National Conference in 1980 on the image of black television families, Tony Brown and Lester Strong, individually, asserted that shows like *The Jeffersons, Good Times, Diff'rent Strokes, Amos 'n Andy,* and *Sanford and Son* were appealing precisely because these images do not disturb or dispute the overall view of black people generally held in the minds of the viewing American audience. Images that are incongruent with established beliefs cause mental tensions. Correct and strong images would be inconsistent with the reasons people watch television: to escape from the sameness of everyday life, and escape to fantasy. Black families, therefore, became "narrow, negative, stereotypical portrayals designed to reflect what television producers and distributors believe the majority of the American market/public imagines black families to be."[2]

10   The theory of the "comforting image" has emerged now among scholars in their effort to analyze and offer explanations for the continuing stereotypical images which characterize American television regarding black family life.[3]

11   This continuing negative portrayal of black people is disconcerting now both to whites and black people, finally. It appears that people are beginning to realize that their neighbors regardless of their skin colorations are much like themselves. They share many of the same experiences, laugh and cry at many of the same atrocities, react similarly to negative and positive influences. Black people, however, are overdue for fair treatment and a change of image in television, as in real life.

12   *The Cosby Show* [is] well on the way to making an impact and to changing the stereotypical image of the Black family on television in the United States.

Notes

1.   Alvin Poussaint. Personal Interview with Judi Moore-Smith. March 1, 1985, Cambridge, MA.

2.   Tony Brown. "Television and the Black Family: The Role of Government", in Anthony Jackson, editor. *Black Families and The Medium of Television*. Ann Arbor: The University of Michigan, 1982, pp. 83–85.

3.   Lester Strong. "Blacks, Television and Ratings", in Anthony Jackson, editor. *Black Families and The Medium of Television*. Ann Arbor: The University of Michigan, 1982, pp. 27–32.

Journal Entry

In what ways is the Huxtable family like your family? How are the Huxtables different from your family?

Questions for Discussion

1.   In the first paragraph of the essay, Cummings lists "all the elements necessary for a successful production." What are they?

2.   In paragraph 2, the author uses three dashes (—). Each of these sets off the end of a sentence. Look at each sentence in which the dash is used and think of another way to punctuate it. How does this change in punctuation change the sentence meanings? Why do you think the author chose to use the dash?

3.   Cummings writes that it is not just the characters' blackness that makes *Cosby* a "black" show but other elements in the show as well. What are they?

4.   Using information from the essay and from your own viewing experience, explain in what ways *Cosby* is not just a "black" show.

5. Critics have charged that *The Cosby Show* is unrealistic. What aspects of the show (if any) do you find unrealistic?

6. Is it possible for one show to portray an entire ethnic group? Should it have to? Should a show like *Cosby* try to portray a particular ethnic group in only a positive light? Why or why not?

7. What other black programs are on television? How are the characters portrayed? How are families presented? What kinds of jobs do the characters have? What are their educational levels? Are there similarities among the black programs? Are there any significant differences?

8. A set of *endnotes* (a list of references from which the author has taken information) appears at the end of the essay. Why do you think the author researched the work of other writers? How does this scholarly technique affect your attitude toward the essay?

Awaiting a Gringo Crumb

Richard Zoglin

About the Reading

The article "Awaiting a Gringo Crumb" originally appeared in the July 11, 1988, issue of *Time* magazine. When the piece appeared, writer Richard Zoglin was optimistic that Hispanics would make advances in the television market during the 1989 season. Unfortunately, such was not the case.

Before You Read

The United States, and particularly the southwestern United States, is experiencing a significant population shift as increasing numbers of individuals of Hispanic descent make up a larger proportion of the population. Yet significant numbers of Hispanic characters or programs rooted in the Hispanic experience have not as yet appeared on network television. Do you think that there would be general (as opposed to exclusively Hispanic) interest in such characters or programs? Or do you think that language differences account for the relative invisibility of Hispanics on television?

As You Read

1. Much of the first part of this article is in fact a list of proposed Hispanic-themed television projects which were turned down. Notice how one example after another reinforces the title "Awaiting a Gringo Crumb" by demonstrating that decision-making power does not rest in Hispanic hands.

2. Watch how this article uses quotes ("Tacos don't get numbers"; "we are waiting for gringos to toss us a crumb"; "we're not on the inside"; "Mr. and Mrs. Producer come home

every night to their Hispanic maid and gardener. That is all they know.") Consider how these quotes, which express strong feelings by and about Hispanics, contribute to the overall tone of the article.

---

1   In 1974, several years before she turned her attention to the decadent doings of wealthy Wasps, *Dynasty* Co-Creator Esther Shapiro brought NBC a script for a much different sort of TV show. Called *Maid in America*, it was a bittersweet movie about a Hispanic girl who goes to work for an upper-middle-class Anglo family. NBC executives praised the script but ultimately turned thumbs down. The reason, Shapiro recalls, was expressed in one blunt comment: "Tacos don't get numbers."

2   Food, fashion and network attitudes have changed since then— but, oddly, not that much. Several Hispanic stars have made it to the medium's mainstream, among them Jimmy Smits, of *L.A. Law*, and A Martinez, the Latino heartthrob of NBC's soap opera *Santa Barbara*. And a few prime-time series, from *Chico and the Man* through *I Married Dora*, have featured Hispanic characters and themes. But in contrast to their achievements in the other arts, Hispanics are still waiting for their *La Bamba* breakthrough on TV.

3   Not that the medium isn't trying. *Trial and Error*, a sitcom starring Mexican-born Comic Paul Rodriguez as the grungy half of a mismatched pair of Hispanic roommates, debuted on CBS in March. But the show drew abysmal ratings and was canceled after just three weeks. *Juarez*, a drama about a Mexican-American lawman in El Paso, was intended to go on ABC's prime-time schedule last January. It was abandoned because of "creative differences" between the network and Writer-Producer Jeffrey Bloom (who had his name removed from the credits when one episode was finally aired in late May). Among the pilots considered for slots on next fall's network schedule were NBC's *The Cheech Show*, a comedy-variety series starring Cheech Marin,

and CBS's *Fort Figueroa*, a drama about the multicultural residents of a run-down Los Angeles apartment building. Both were turned down.

4   The lone Latino breakthrough on the networks for next season: Benjamin Bratt, the part-Hispanic actor who starred in *Juarez*, will play one of the leads in *Knightwatch*, a new ABC series about a community crime-fighting group. "It's absurd that we don't have one half-hour of Hispanic-themed programming on network television," complains Marin. "We can make stuff as bad as the stuff that's on." Says Rodriguez: "There is no lack of talent in our community, but we are waiting for gringos to toss us a crumb."

5   Why hasn't the large Hispanic community—which watches 32% more TV than the rest of the population, according to a survey commissioned by Univision, a Spanish-language network—been courted more aggressively by mainstream TV? One reason may be the proliferation of Spanish-language TV stations (130 outlets broadcasting full or part time in Spanish), which have siphoned off a portion of the available audience. The Nielsen ratings, some charge, have long underestimated the Spanish-speaking audience, thus giving the networks less incentive to program for it. Equally problematic is the dearth of Hispanic writers and producers who have the experience or clout to get their projects made. "We're not on the inside, working, developing our craft," says Eduardo Cervantes, a vice president of current programs at Columbia Pictures Television and one of the few Hispanics in a top studio position. Most so-called Hispanic shows are written by Anglos, and as a result depend heavily on outsiders' stereotypes. "Mr. and Mrs. Producer," says Rodriguez, "come home every night to their Hispanic maid and gardener. That is all they know."

6   Network executives insist that they are receptive, even eager, for shows dealing with Hispanic characters and culture. "Everyone is dying to come up with a Hispanic show," asserts Thomas Murphy, chairman of Capital Cities/ABC. "It would be good for the Spanish-speaking population and for the network." What is needed most is a successful series that would encourage

TV's favorite pastime: imitation. Says Norman Lear, whose *a.k.a. Pablo* (also starring Rodriguez) had a short run in 1984: "As soon as a TV hit comes along, they'll copy it 100 times."

———————

Journal Entry

Write a brief proposal (one paragraph would be long enough) of your own for a new television show which would feature an ethnic minority not currently portrayed or which you consider to be under-represented on television today. Keeping in mind what kinds of shows you think people like to watch, consider what kind of show you would make (police, drama, or comedy) for example, what group would be featured, what jobs the characters would hold, where the show would be set, and so on.

Questions for Discussion

1. If you have watched any of the canceled shows mentioned in the article, why do you think they failed?

2. What does Esther Shapiro mean when she says, "Tacos don't get numbers"? Why do you think Hispanic shows have not done well in the past?

3. Do you think that Spanish-language networks help or hinder the mainstreaming of Hispanic television shows? Explain.

4. What other groups are "left out" of the television lineup? How do you account for their absence?

5. Paragraph 3 begins with the assertion "Not that the medium isn't trying." Notice that this assertion contains two negatives. How does this sentence fragment introduce the paragraph effectively? Does the remainder of the essay support the idea that television is trying to include Hispanic programming?

6. Zoglin notes that the series *Trial and Error* aired for only three weeks before it was canceled. Do you think networks should make exceptions for breakthrough shows and give them more time to catch on than they give other shows? Should television practice a sort of "series Affirmative Action"?

7. Notice that paragraph 3 describes the reasons for a cancelled program as "creative differences." This catch-all term could suggest a number of reasons for cancellation. By enclosing the phrase within quotation marks, the author expects the reader to *infer* (to find or see) further meanings in the text. What ideas does "creative differences" suggest to you?

8. The article mentions Jimmy Smits and A Martinez, Hispanics who have succeeded in breaking into mainstream television. Do you think we need to have primarily Hispanic or primarily black shows, or should all shows include people of every ethnic group? Explain.

9. This article did not appear under a *byline* (the author's name). After reading the article, do you think that the author is Hispanic or not? Why?

TIME FOR SOME REAL-LIFE TV DADS?

Joe Rhodes

About the Reading

This article appeared in the "TV Times" section of the *Los Angeles Times*. In the piece, Joe Rhodes examines images of fatherhood which have been presented on television. Rhodes concludes that television's idealized view of fathers is finally beginning to change.

Before You Read

The question which forms the title for this article might be read in several ways: Is it finally time for some real-life dads? Is there ever a time for some real-life dads? Do real-life dads have/ need/ deserve time? The point of an ambiguous, or somewhat unclear, title is that the reader is offered the possibility of interpreting it in several different ways. A title which asks a question also intends to arouse the reader's curiosity or cause the reader to look at a subject in a new light. In this case, it also implies the comparison of real-life dads and images of fathers which is the basis for the essay.

As You Read

1. Notice the style in which Rhodes constructs his essay. Because his paragraphs are extremely short, he is able to move briskly from one example to the next. In spite of giving plenty of specific examples, notice that Rhodes is clearly writing from his own observations, without using expert opinions or research findings. In consequence, the overall feeling of his essay is fairly light-hearted, in spite of the fact that his subject of parents who can't measure up to images is serious.

2. Watch the conversational techniques which Rhodes employs. For example, he uses a number of questions, exclamation marks, and parenthetical asides (comments enclosed in parentheses). These devices allow him to "talk" directly to the reader and fit nicely with the "trip down memory lane" style of the essay.

---

1   It took me 35 years to figure this out, but I finally understand why parents have always worried about their kids watching too much television. It's not the violence or the sex or even the fear that they'll try to comb their hair like Ted Koppel. No, it's something much scarier than that.

2   Parents are afraid that their kids will start comparing them to the parents on TV. Particularly, the fathers. Go on, admit it. Wouldn't you rather have been raised by a TV dad?

3   For one thing, TV dads never went to work, at least not in the '50s and early '60s. And I'm not just talking about Ozzie Nelson here.

4   Robert Young, Jim Anderson on "Father Knows Best," was supposed to be an insurance salesman, but he was home every night before supper. And Carl Betz, from "The Donna Reed Show," was Dr. Alex Stone, a pediatrician whose phone never rang after sunset. What, babies never had ear infections in Hilldale?

5   And what about Fred MacMurray on "My Three Sons"? Steve Douglas was an aviation engineer who spent all his time smoking a pipe and reading the newspaper while Bub or Uncle Charley did the dishes and scrubbed the floors.

6   Because they had plenty of free time, TV dads were always good at giving advice, solving problems and explaining the meaning of life.

7   TV dads hardly ever yelled, even when their kids did something really stupid like putting the dog in the washing machine. You never once heard Ward Cleaver say to the Beaver, "Stay right there, you little punk. I'm going to get my belt!"

8   Instead he said things like (and this is an actual piece of "Leave It to Beaver" dialogue): "I don't care what kind of trouble you may get into in life, you don't ever need to be afraid to come to your parents and tell them."

9   Man, real-life fathers never said stuff like that! But TV dads did all the time. Remember on "The Andy Griffith Show" when Opie killed a bird with his slingshot? His father, Sheriff Andy Taylor, didn't chase him or beat him or lock him up in jail. Andy Taylor, the quintessential TV dad, had a heart-to-heart talk with his son.

10   "I'm not going to give you a whipping," Andy said, opening the bedroom window. "Do you hear that? That's them young birds chirping for their mama that's not coming back. You just listen to that awhile."

11   There used to be plenty of other ways to tell TV dads from the real ones. Real dads wore short-sleeved dress shirts with sweat stains under the arms. TV dads—everyone from Rob Petrie to Clifford Huxtable—wore sweaters. Certainly, there were exceptions. Jed Clampett and Herman Munster, fashion daredevils that they were, went with jackets, regardless of the occasion.

12   But that's beside the point, which is that shows about fatherhood always have been an integral part of television programming, turning up even more frequently than professional wrestling. You don't believe me? Look at these titles from network shows:

13   "Father Knows Best." "Professional Father." "Bachelor Father." "Make Room for Daddy." "Father of the Bride." "The Feather and Father Gang." "The Courtship of Eddie's Father." "Wait Till Your Father Gets Home." "My Two Dads." "Major Dad." "The Father Dowling Mysteries." (No, wait. Forget about that last one.)

14   And I haven't even mentioned, "Zorro and Son," or for that matter, the most influential TV dad of them all.

15   Archie Bunker.

16   He called people names. He hated his job. He yelled at his wife and didn't understand his only child. He had gas. You could look at Archie Bunker and, theoretically, decide that your own old man might not be so bad after all.

17   These days, there are plenty of TV dads that you'd just as soon avoid. Al Bundy and Homer Simpson leap immediately to mind. And look at Tony Danza's daughter on "Who's the Boss?" Her dad is a maid. How must that be?

18   Let's not even start with all these mutant makeshift families springing up, orphans being raised by millionaires, single guys stuck with a daughter that one of them might have fathered. Ward Cleaver wouldn't know where to begin.

19   But not everyone went off the deep end. The '80s did give us some stable TV dads. There was Steven Keaton of "Family Ties" and, of course, there's "The Cosby Show." But, sweater or not, "Cosby's" Cliff Huxtable is a long way from Ozzie Nelson. Ozzie never would have said to Ricky what Cliff once said to his son, Theo: "I brought you into this world and I can take you out of it."

20   So take heart, real-life dads. Maybe you've still got a chance.

Journal Entry

What television dad would you most (or least) want to have as your own father? Why?

Questions for Discussion

1. Why might people, as Rhodes suggests, "rather have been raised by a television dad"? What characteristics were shared by television dads of the 50s and 60s?

2. How might the television view of fathers have affected viewers' attitudes towards their own fathers or their own parenting skills?

3. Who are Jed Clampett and Herman Munster? What is funny about Rhodes terming them "fashion daredevils"? (If you don't know, ask someone who watched television in the 60s or watch a rerun on Nickelodeon.)

4. Which of the shows mentioned in the essay are you familiar with? How does Rhodes' use of numerous examples
   contribute to the essay?

5. How would you describe Cliff Huxtable on *The Cosby
   Show*? Do you agree with Rhodes that real-life dads should
   "take heart" from Cliff? Why or why not?

6. How would you describe today's television dads? Consider
   their jobs, their behavior, and their interaction with family
   members, friends, neighbors and coworkers.

7. To what extent do you think today's television dads are
   realistically portrayed? Explain.

8. Look at the title of the article. Why does it end in a question
   mark? How would the meaning be changed if it ended in no
   punctuation at all? How would the meaning be changed if
   the title was "Time for Some Real-Life TV Dads!"?

SIN, SUFFER, AND REPENT

Donna Woolfolk Cross

About the Reading

In this selection taken from *Mediaspeak: How Television Makes Your Mind Up*, Donna Woolfolk Cross examines the curious "vision of morality and American family life" which appears in television soap operas.

Before You Read

Soap operas—which got their name because they were sponsored by manufacturers of soap products—originated as radio drama in the 1930s, when radio provided entertainment for people who were anxious for even temporary relief from the poverty and stress caused by the Great Depression. As Cross points out in this article, today millions of Americans watch one or more soaps on a regular basis—sometimes to the point of confusing the reality of the soap opera with the reality of daily life. Soaps have always sent the message that no matter how terrible people's problems, their families will help to sustain them.

As You Read

1. The thesis of this essay appears in the final paragraph. In leading up to her assertion that "under the surface of romantic complications, soap operas sell a vision of morality and American family life, of a society where marriage is the highest good, sex the greatest evil, where babies are worshipped and abortion condemned, where motherhood is exalted and children ignored," notice how Cross uses supporting details such as dialogue and events from actual soap opera plot lines in order to persuade her readers of the validity of her interpretation.

275

2. Cross clearly has a sense of humor, as her stories about Susan Lucci's experiences with soap opera viewers and Cross' own comments such as "Husbands, weak-minded souls. . ." reveal. Watch how she pokes fun at the unbelievable qualities of soap operas while at the same time writing a serious essay about their impact on American life, morality, and culture.

———————

Soap operas reverse Tolstoy's famous assertion in Anna Karenina *that "Happy families are all alike; every unhappy family is unhappy in its own way." On soaps, every family is unhappy, and each is unhappy in more or less the same way.*

—Marjorie Perloff

It is the hope of every advertiser to habituate the housewife to an engrossing narrative whose optimum length is forever and at the same time to saturate all levels of her consciousness with the miracle of a given product, so she will be aware of it all the days of her life and mutter its name in her sleep.

—James Thurber

1   In July 1969, when the entire nation was glued to television sets watching the first man walk on the moon, an irate woman called a Wausau, Wisconsin, TV station to complain that her favorite soap opera was not being shown that day and why was that. The station manager replied, "This is probably the most important news story of the century, something you may never again see the equal of." Unimpressed, the lady replied, "Well, I hope they crash."

2   One can hardly blame her. For weeks, she had been worrying that Audrey might be going blind, that Alice would marry that scoundrel Michael, and that Dr. Hardy might not discover his patient Peter to be his long-lost natural son before the boy died of

a brain tumor. Suddenly, in the heat of all these crises, she was cut off from all information about these people and forced to watch the comings and goings of men in rubber suits whom she had never met. It was enough to unhinge anybody.

3   Dedicated watchers of soap operas often confuse fact with fiction.[1] Sometimes this can be endearing, sometimes ludicrous. During the Senate Watergate hearings (which were broadcast on daytime television), viewers whose favorite soap operas were pre-empted simply adopted the hearings as substitute soaps. Daniel Shorr reports that the listeners began "telephoning the networks to criticize slow-moving sequences, suggesting script changes and asking for the return of favorite witnesses, like 'that nice John Dean.'"

4   Stars of soap operas tell hair-raising stories of their encounters with fans suffering from this affliction. Susan Lucci, who plays the promiscuous Erica Kane on "All My Children," tells of a time she was riding in a parade: "We were in a crowd of about 250,000, traveling in an antique open car moving ver-r-ry slowly. At that time in the series I was involved with a character named Nick. Some man broke through, came right up to the car and said to me, "Why don't you give *me* a little bit of what you've been giving Nick?" The man hung onto the car, menacingly, until she was rescued by the police. Another time, when she was in church, the reverent silence was broken by a woman's astonished remark, "Oh my god, Erica prays!" Margaret Mason, who plays the villain-ous Linda Anderson in "Days of Our Lives," was accosted by a woman who poured a carton of milk all over her in the super-market. And once a woman actually tried to force her car off the Ventura Freeway.

5   Just as viewers come to confuse the actors with their roles, so too they see the soap image of life in America as real. The National

---

[1] Contrary to popular belief, soap operas are not the harmless pastime of lonely housewives only. Recent surveys show that many high school and college students, as well as many working and professional people, are addicted to soaps. A sizable chunk of the audience is men. Such well-known people as Sammy Davis, Jr., Van Cliburn, John Con-nally, and Supreme Court Justice Thurgood Marshall admit to being fans of one or more soap operas.

Institute of Mental Health reported that a majority of Americans actually adopt what they see in soap operas to handle their own life problems. The images are not only "true to life"; they are a guide for living.

6   What, then, is the image of life on soap operas? For one thing, marriage is touted as the *ne plus ultra* of a woman's existence. Living together is not a respectable condition and is tolerated only as long as one of the partners (usually the woman) is bucking for eventual marriage. Casual sex is out; only the most despicable villains engage in it: "Diane has no respect for marriage or any of the values we were brought up with. She's a vicious, immoral woman." Occasionally, a woman will speak out against marriage, but it's clear that in her heart of hearts she really wants it. Women who are genuinely not interested in marriage do not appear on soap operas except as occasional caricatures, misguided and immature in their thinking. Reporter Martha McGee appeared on "Ryan's Hope" just long enough to titillate the leading man with remarks like, "I don't know if you're my heart's desire, but you're sexy as hell." Punished for this kind of heretical remark, she was last seen sobbing brokenly in a telephone booth.

7   No, love and marriage still go together like a horse and carriage in soap operas, though many marriages don't last long enough for the couple to put away all the wedding gifts. As Cornell professor Rose Goldsen says, this is a world of "fly-apart marriages, throwaway husbands, throwaway wives." There is rarely any clear logic behind the dissolution of these relationships; indeed, the TV formula seems to be: the happier the marriage, the more perilous the couple's future. A blissful marriage is the kiss of death: "I just can't believe it about Alice and Steve. I mean, they were the *perfect* couple, the absolute *perfect* couple!"

8   Most marriages are not pulled apart by internal flaws but by external tampering—often by a jealous rival: "C'mon, Peter. Stay for just one more drink. Jan won't mind. And anyway, the night's still young. Isn't it nice to be together all nice and cozy like this?"

9   Often the wife has willfully brought this state of affairs on herself by committing that most heinous of all offenses: neglecting her man. "NHM" almost always occurs when the woman

becomes too wrapped up in her career. Every time Rachel Corey went to New York City for a weekend to further her career as a sculptress, her marriage tottered. At this writing, Ellen Dalton's marriage to Mark appears to be headed for big trouble as a result of her business trip to Chicago:

Erica: I warned you, Ellen, not to let your job interfere with your marriage.

Ellen: I have tried to do my best for my marriage *and* my job . . . Mark had no right to stomp out of here just now.

Erica: Don't you understand? He just couldn't take any more.

Ellen: What do you mean?

Erica: It's not just the trip to Chicago that Mark resents. It's your putting your job before having a family.

Ellen: I demand the right to be treated as an equal. I don't have to apologize because I don't agree to have a child the minute my husband snaps his fingers. I'm going to Chicago like a big girl and I'm going to do the job I was hired to do. (stalks out the door)

Erica: (musing to herself) Well, I may be old-fashioned, but that's no way to hold onto your man.

10 Career women do appear frequently on soap operas, but the ones who are romantically successful treat their careers as a kind of sideline. Female cardiologists devote fifteen years of their lives to advanced medical training, then spend most of their time in the hospital coffee shop. One man remarked to a career woman who was about to leave her job, "Oh Kate, you'll miss working. Those long lunches, those intimate cocktail hours!" Women residents apparently schedule all their medical emergencies before dinnertime, because if they should have to stay late at the hospital, it's the beginning of the end for their marriages. It's interesting to speculate how they might work this out:

Nurse: Oh my God, Dr. Peterson, the patient's hemorrhaging!

Dr. Peterson: Sorry, nurse, it'll have to wait. If I don't get my meat loaf in by a quarter to six, it'll never be ready before my husband gets home.

11   Husbands, weak-minded souls, cannot be expected to hold out against the advances of any attractive woman, even one for whom they have contempt, if their wives aren't around. Meatloafless, they are very easily seduced. The clear suggestion is that they could hardly have been expected to do otherwise:

> "Well, after all, Karen, you weren't around very much during that time. It's not surprising that Michael turned to Pat for a little comfort and understanding."

12   If, in the brief span of time allotted to them, a couple manage to have intercourse, the woman is certain to become pregnant. Contraception on soap operas is such a sometime thing that even the Pope could scarcely object to it. The birthrate on soaps is eight times as high as the United States birthrate; indeed it's higher than the birthrate of any underdeveloped nation in the world. This rabbitlike reproduction is fraught with peril. One recent study revealed that out of nineteen soap opera pregnancies, eight resulted in miscarriages and three in death for the mother. Rose Goldsen has estimated that the odds are 7 to 10 against any fetus making it to full term, worse if you include getting through the birth canal. Women on soap operas miscarry at the drop of a pin. And of course, miscarriages are rarely caused by any defect with mother or baby: again, external forces are to blame. Often, miscarriage is brought on by an unappreciative or unfaithful mate. For example, on "Another World," Alice, the heroine, suffered a miscarriage when her husband visited his ex-wife Rachel. One woman lost her baby because her husband came home drunk. This plot twist is no doubt particularly appealing to women viewers because of the instant revenge visited upon the transgressing mate. They can fantasize about similar punishment for husbandly malfeasance in their own lives—and about his inevitable guilt and repentance:

> *Husband:* (stonily) Jennifer, these potatoes are too gluey. I can't eat this!
> *Wife:* (clutches her belly) Oh no!

Husband: What? What is it?

Wife: It's the baby! Something's wrong—call the doctor!

Husband: Oh my God, what have I done?

Later, at the hospital:

Doctor: I'm sorry, Mr. Henson, but your wife has lost the baby.

Husband: (brokenly) I didn't know, I didn't know. How could I have attacked her potatoes so viciously with her in such a delicate condition.

Doctor: Now, now. You mustn't blame yourself. We still don't know exactly what causes miscarriages except that they happen for a complicated set of physical and emotional reasons.

Husband: Oh, thank you, Doctor.

Doctor: Of course, carping about the potatoes couldn't have helped.

13   Miscarriage is effective as a punishment because it is one of the very worst things that can happen to a woman on a soap opera. In the world of soaps, the one thing every good and worthwhile woman wants is a baby. Soap operas never depict childless women as admirable. These "real people" do not include women like Katharine Hepburn, who once announced that she never wanted to have children because "the first time the kid said no to me, I'd kill it!" Childless women are either to be pitied, if there are physical reasons that prevent them from getting pregnant, or condemned, if they are childless by choice.

14   Second only to neglecting her man in her hierarchy of female crime is having an abortion. No admirable character *ever* gets an abortion on a soap opera. Occasionally, however, a virtuous woman will consider it, usually for one of two reasons: she doesn't want the man she loves to feel "trapped" into marrying her; or she has been "violated" by her husband's best friend, a member of the underworld, or her delivery boy, who may also be her long-lost half brother. But she always "comes around" in the end, her love for "the new life growing inside me" conquering her misgivings. If the baby should happen to survive the perilous journey through the birth canal (illegitimate babies get miscarried at a far higher rate than legitimate ones), she never has any regrets. Why should she?

Babies on soap operas never drool, spit up, or throw scrambled eggs in their mothers' faces. Babyhood (and its inevitable counterpart, motherhood) is "sold" to American women as slickly as soap. Kimberly, of "Ryan's Hope," is so distressed when she finds out she is pregnant that she runs away from home. She has the baby, prematurely, while alone and unattended on a deserted houseboat. It is a difficult and dangerous birth. But once the baby is born, Kimberly is all maternal affection. "Where is she?" she shouts. "Why won't they let me see my little girl?" By the end of the day, she announces, "If anything happens to this baby, I don't know what I'll do!"

15   Mothers are never tired, sleepless, or discouraged. Radiant, they boast about the baby's virtues:

Well, he's just the smartest, best little baby in the whole wide world!

He looks just like his daddy—those big blue eyes, that enchanting smile!

Look at her little hands and feet. Have you ever seen anything more adorable! And she's good as gold—really, no trouble at all. She's Mommy's precious little princess, aren't you, darling?

16   One producer of a (now defunct) soap opera actually wanted, as a promotion gimmick for one of the plotlines, to give away one baby a week as a prize! The idea was abandoned only because of the lack of cooperation from adoption agencies.

17   After the age of about ten months, children are of no interest in soap operas unless they are hit by a car or contract a fever of unknown origin, in which case they occasion a lot of hand-wringing and pious sentiments from all the adults. If the producers cannot arrange any such misfortune, the rule is that children are not seen or heard. Having a young child around would interrupt the endless raveling of the sleeve of romance. It won't do to have little Bobby need to go on the potty or have his nose blown in the middle of the adults' complicated lives, which have, as one critic says, "all the immediacy of a toothache and the urgency of a telegram."

18   You may hear a good deal of pious talk about a young child's
need for stability and love, but usually only when a couple's
marriage is on the rocks. Children on soap operas still go to sleep
at night having no idea whether one or both of their parents will
be around in the morning—a situation which brings to mind
Lady Bracknell's remark in *The Importance of Being Earnest*:
"Losing one parent might be regarded as a misfortune; losing two
seems like carelessness."

19   Children on soap operas are secondary. Because they serve
largely as foils for the adult characters, their development does
not follow the slow, steady pattern of the rest of the action.[2] Their
growth is marked by a series of sudden and unsettling metamorphoses as new and older juvenile actors assume the roles. On
Tuesday, little Terence is cooing in his cradle. On Monday next,
he is the terror of the Little League. By Thursday, his voice begins
to change. Friday night is his first date. He wakes up on Monday a
drug-crazed teenager, ready to be put to use creating heartbreak
and grief for his devoted mother and her new husband. He stays
fifteen years old for about two to five years (more if he managed
to get into lots of scrapes), and then one day he again emerges
from the off-camera cocoon transformed into a full-fledged adult,
with all the rights, privileges, pain, and perfidy of that elite corps.
And so the cycle continues.

20   Under the surface of romantic complications, soap operas sell a
vision of morality and American family life, of a society where
marriage is the highest good, sex the greatest evil, where babies
are worshipped and abortion condemned, where motherhood is

---

[2] The pace of many soap operas has picked up considerably in the last few years, as
audience surveys have revealed a strong viewer interest in action-and-adventure stories.
Before 1980, however, plot movement on the soaps was glacierlike, and on the earliest
soaps, almost imperceptible. James Thurber claimed that it took one male character in
a soap three days to get an answer to the simple question, "Where have you been?" He
wrote, "If . . . you missed an automobile accident that occurred on a Monday broadcast,
you could pick it up the following Thursday and find the leading woman character still
unconscious and her husband still moaning over her beside the wrecked car. In one
program . . . [a character] said, 'It doesn't seem possible to me that Ralph Wilde arrived
here only yesterday.' It should not have seemed possible to anyone else, either, since Ralph
Wilde had arrived, as mortal time goes, thirteen days before."

exalted and children ignored. It is a vision of a world devoid of social conflict. There are hardly any short-order cooks, bus driv-ers, mechanics, construction workers, or farmers on soap operas. Blue-collar problems do not enter these immaculate homes. No one suffers from flat feet or derrière spread from long hours spent at an unrewarding or frustrating job. The upwardly mobile professionals who populate soap operas love their work, probably because they are hardly ever at it—one lawyer clocked in at his office exactly once in three months. Their problems are those of people with time on their hands to covet the neighbor's wife, track down villains, betray friends, and enjoy what one observer has called "the perils of Country Club Place."

Journal Entry

Pick one to write about:

1. If you watch soap operas, briefly describe your favorite show (where is it set, where does most of the action take place, what kinds of stories provide the focus, what are the main characters like?).

2. If you watch soap operas, briefly describe your favorite character (job, family status, personality, looks, education, and so on).

3. If you do not watch soap operas, briefly explain why you do not watch them.

Questions for Discussion

1. The two quotes at the beginning of the essay are called *epigraphs*. How do they relate to the material in the essay itself? Do they add anything to the essay? Why or why not?

2. The essay itself begins with an anecdote (a short, true story). How effective do you find this introduction? What points are raised in the story about the Wisconsin viewer?

3. Cross spends a great deal of time discussing the confusion of fact with soap opera fiction. What specific examples does she give to illustrate this confusion? Why do you think she wants to make this point before she brings up the image of life presented by soap operas?

4. The essay focuses only on one aspect of life in the soaps: morality and family life. According to Cross, what view of family life and morality is presented in soaps? Do you agree with her assessment?

5. What aspects of life presented on soaps are not discussed in this essay? Do you think they are presented realistically? Why or why not? Give examples to support your answer.

6. One aspect of soap operas which has received some attention lately is their depiction of minority groups. How are minorities represented in soap operas, if they are present at all (in what jobs? as villains? as educated professionals? what type of family life?)?

7. Cross' essay uses the academic device of *discursive footnotes* (notes at the foot of the page—hence the name "footnotes"—which provide additional information). Why do you think she puts this information in a note rather than in the text itself? How does her use of this academic device help to make a "popular" subject a "serious" one?

FROM "HOW TV VIOLENCE DAMAGES YOUR CHILDREN"

Victor B. Cline

About the Reading

A psychotherapist, Victor B. Cline has written extensively on the topics of television and motion pictures. The piece which follows was excerpted from a longer article which appeared in *The Ladies Home Journal.* As a result of his findings about the effects of televised violence on children, Dr. Cline decided that his own children would not watch television at all, and the family gave up television for a period. While they later began viewing selectively (though never on school nights), says Cline, television was "now just not a major part of our lifestyle."

Before You Read

Television, even violence portrayed on television, has become so much a part of American daily life that many people take it for granted and don't give much thought to it. The title of this article, however, suggests its author's point of view and prepares you to read an essay which not only holds a strong opinion but which will show you how Cline believes that damage is being done. What effect does the title have on you, especially since it asserts that damage is being done to *your* children, as opposed to children in general? Is this an argument that you've heard before and have become indifferent to? Or is this a new or shocking thought?

As You Read

1. Because Cline hopes to jolt the reader into awareness, he uses a number of techniques which are designed to catch your attention. Watch how he begins the essay with a series

of "items"—facts which go beyond the question of whether television violence may have a damaging influence on young viewers and drive home Cline's point that it does.

2. Cline assembles an impressive array of cases, research outcomes, and expert opinions. Notice how he uses evidence which leads to his powerfully stated conclusion that "the responsibility for effecting change rests with every adult citizen. Meaning you. Meaning me. Meaning us."

---

1   *Item*: Shortly after a Boston TV station showed a movie depicting a group of youths dousing a derelict with gasoline and setting him afire for "kicks," a woman was burned to death in that city—turned into a human torch under almost identical circumstances.

2   *Item*: Several months ago, NBC-TV presented in early-evening, prime viewing time a made-for-TV film, *Born Innocent*, which showed in explicit fashion the sexual violation of a young girl with a broom handle wielded by female inmates in a juvenile detention home. Later a California mother sued NBC and San Francisco TV station KRON for $11,000,000, charging that this show had inspired three girls, ages 10 to 15, to commit a similar attack on her 9-year-old daughter and an 8-year-old friend three days after the film was aired.

3   *Item*: A 14-year-old boy, after watching rock star Alice Cooper engage in a mock hanging on TV, attempted to reproduce the stunt and killed himself in the process.

4   *Item*: Another boy laced the family dinner with ground glass after seeing it done on a television crime show.

5   *Item*: A British youngster died while imitating his TV hero, Batman. The boy was hanged while leaping from a cabinet in a garden shed. His neck became caught in a nylon loop hanging from the roof. His father blamed the TV show for his death—and for encouraging children to attempt the impossible.

6 These are just a sampling of many well-documented instances of how TV violence can cause antisocial behavior—instances that are proving that TV violence is hazardous to your child's health.

7 TV broadcasters can no longer plead that they are unaware of the potential adverse effects of such programs as *Born Innocent*. During the last decade, two national violence commissions and an overwhelming number of scientific studies have continually come to one conclusion: televised and filmed violence can powerfully teach, suggest—even legitimatize—extreme antisocial behavior, and can in some viewers trigger specific aggressive or violent behavior. The research of many behavioral scientists has shown that a definite cause-effect relationship exists between violence on TV and violent behavior in real life. . . .

"Monkey See, Monkey Do"

8 Much of the research that has led to the conclusion that TV and movie violence could cause aggressive behavior in some children has stemmed from work in the area of imitative learning or modeling which, reduced to its simplest expression, might be termed "monkey see, monkey do." Research by Stanford psychologist Albert Bandura has shown that even brief exposure to novel aggressive behavior *on a one-time basis* can be repeated in free play by as high as 88 percent of the young children seeing it on TV. Dr. Bandura also demonstrated that even a single viewing of a novel aggressive act could be recalled and produced by children six months later, without any intervening exposure. Earlier studies have estimated that the average child between the ages of 5 and 15 will witness, during this 10-year period, the violent destruction of more than 13,400 fellow humans. This means that through several hours of TV-watching, a child may see more violence than the average adult experiences in a lifetime. Killing is as common as taking a walk, a gun more natural than an umbrella. Children are thus taught to take pride in force and violence and to feel ashamed of ordinary sympathy.

9 According to the Nielsen Television Index, preschoolers watch television an average of 54 hours a week. During one year, children of school age spend more time in front of a TV set than they

do in front of a teacher; in fact, they spend more time watching TV than any other type of waking activity in their lives.

10   So we might legitimately ask, What are the major lessons, values and attitudes that television teaches our children? Content analyses of large numbers of programs broadcast during children's viewing hours suggest that the major message taught in TV entertainment is that violence is the way to get what you want.

Who are the "Good Guys"?

11   Another major theme that many TV studies have shown to occur repeatedly is that violence is acceptable if the victim "deserved" it. This, of course, is a very dangerous and insidious philosophy. It suggests that aggression, while reprehensible in criminals, is acceptable for the "good guys" who have right on their side. But, of course, nearly every person feels that he or she is "right." And often the "good guys" are criminals whom the film happens to depict sympathetically, as in *The Godfather*. Who is "good" and who is "bad" merely depends on whose side you're on.

12   Studies by McLeod and Associates of boys and girls in junior and senior high school found that the more the youngster watched violent television fare, the more aggressive he or she was likely to be. Other studies revealed that the amount of television violence watched by children (especially boys) at age 9 influenced the degree to which they were aggressive 10 years later, at age 19.

13   The problem becomes increasingly serious because, even if your child is not exposed to a lot of media violence, the youngster still could become the *victim or target* of aggression by a child who is stimulated by the violence that he or she sees on TV.

14   And criminals are too frequently shown on TV as daring heroes. In the eyes of many young viewers, these criminals possess all that's worth having in life—fast cars, beautiful, admiring women, superpotent guns, modish clothes, etc. In the end they die like heroes— almost as martyrs—but then only to appease the "old folks" who insist on "crime-does-not-pay" endings.

15   The argument that you can't get high ratings for your show unless it is hyped up with violence is, of course, not true—as 20 years of *I Love Lucy* and, more recently, *All in the Family, Sanford*

and Son, The Waltons and scores of other shows have demonstrated. Action shows featuring themes of human conflict frequently have appeal, yet even they needn't pander to the antisocial side of man's nature or legitimatize evil.

16   The hard scientific evidence clearly demonstrates that watching television violence, sometimes for only a few hours, and in some studies even for a few minutes, can and often does instigate aggressive behavior that would not otherwise occur. If only 1 percent of the possibly 40,000,000 people who saw *The Godfather* on TV were stimulated to commit an aggressive act, this would involve 400,000 people. Or if it were only one in 10,000, it would involve 4,000 people—plus their victims.

17   Some parents believe that if their children are suitably loved, properly brought up and emotionally well-balanced, they will not be affected by TV violence. However, psychiatrist Frederic Wertham responds to this by noting that all children are impressionable and therefore susceptible. We flatter ourselves if we think that our social conditions, our family life, our education and our entertainment are so far above reproach that only emotionally sick children can get into trouble. As Dr. Wertham points out, if we believe that harm can come only to the predisposed child, this leads to a contradictory and irresponsible attitude on the part of adults. Constructive TV programs are praised for giving children constructive ideas, but we deny that destructive scenes give children destructive ideas.

18   It should also be noted that the "catharsis theory" in vogue a few years ago, which suggested that seeing violence is good for children because it allows them vicariously to discharge their hostile feelings, has been convincingly discarded. Just the opposite has been found to be true. Seeing violence stimulates children aggressively; it also shows them how to commit aggressive acts.

19   The author of this article has conducted research studying the "desensitization" of children to TV violence and its potential effects.

20   In our University of Utah laboratories, we set up two six-channel physiographs which had the capacity to measure emotional responsiveness in children while they watched violent TV shows.

When most of our subjects saw violent films, those instruments measuring heart action, respiration, perspiration, etc., all hooked up to the autonomic nervous system, did indeed record strong emotional arousal. We studied 120 boys between the ages of 5 and 14. Half had seen little or no TV in the previous two years (hence had seen little media violence), and the other half had seen an average of 42 hours of TV a week for the past two years (hence a lot of violence). As our violent film, we chose an eight-minute sequence from the Kirk Douglas prizefighting film, *The Champion*, which had been shown many times on TV reruns, but which none of the boys tested had ever seen. We considered other, more violent films, but they were too brutal, we felt, to be shown to children— even for experimental purposes. The boxing match seemed like a good compromise. Nobody was killed or seriously injured. Nothing illegal occurred. Yet the fight did depict very graphically human aggression that was emotionally arousing.

21   These two groups of boys watched our film while we recorded their emotional responses on the physiograph. The results showed that the boys with a history of heavy violence watching were significantly less aroused emotionally by what they saw—they had become habituated or "desensitized" to violence. To put it another way, our findings suggested that the heavy TV watchers appeared to be somewhat desensitized or "turned off" to violence, suggesting the possibility of an emotional blunting or less "conscience and concern" in the presence of witnessed violence. This means that they had developed a tolerance for it, and possibly an indifference toward human life and suffering. They were no longer shocked or horrified by it. It suggested to us the many instances of "bystander apathy," in which citizens in large urban areas have witnessed others being assaulted, yet did not come to their rescue or try to secure aid or help. Or incidents such as the My Lai massacre, in which American soldiers killed Vietnamese civilians. This suggests an unfeeling, indifferent, noncaring, dehumanized response to suffering or distress.

22   In any event, our research has presented the first empirical evidence that children who are exposed to a lot of TV violence do to some extent become blunted emotionally or desensitized to it.

23   Since our children are an important national resource, these
findings suggest that we should teach them wisely. The kinds of
fantasies to which we expose them may make a great deal of difference as to what kinds of adults they become, and whether we will
survive as a society. . . .

24   The evidence is clear: a child's mind can be polluted and corrupted just as easily as his body can be poisoned by contaminants
in the environment. Children are essentially powerless to deal
with such problems. This means that the responsibility for effecting change rests with every adult citizen. Meaning you. Meaning
me. Meaning us.

Journal Entry

1. List (as well as you can remember) the television shows you
   have watched in the last week.

2. Add up the number of hours you spent in front of television watching these shows.

3. List at least three things you could have done with this
   time instead of watching television.

4. If you had it to do over again, would you have spent your
   time watching television? Why or why not?

Questions for Discussion

1. What attention-getting advice does Cline use to open his
   essay? Do you find it effective? Why or why not?

2. Paragraphs 8, 9, 16, and 20 use statistics. How does the use
   of statistics help to convince the reader?

3. In paragraph 18, Cline discusses the "catharsis theory."
   What is a catharsis?

4. What does Cline mean by the "desensitization" of children to television violence? What does it mean to be desensitized to something? Why, in this case, is such desensitization harmful?

5. This article deals with the negative effects of television violence on children. Can you think of other negative effects of television viewing on children and on their families?

6. Television is not all bad. What positive effects can television have on viewers, particularly young viewers?

7. Notice how Cline ends his article with the use of sentence fragments and the device of repetition. What effect does the line "Meaning you. Meaning me. Meaning us." have on the reader?

8. Look through the essay for statements which appeal to the reader's emotions, such as "Since our children are an important national resource . . ." (paragraph 23). Make a list of emotions to which Cline appeals in the essay. How does appealing to these various emotions help persuade the reader of Cline's point that television violence is damaging to children?

MTV ROCKS (AND ROLLS) AMERICAN YOUTH

James L. Hall

About the Reading

James L. Hall is Associate Professor of Radio, Television, and Film at the University of Southern Mississippi, Hattiesburg. In the following piece, which appeared in the November 1989 issue of *USA Today*, Dr. Hall examines whether MTV is "communicating potentially harmful, suggestive content to its audience."

Before You Read

The music video is a relatively new concept in entertainment. In fact, MTV has become so popular that not only has its success inspired other music video stations, such as VH1, but music videos are now appearing on television stations which specialize in "regular" programming, and large record stores are stocking music videos for purchase and home viewing (the innovative packaging and marketing of Madonna's "Justify My Love" was a ground-breaking example of this trend). Clearly, music videos do more than simply provide a visual parallel to song lyrics. What do you think are the qualities of music videos which attract such large audiences?

As You Read

1. Hall's thesis about MTV, which follows a brief historical survey of controversies over popular music, is that "From the very first week of cablecasting, its almost-anything-goes programming policy has produced far-reaching effects on the way concerned citizens view rock music in general and that segment of the recording industry in particular."

Because this essay attempts to raise public consciousness about the effects of MTV, notice that Hall uses a number of hard-hitting techniques to stress the urgency of gaining awareness: he provides a checklist of key questions in order to judge "potentially harmful" effects of music video content, and he quotes a number of professional opinions and studies which support the idea that music videos are not merely "potentially" but in fact harmful.

2. Look at the level of vocabulary which Hall uses in this article. The popular subject of music videos might at first seem to be at odds with such phrases as "engendered myopic examination." Note Hall's language as you read, considering its effect on the reader, and thinking about the audience he is writing for.

---

1   Changes in musical form always have produced controversy. In the mid-1950's, obscure black entertainers hit the white-dominated pop charts by making a transition from the traditional rhythm and blues music to the more universally popular rock and roll. Eyebrows raised when Etta James sang "The Wallflower" ("Roll With Me Henry"), which left little to the imagination. The Clovers had their problems with "Honey Love," in which suggestive lyrics expressed a yearning for lovemaking. As a dance craze, the jitterbug matched the beat of rock and roll with the "dirty bop" and caused a cry of concern. The so-called African beat sent American youth into a dance frenzy and their parents into a tizzy while Bo Diddley moaned almost unintelligible lyrics about "I'm a Man." Little Richard quickly rose to stardom with such controversial songs as "Long Tall Sally" and "Tutti Frutti." It was the beat that prompted Elvis Presley's hip gyrations on the nationally ranked "Ed Sullivan Show" and caught the imagination of a group of Liverpool teenagers who later called themselves "The Beatles." The same beat attracted American young people.

2   Over the last 30 years, rock and roll has produced consider-
able discussion and debate. Questionable content, from dirty
words to obscenities, and so-called "lewd" performances, from
Presley to The Beastie Boys, have generated controversy. Even a
complex "message system" has produced significant concern;
supposedly heard only if the record is played in reverse, listeners
reputedly hear references to drugs, sex, violence, and occult
information. Primarily because of its use of suggestive lyrics,
rock and roll music has been the target of attacks from concerned parents, teachers, and churchmen. MTV's completely
new dimension for viewing rock stars in the privacy of the home
has intensified the controversy. From the very first week of
cablecasting, its almost-anything-goes programming policy has
produced far reaching effects on the way concerned citizens view
rock music in general and that segment of the recording industry in particular.

3   Two types of rock music videos have evolved: performance
videos, in which filming occurs during a live, or simulated, stage
performance: and concept videos, in which artists supplement
their lyrics with settings and actions specifically designed to create
moods for video viewers. Concept videos have been described as
"video minimovies"; "surrealistic visual riffs in a song"; "production numbers soaked in blotter acid" [LSD]; "three-minute visual fantasies"; "narrative mini-melodramas"; and "short bursts of
sensual energy." The concept video has received greater attention
because its content has been more controversial. Pat Aufderheide,
cultural editor of In These Times, attributes "the success of MTV
[to the] understanding that the channel offers not videos but environment, a context that creates mood. These are fascinating
and disturbing elements of a form that becomes not only a way of
seeing and hearing but of being. Music videos invent the world they
represent."

4   The techniques of the concept videos have produced criticism
focused on both MTV and individual videos. Media analysts concerned about the potentially harmful effects of the questionable
content of MTV have posed seven key questions:

- What effect does the programming have on impressionable younger children?
- Are the video productions scripted with the goal of communicating the lyrics of the songs to the audience?
- Are the visual images part of a complex communication system known only to the rock subculture?
- Is there a dominance of sex and violence in rock music videos?
- Is the occult a significant part of rock lyrics?
- Are women portrayed as inferior?
- Is there a cause-and-effect relationship between the presentation of a rock video production and the purchase of its single or album?

5   Influenced by extensive media coverage and public outcry against the "bizarre" subject matter of music videos, researchers attempted to determine whether or not the criticism was justified. Barry Sherman and Joseph Dominick of the University of Georgia found that concept videos are "violent, male-oriented, and laden with sexual content." Their investigations showed that sex and violence are often attributes of performance videos as well. In a predominantly white, male world, MTV featured proportionately more male characters than the other music video programming sources. University of North Carolina researchers Jane Brown and Kenneth Campbell reported that, when women and blacks do appear, they are usually in the background, and women often appear in passive and solitary activity or in attempts to gain attention of men who ignore them. Perhaps the most significant Brown and Campbell finding was that youth rely on MTV as a part of their political awareness. They are, in effect, "a community of viewers" and, like any organized subculture, enjoy a common ground connection.

6   For some youths, MTV may prompt an interplay of music, performers, and viewpoints. Sexual content does exist, even if it is implied more often than overtly displayed (flirtation accounts for more than half of the sexual contact). Aggressive behavior

frequently appears in music videos: 72% of the music videos sampled presented hand-to-hand combat, the most common kind of aggression shown in this type of programming. The often-quoted National Coalition on Television Violence (NCTV) analyzed 518 videos, totaling 100 hours of programming. The results, which included both acts and threats of violence, indicated significant aggression in 40% of the videos; 39% of the violent acts were sexually related. The NCTV found acts and threats of violence occurring in both the videos and the lyrics of the songs.

7   Although young people both listen to and watch the videos, they have a distinct preference for the visual imagery of concept videos in which artists interpret the lyrics. In rock music, suggestiveness begins with the lyrics. Inevitably, MTV's transformation of those same rock lyrics into high stylized video productions engendered myopic examination. The indictment of MTV parallels the concerns expressed by the Senate Commerce Committee during a special Congressional hearing on pornographic rock music.

8   Why do parents consent to pay the extra premium charge to bring MTV into their homes in the first place? By shrewdly including MTV in an attractive list of cable services and channels, cable operators make the network part of a package parents prefer. Inasmuch as cable is a contracted consumer service, cable operators justify the inclusion of "questionable" programming on the grounds that it is not meant for general public viewing.

9   If MTV is communicating potentially harmful, suggestive content to the youth of America, then the indictment of this programming genre appears justified. Throughout the period of additional research and investigation, concerned parents must take decisive steps in monitoring MTV and concept videos. The alternative is an indictment of permissive parents who consent to the inclusion of MTV in a cable premium package.

———————

Journal Entry

Assume that you are the parent of a child between the ages of 11 and 18. Watch a music video and note all objections you might possibly have to the content: lyrics, storyline, level of violence, treatment of women, physical movements, and so on. Title your entry with the title of the video and the name of the group.

Questions for Discussion

1. This essay begins with a brief historical overview of objections to rock and roll music over the past 30 years. How effective is this opening? Why?

2. Hall identifies two distinct types of music videos. What are they, and how do they differ? Which one appears to be the more disturbing to critics?

3. What is the effect on the reader of the checklist in paragraph 4? Why do you think that Hall includes this checklist in his essay?

4. Do you think it is important to look closely at a new medium like music television? Why or why not? If you were a researcher, what questions do you think you should ask about this medium and the videos on it?

5. Hall ends his essay by focusing on the inclusion of MTV in package cable deals. Why is this point important to the debate about MTV?

6. Who are the primary consumers of MTV? Why do you think MTV is aimed at this particular group? Can you think of any other stations that are aimed at specific groups only? What do you think of this practice?

7. MTV obviously sells music—albums, singles, CDs, cassettes. But what else does it sell? Consider such areas as fashion, lifestyle, and ideas. What attitudes does MTV promote?

8. List all of the different sources from which Hall draws information on widespread concern about the possible harmful effects of music videos. How likely is the reader to be persuaded of Hall's points not merely by the information which he presents in the essay but also by the sources from which he draws?

9. In paragraph 7, Hall uses a transition sentence which reminds the reader that "young people both listen to and watch the videos" but he then argues that visuals are more powerful than even suggestive lyrics. How does his use of a transition help to make his point more forcefully?

10. Hall begins paragraph 8 with a *rhetorical question* —a question which does not require an answer from the reader, but which the writer will go on to answer within the paragraph. Why is this an effective device at this point in the article?

MONEY FOR NOTHING

Mark Knopfler

About the Reading

The lyrics of Dire Straits' "Money for Nothing," which are reproduced here from the 1985 album *Brothers in Arms*, form one element of a music video featuring the group performing the song. The video is enhanced by computer graphics and shows two robotlike men acting out the lyrics while the band is shown singing the song. Interestingly, the music video itself illustrates the point it is trying to make—at the same time it *is* music television (MTV) and it *is about* MTV.

Before You Read

Almost all of us have found ourselves singing along with a popular song, even when we haven't given much thought to the content of the lyrics. Yet, there is a great deal of disagreement about rock lyrics—some people say that they are meaningless and difficult to hear and understand in any case, while others argue that rock lyrics are so important in terms of reflecting social views and values as to be worth studying quite apart from the music that they are set to. Have you ever read lyric sheets packaged with music products? Why do you think that they are included?

As You Read

1. Notice that the words to "Money for Nothing" are arranged in stanzas (grouped thoughts which act much like paragraphs) which might remind you of poetry. Consider the effect that the arrangement of the lyrics has on you as you read.

2. From the first line of these lyrics, the reader "hears" the voice of the speaker. Notice the power of that voice not only to observe MTV performers but also to make judgments about them.

———————

1 Now look at them yo-yo's that's the way you do it
You play the guitar on the MTV
That ain't workin' that's the way you do it
Money for nothin' and chicks for free
Now that ain't workin' that's the way you do it
Lemme tell ya them guys ain't dumb
Maybe get a blister on your little finger
Maybe get a blister on your thumb

2 We gotta install microwave ovens
Custom kitchen deliveries
We gotta move these refrigerators
We gotta move these colour TV's

3 See the little faggot with the earring and the makeup
Yeah buddy that's his own hair
That little faggot got his own jet airplane
That little faggot he's a millionaire

4 We gotta install microwave ovens
Custom kitchen deliveries
We gotta move these refrigerators
We gotta move these colour TV's

5 I shoulda learned to play the guitar
I shoulda learned to play them drums
Look at that mama, she got it stickin' in the camera
Man we could have some fun
And he's up there, what's that? Hawaiian noises?

Bangin' on the bongoes like a chimpanzee
That ain't workin' that's the way you do it
Get your money for nothin' get your chicks for free

6   We gotta install microwave ovens
Custom kitchen deliveries
We gotta move these refrigerators
We gotta move these colour TV's, Lord

7   Now that ain't workin' that's the way you do it
You play the guitar on the MTV
That ain't workin' that's the way you do it
Money for nothin' and your chicks for free
Money for nothin' and chicks for free

Journal Entry

After reading "Money for Nothing," put the lyrics into your own words as if you are telling one of your friends what the song says.

Questions for Discussion

1. What is the theme (main point) of "Money for Nothing"? How does the title relate to this theme?
2. What concrete images (names of *things*) are included in the lyrics? Taken as a group, what do these items suggest to you about American culture?
3. Is there a recognizable pattern of rhyme in the lyrics? What words and lines are repeated? What is the effect of this repetition?
4. From the lyrics, how would you describe the speaker? Is the speaker male or female? What kind of job does the speaker have? What values?

5. How would you describe the speaker's tone (happy, sarcastic, angry, resentful)? Why?

6. Do you share the speaker's view of MTV performers? Why or why not? Do performers get "Money for Nothing"? Should they get paid the large amounts of money they receive? Why or why not? Do they deserve the public's adulation? Why or why not?

TOONED ON!: AMERICA
FLIPS FOR CARTOONS

David S. Wilson

About the Reading

David S. Wilson is a freelance writer based in Los Angeles. In this article, which appeared in *TV Guide*, Wilson takes a look at the upsurge in cartoon popularity and programming. He examines the reasons for cartoon popularity today and explores the tactics that production companies use to attract a larger share of the cartoon audience.

Before You Read

Think back to your childhood—do you remember watching cartoons on Saturday mornings and/or after school? If you do, can you remember what kind of cartoons you enjoyed (G.I. Joe, Bugs Bunny)? Even if you were not a cartoon-watcher in childhood, think about the qualities of cartoons which appeal to children in particular.

As You Read

1. In examining America's fascination with cartoons, Wilson cites a number of statistics; in fact, almost every paragraph contains a statistic of some kind. Watch how Wilson uses these facts to support his main point—that cartoons are not only popular, but highly profitable.

2. In addition to using facts and figures in support of his main ideas, Wilson also uses a number of allusions, or references, to popular cartoon characters and to entertainment figures from George Carlin to Steven Spielburg. Watch how Wilson's use of allusions enables him to persuade the reader that he is not simply theorizing, but that he has

done some research and that he really does know a great deal about his subject.

―――――――――――

1   Don't look now but bears, ducks, turtles, cwazy wabbits, Peter Pan, Captain Planet and Bart Simpson are all taking over your TV screen.

2   What's up, doc? An explosion of cartoon programming involving Hollywood talent as diverse as New Kids on the Block, Roseanne Barr and Steven Spielberg. Animated shows, which used to be confined to the Saturday morning and weekday-afternoon ghettos, are now beginning to migrate to prime time, and they're becoming more costly and sophisticated in the process. . . .

3   There are a number of theories explaining the current animation avalanche. The pop-sociological view is that aging baby boomers are nostalgically seeking to recapture the cartoon memories of their childhood—while keeping their own kids entertained. In short, grown-ups are fueling the toon boom. Fox estimates that 94 percent of the audience for its breakaway hit *The Simpsons* is over 18. . . .

4   Another reason why cartoons are so popular is that, technically, they're better than ever. There's been a revolution in the razzle-dazzle that animation can now achieve, giving it the necessary leg-up to attract special-effects-jaded audiences.

5   From an industry perspective, though, there is really only one explanation needed: money. The success of "Who Framed Roger Rabbit"—$153 million at the box office in 1988—gave cartoon-based entertainment projects new financial cachet. Then the merchandising bonanza of "Teenage Mutant Ninja Turtles," with its $650 million in T-shirts, lunch boxes and other paraphernalia, proved cartoon characters' incredible marketing potential. Anyone who has been to a mall knows who the current merchandising kingpin is. Bart Simpson—and Simpsonia in general—will produce $200 million in sales this year. Overall, cartoon-character licensing is a $12-billion-a-year industry.

6   Ironically, it may have been an overemphasis on merchandising that killed an earlier wave of '80s cartoon programming. Kids eventually tired of the *Masters of the Universe*-style series, where it seemed storyline, character and animation art were afterthoughts to action figures and pajamas. Part of the difference now is the price tag, ballooning as high as $400,000 per episode for the quality animation of Disney or Warner Bros. projects. More consideration is also being given to other on-screen values: less violent storylines and more sympathetic characters. . . .

7   One favorite tactic a production company uses in getting an edge on the competition is to build its animated series around a known celebrity or property. George Carlin, a costar of the 1989 film "Bill & Ted's Excellent Adventure," lends his voice to CBS's Saturday morning cartoon adaptation. Also on Saturdays, comedian Howie Mandel stars in *Bobby's World* on Fox, Roseanne Barr lends her younger image (but not her voice) to *Little Rosey* (ABC) and the rock group New Kids on the Block appears in person and in animation for their ABC show.

8   The winner in the celebrity sweepstakes, however, is Ted Turner's *Captain Planet and the Planeteers*, an ecology-minded cartoon series. Hoping to stand out on Sunday mornings on TBS and in syndication, the show has landed the vocal talents of well-known stars, including Sting, Dean Stockwell and Whoopi Goldberg, who incidentally is reportedly developing her own animated program. For *Planet*, there's even environmentally sound merchandising—toys with recyclable packaging.

9   It isn't just cartoon shows, though, that are battling for your kids' attention—it's the cartoon commercials *within* them. Popeye characters are pitching products in TV spots for Proctor & Gamble, while Warner Bros. is tying Bugs Bunny's 50th birthday this year to a big ad campaign promoting the idea of using commercial spokestoons, who don't talk back to directors, display embarrassing public behavior or demand big raises. . . .

10   Even Steven Spielberg, undisputed master of live-action blockbusters, has leaped enthusiastically aboard the toon wagon. "As the dollar shrinks and movies cost more, my imagination is becoming less and less affordable," he says. "So I've turned to

animation as a way to free it up. In animation, anything can happen."

———————

Journal Entry

"Tie-ins" are not a new concept in American merchandising; many American television shows have inspired manufacturers to create items associated with them.

Draw a line down the middle of your journal page. On the left side of the page, list all of the "tie-in" products that you can remember from television characters or shows from your childhood (these might be items that you had or wished to have). On the right side, list as many current television programs which are associated with "tie-ins" as you can think of.

After looking over your list, write a paragraph explaining your opinion about "tie-ins." Why do people buy them? How do you feel about buying them?

Questions for Discussion

1. What reasons does Wilson give for the "current animation avalanche"? Do you agree with him? Can you think of other reasons?

2. What tactics for attracting viewers does Wilson describe in the essay? Can you think of others?

3. Wilson cites the *Teenage Mutant Ninja Turtles* (TMNT) cartoon show as an example of a show which is closely tied to product marketing; in fact, in this case the products were developed first and then the show was developed to sell the products. What is your attitude toward this practice?

4. A great deal has been written lately about the use of cartoon characters to sell products like candy bars and hamburgers that are unrelated to their shows. What do you think of this

practice? Is it successful? Could it backfire? Does it manipu-
late people, especially children?

5. Wilson suggests that cartoons are moving toward "less violent storylines and more sympathetic characters." Do you
   agree? Give examples to support your answer.

6. Like *Captain Planet and the Planeteers*, a number of cartoons today have a message for children. Some cartoons
   show important lessons in the story itself and others are
   followed by a spot in which one of the characters gives children advice. What do you think of this practice? Should
   children be learning values from cartoons? Given the nature
   of most cartoon shows, what negative values might they be
   learning at the same time?

7. Wilson notes that 94 percent of those who watch *The
   Simpsons* are over 18. Why do you think this runaway
   hit has such appeal to the American public, especially
   grownups? Can you think of other cartoons that seem to
   be aimed at adult audiences (consider subject matter, language, etc.)? Should children be watching these shows?
   Why or why not?

SUGGESTIONS FOR WRITING

Assignment 1

Write an essay in which you examine how children, mothers,
or grandparents are portrayed on television. Be sure to include
in your essay a number of specific examples from actual television shows to illustrate the points you make.

Strategies for Prewriting and Planning: Before you begin this
assignment, reread "Time for Some Real-Life TV Dads?." Then,
watch several family television shows and pay close attention to
the way various family members are portrayed. You should take

notes on the programs as you watch. After viewing these shows and reviewing your notes, decide which group (children, mothers, or grandparents) you want to focus on. Before you begin to write your essay, decide on a strategy. For example, if you have watched reruns of old television programs on Nickelodeon, you may wish to compare television mothers of today to television mothers of the past. Or, if you have watched several contemporary programs, you may wish to discuss the unrealistic portrayal of children on television, choosing several criteria on which to focus, such as respect for authority, behavior at school, talents, and so on. You may find that you need to go back and watch additional programs to get enough specific examples to make a convincing essay.

Assignment 2

Write an essay in which you examine advertising and children's television. Discuss some aspect of television advertising directed toward children and develop your own policy for this sort of advertising. Use specific examples of advertising which you would consider suitable and/or unsuitable.

Strategies for Prewriting and Planning: Watch at least one hour of children's television programming on a commercial television station. Pay close attention to the advertising shown during and between programs and take notes both on the frequency of ads and on the types of ads and the products which are being advertised. For whom are the products intended (for children, or for adults and children, with children being used to persuade adults to buy products)? What devices do the advertisers use to sell products (music, a group of happy children, larger-than-life product displays, and so on)? Does the product have a slogan, a logo, a spokesperson or spokescharacter which makes the product easily identifiable? To help plan your essay, ask yourself the following questions. What successfully sells things to children? What do you think of the methods used on television to sell products to children? Should such advertising be restricted? Use the answers to some or all of these questions to develop a thesis for your essay.

Assignment 3

Write an essay in which you analyze an MTV video of your choice. Use specific elements from the video to develop your essay.

Strategies for Prewriting and Planning: Reread "MTV Rocks (and Rolls) American Youth" and note the criteria which Hall uses to examine music videos. Then, choose an MTV video which you find especially interesting or powerful or objectionable. If you have a video recorder, you may wish to tape the video you have selected. As you watch the video, take notes on elements which you consider to be important in creating the video's mood—consider the song lyrics, the music itself, the visual effects, the storyline, and the level of reality and fantasy of the video. You may also wish to consider the values portrayed in the video, perhaps considering the treatment of women, the level of violence, aspects of sexuality, and so forth.

Assignment 4

Write an essay analyzing a currently popular black television program other than *The Cosby Show*.

Strategies for Prewriting and Planning: After reading "*The Cosby Show* and the Changing Image of the Black Family on Television," watch other "black" television programs. As you watch, look for the symbols which Cummings identifies, for stereotypical portrayals, for images of black men, women, or families, for socioeconomic status or level of education. Select one program to write about. Based on your critical viewing, choose several criteria, such as those listed above, to discuss the show's treatment of blacks. You may wish to evaluate whether or not this program contributes to stereotypical views. Or, you may wish to argue that this is not a "black" show at all. Whatever points you choose to make in your analysis, be sure to use specific examples from the program as support.

Assignment 5

Write an essay in which you analyze the portrayal of modern-day American life in a popular television show. Discuss whether the show and its characters provide an accurate reflection of American life and why they do or do not.

Strategies for Prewriting and Planning: Choose a *popular* television program as *The Simpsons* or *Full House*. Watch the show as if you had just arrived in the United States and it is the first television program you have seen. What would the program tell you about modern-day America, its concerns, and its values? As you watch the program, take notes on how characters dress, act and interact, where they work, what they think and worry about, what they do for recreation, how their families are structured, where and how they live, and so on. Notice also the larger concerns portrayed in the program, including ethnic representations, current and historical events, and social issues. After looking over your notes, formulate a thesis which reflects the view of American life your program presents.

Assignment 6

After reading "How TV Violence Damages Your Children," write an essay in which you apply Cline's arguments about the harmful effects of television violence on children.

Strategies for Prewriting and Planning: Watch at least one hour of afterschool or weekend cartoon programming for children. As you watch, take notes on the level of violence presented.

What kinds of violence do you see? Toward whom is it directed? How frequently do violent acts occur? What consequences does this violence have for the perpetrator and the victim? Is violence presented as humorous? What lessons might children be learning from the violence they see? Use your observations to provide examples proving that Cline's analysis is right.

Assignment 7

Opinions about television are divided. Take a stand of your own on this issue and argue either that television is a positive influence on society or that it is a negative influence on society.

Strategies for Prewriting and Planning: After reading the selections in this chapter and spending some time watching television, decide which stand you will take. Be sure to stick to one stand, either positive or negative—do not mix the two. List all of the reasons that support your stand. For example, you may feel that television is positive because it educates viewers, or you might find television a negative influence because of the violence it portrays. Then, use specific examples from your reading and viewing to support your reasons. These examples should consist of references to readings, and to specific shows or types of shows, perhaps to particular episodes.

7

UTILIZING THE TECHNIQUES OF LIBRARY RESEARCH: WRITING AN ANNOTATED BIBLIOGRAPHY

During your college career, a number of your instructors will expect you to be familiar with the techniques of library research. In order to locate material for a speech class, for instance, you may need to be able to locate an article or articles in newspapers or magazines. Your history professor may require you to locate a book on a famous person or an important historical period or movement. Or, you may be asked to explore in depth a subject brought up in class lecture or discussion by writing a research paper which includes a list of all of the sources you have consulted.

In order to complete these types of assignments, you will need to know

1. How to find articles on a particular topic in newspapers and magazines and how to get the important information from the articles when you find them;

2. How to locate books on a topic and how to summarize the information in them;

3. How to give credit for ideas you borrow from someone else; and

4. How to record information about your sources in a pre-scribed format so that someone else who wishes to consult one of your sources could do so easily.

This chapter outlines a research project called an *annotated bibliography*. By completing this project, you will gain experience in all of these areas of library research. In addition, you will get a chance to look in more depth into one area of the broad topics of advertising, television and heroes, all of which have been ad-dressed in this book.

ANNOTATED BIBLIOGRAPHY

A bibliography is a list of materials (books, magazine articles, and so on) on a specific topic. An *annotated* bibliography includes commentary on each of the materials listed. This commentary usually consists of a summary of content and an evaluation of the source.

Assignment

1. Assume that you have been hired by your instructor as a research assistant. Your instructor is preparing to write an article on one of the topics below, but does not have time to research all of the materials in the college library on this topic. Your job is to locate sources that could be used in writing the article and provide the instructor with full docu-mentation, a summary of contents, and an evaluation of use-fulness for each source. You must present this information in the form of an annotated bibliography.
2. Choose *one* of the following general topics:

   Television

   Heroes/Heroines

   Advertising
3. Locate *one* encyclopedia article and *one* book on the general topic.

4. After skimming your sources from #3, you will be ready to limit your topic further. Suggested limited topics appear below:

    A. **Television:** television violence, minorities in television, children and television, women in television, sex in television, television and politics.

    B. **Heroes/Heroines:** select an American living today whom you consider a hero or heroine. You may choose an innovator in education, a businessman, an entertainer, an activist, a writer, a politician.

    C. **Advertising:** television advertising, political advertising, advertising for a particular type of product (cigarettes, beer, cosmetics, and so on), consumer behavior, marketing research.

5. After you have limited your topic, locate *two* magazine articles and *one* newspaper article which focus on your limited topic.

6. Now you are ready to take notes on your sources. Be sure to record all of the information you will need for your bibliographic *citation* (listing) at the top of your notes. In order to avoid *plagiarism*, that is, copying a writer's words or borrowing the writer's ideas without giving proper credit, notes should be in *your* words, not those of the author. Any key words or phrases borrowed from the original source should be enclosed in quotation marks (" ") and the page noted in parentheses ( ) immediately after the quote.

7. From your notes, you will prepare your annotated bibliography, allowing one double-spaced typed page per source. At the top of the page, give the bibliographic data in proper MLA format (see pages 321 to 323). Follow the citation examples exactly, including capitalization, period and comma placement, and indentation.

    After you have written the bibliographic citation, write a one- or two-paragraph summary of the article or book. If you refer to the author of the article in writing your summary, the first time you do so you should use his or her full name; thereafter, use the last name only.

Next, write a paragraph in which you *evaluate* the source. In preparing your evaluation, ask yourself the following questions: What information in this source might be useful to your instructor? What limitations, if any, does the source have? What, if anything, is particularly different or interesting in this source?

8. Type your entry for each source on a separate page, double spacing and leaving a one-inch margin on each side. Each entry must include citation, summary and evaluation (see sample on page 320, which is based on the article "Children Who Dress for Excess" which appears in Chapter 1). Place your pages in alphabetical order based on the first word in each bibliographic citation. Make a cover page which includes a title (may be same as limited topic), your name, and course information and date (see sample on page 319). Staple all pages together in the upper left corner.

Advertising: Consumer Behavior

By
Maria Alvarez

English A
Dr. Jones
May 2, 1991

Harris, Ron. "Children Who Dress for Excess." Los
    Angeles Times 12 Nov. 1989: A1+.

   This article is about children who are obsessed
with wearing expensive name-brand clothing. Ron
Harris gives examples of children who have even
been killed for their costly clothes. According
to Harris, there are several reasons for this
clothing fixation. One is advertising directed
toward kids; clothing ads make kids feel that
they must wear a particular shoe or jacket to be
worthwhile people. This feeling is reinforced
by peer pressure. In some cases, says Harris,
students who wear no name clothes are "ridiculed,
scorned and sometimes even ostracized by their
classmates" (A26). The problem is worsened by
parents who indulge their children, buying them
everything they ask for.
   Some schools have begun to try to correct this
problem, and educators at other schools wish
parents would learn to say "no" to their kids. Some
schools have adopted "exclusionary" dress codes
(A1) while others now require students to wear
uniforms. Though a lot of parents seem upset by
their kids' emphasis on material goods, in most
cases, the article points out, the kids learned
this behavior from their parents.
   This article is a good source of information on
the behavior of young consumers and the way they
are manipulated by the media and advertisers. The
specific examples Harris gives of kids' behavior,
such as killing for shoes or refusing to enter
discount stores, are very interesting.

In scholarly writing that involves researching the ideas of others, it is the practice that all information about source materials be presented in a particular format. That is, it should be arranged in a particular order, and punctuated, indented, and underlined in a certain way. This format may vary from one discipline to another, with science using one format and English another. In any case, instructors will specify which format they want you to use. The important thing is to be able to find the information you need to include for each source and to be able to follow models for arranging this information. The model given below reflects the format put out by the Modern Language Association (MLA) and used in English classes. This is the format you will use in preparing your annotated bibliography.

MLA FORMAT FOR BIBLIOGRAPHIC ENTRIES

Book

A Book with One Author

Jefferson, Nadia. <u>Advertising and Buyer Manipulation: You Are What You Buy.</u> New York: Viking, 1985.

The author's last name is given first, followed by a comma, then the author's first name, and finally a period. The title of the book (including any subtitle, such as "You Are What You Buy") is underlined and followed by a period. The city of publication is followed by a colon, the publisher's name and a comma, and the date of publication. The entire entry ends with a period. The publication information can be found on the title page and copyright page at the beginning of the book. All lines *except the first* are indented 5 spaces.

A Book with Two or Three Authors

Samuels, Joseph, and Laura Rodriguez. <u>Conning the Consumer.</u> Boston: Holt, 1979.

Only the first author's name is given with the last name first. The second author's name is not reversed. The names of each author are separated by a comma.

Encyclopedia

A Signed Encyclopedia Article

Smith, Arturo. "Advertising." Encyclopedia of the Americas. 1980 ed.

The title of the encyclopedia article is followed by a period and enclosed in quotation marks. The title of the encyclopedia is underlined and followed by a period. For an encyclopedia it is unnecessary to give page numbers, but it is important to include the year of publication.

An Unsigned Encyclopedia Article

"Advertising." Collegiate Encyclopedia. 1980 ed.

Sometimes articles in encyclopedias are not signed. In this case, you begin your entry with the title.

Magazine

An Article in a Monthly Magazine

Melbourne, Sofia. "Predicting Consumer Reaction." Psychology Today
    May 1988: 26–29.

For an article in a monthly magazine, the article title is followed by a period and enclosed in quotation marks. The name of the magazine is underlined and followed by the month and year of publication, a colon, the numbers of the pages on which the article appears, and a period.

An Article in a Weekly Magazine

Teinowitz, Ira. "Jest Plain Offensive: Touchy Consumers Howl at 'Slurs'
    in Ads." Advertising Age 17 July 1989: 3+.

An article in a weekly magazine is treated the same as an article in a monthly magazine with the exception of the date. The date for a weekly magazine consists of the day, then the month, then the year. If the article appears on pages that are not in sequence, give only the first page number followed by a plus sign (+).

Newspaper

A Signed Article in a Daily Newspaper

Harris, Ron. "Children Who Dress for Excess." <u>Los Angeles Times</u> 12
     Nov. 1989: A1+.

An article in a daily newspaper is treated like an article in a weekly periodical except that the section, as well as the page numbers, follows the date. If the sections are lettered, they appear as above; if they are numbered, the following format is used: sec. 1: 1+ (see example below).

An Unsigned Article in a Daily Newspaper

"Shopaholics." <u>Wilmington Herald</u> 19 May 1990, sec. 2: 1.

Entries for unsigned articles begin with the title of the article.

Editorial

A Signed Editorial

Newsome, Tom. "Disgraceful Behavior." Editorial. <u>Midvale Times</u> 13
     June 1990, sec. 1: 11.

A signed editorial is treated like a signed newspaper article with the addition, after the title, of the word "Editorial." The word "Editorial" is not placed in quotation marks, nor is it underlined.

An Unsigned Editorial

"Monkey See, Monkey Do." Editorial. <u>Eastside News</u> 20 Aug. 1990: B19.

When the editorial is unsigned, the title is given first.

Note: If you find a source that does not seem to fit into any of these models, consult your instructor or *The MLA Handbook* or your reference librarian.

EXERCISE: USING PROPER
MLA BIBLIOGRAPHIC FORM

Instructions: Following the models provided in this chapter, put the following bibliographic information into the proper MLA format.

1. **Book**
   Title: Student's Guide to Survival
   Author: Mel Martinez   Date of Publication: 1982
   Publisher: Wizard Press   Place of Publication: Boston

2. **Newspaper**
   Article Title: Youth Dies—Too Much Studying Blamed
   Author: no author given
   Newspaper Title: Westchester Times   Page: 2
   Date: Monday, December 10, 1990   Section: B

3. **Monthly Magazine**
   Article Title: Wildest Campus Weekends
   Author: Marjorie Coed   Pages: 23–24
   Magazine Title: Campus Life   Volume Number: 12
   Date: November 1989

4. **Encyclopedia**
   Article Title: Education   Author: Joseph Wiseman
   Encyclopedia: World Book Encyclopedia   Edition: 1985

5. **Weekly Magazine**
   Article Title: The Fine Art of Procrastination
   Author: DeWitt Tomorrow   Pages: 45+
   Magazine Title: Self   Date: May 23, 1990

ACKNOWLEDGMENTS

Melbourne S. Cummings, "The Changing Image of the Black Family on Television" from the *Journal of Popular Culture*, Vol. 22:2, Fall 1988. Copyright (c) 1988 by Journal of Popular Culture. Reprinted by permission.

Mary Crow Dog with Richard Erdoes, *Lakota Woman* by Mary Crow Dog with Richard Erdoes. Copyright (c) 1990 by Mary Crow Dog with Richard Erdoes. Reprinted by permission of the Grove Press.

Amy Ehrlich, "Jack and the Bean Stalk" from *The Random House Book of Fairy Tales*, adapted by Amy Ehrlich. Text copyright (c) 1985 by Amy Ehrlich. Reprinted by permission of Random House, Inc.

Pete Engardio with Walecia Konrad, Ronald Grover, Jo Ellen Davis and Loris Therrien, "Fast Times on Avenida Madison" reprinted from the June 6, 1988 issue of *Business Week* by special permission. Copyright (c) 1988 MacGraw-Hill, Inc.

Jules Feiffer, "Faster Than an Express Train" from *The Great Comic Book Heroes* by Jules Feiffer. Copyright (c) 1965 by Jules Feiffer. Used by permission of Doubleday, a division of Bantam Doubleday Dell Publishing Group, Inc.

Denise Fortino, "Why Kids Need Heroes" from *Parents* Magazine, November 1984. Copyright (c) 1984 by Denise Fortino. Reprinted by permission.

Richard L. Gordon, "Ads, Violence and Values" from *Advertising Age*, April 2, 1990. Reprinted with permission from Advertising Age, April 2, 1990. Copyright (c) 1990 Crain Communications, Inc.

James L. Hall, "MTV Rocks (and Rolls) American Youth" from *USA Today* Magazine, November 1989. Reprinted from USA Today Magazine by the Society for the Advancement of Education. Reprinted by permission.

Ron Harris, "Children Who Dress for Excess" from *Los Angeles Times*, November 12, 1989. Copyright (c) 1989 by Los Angeles Times Syndicate. Reprinted by permission.

Roger Hoffman, "The Dare" from *The New York Times*, March 23, 1986. Copyright (c) 1986 by The New York Times Company. Reprinted by permission.

Peter Homans, "The Western: The Legend and the Cardboard Hero." Copyright 1980 by Peter Homans. Reprinted by permission of the author.

Langston Hughes, "Salvation" from *The Big Sea*. Copyright (c) 1940 by Langston Hughes. Renewal copyright (c) 1968 by Arna Bontemps and George Houston Bass. Reprinted by permission of Hill and Wang, a division of Farrar, Straus and Giroux, Inc.

Mark Knopfler, "Money for Nothing" from *Brothers In Arms*, Warner Brothers, 1985. Reprinted by permission of Almo Irving Music Publishing, Inc.

Dawn Ann Kurth, "Bugs Bunny Says They're Yummy" from *The New York Times*, 1972. Copyright (c) 1972 by The New York Times Company. Reprinted by permission.

Marcus Mabry, "A Long Way From Aunt Jemima" from *Newsweek*, August 14, 1989. Copyright (c) 1989 by Newsweek, Inc. All Rights Reserved. Reprinted by permission.

Gloria Naylor, "Mommy, What Does 'Nigger' Mean?" from *The New York Times*, February 20, 1986. Copyright (c) 1986 by The New York Times Company. Reprinted by permission.

Holly Peck, "The Military: Is It for Real?" Reprinted by permission.

Americo Peredes, "The Rabbit and the Coyote" from *Folktales of Mexico* edited by Americo Peredes. Copyright (c) 1970 by The University of Chicago Press. Reprinted by permission.

John Pete, "Winabijou Looks for the Wolf" told by John Pete and translated by George Cadotte from *Folktales Told around the World*, edited by Richard M. Dorson. Copyright (c) 1975 by The University of Chicago Press. Reprinted by permission.

Joe Rhodes, "Time for Some Real-Life T.V. Dads?" from the *Los Angeles T.V. Times*, June 17–23, 1990. Copyright (c) 1990 by Joe Rhodes. Reprinted by permission of the author.

John Schwartz with Dorothy Wang and Nancy Matsumoto, "Tapping into a Blossoming Asian Market" from *Newsweek*, September 9, 1987. Copyright (c) 1987 by Newsweek, Inc. All rights reserved. Reprinted by permission.

Jeffrey Schrank, "Advertising Claims" adapted from DECEPTION DETECTION. Copyright (c) 1975 by Jeffrey Schrank. Reprinted by permission of Beacon Press.

Sophronia Scott, "It's a Small World after All" from *Time* Magazine, September 25, 1990. Copyright (c) 1989 by Time Warner, Inc. Reprinted by permission.

Pretty Shield, "A Woman's Fight" from PRETTY SHIELD: MEDICINE WOMAN OF THE CROWS by Frank Linderman. Copyright (c) 1932 by Frank B. Linderman. Reprinted by permission of HarperCollins Publishers.

Ira Teinowitz, "Just Plain Offensive: Touchy Consumers Howl at 'Slurs' in Ads" from *Advertising Age*, July 17, 1989. Reprinted with permission from Advertising Age, July 17, 1989. Copyright (c) 1989 Crain Communications, Inc.

Randall Williams, "Daddy Tucked the Blanket" from *The New York Times*, July 10, 1975. Copyright (c) 1975 by The New York Times Company. Reprinted by permission.

E.M. Wilmot-Buxton, "The Story of Balder the Beautiful" from *The Junior Classics: Myths and Legends*. Copyright (c) 1938 and 1948 by Collier Publishers. Reprinted by permission of Collier Publishers.

David S. Wilson, "Tooned On!" from *T.V. Guide*, June 9, 1990. Copyright (c) 1990 by the *Los Angeles Times Syndicate*. Reprinted by permission.

Elizabeth Wong, "The Struggle to Be an All-American Girl." Copyright (c) Elizabeth Wong. Reprinted by permission.

Richard Zoglin, "Awaiting a Gringo Crumb" from *Time* Magazine, July 11, 1988. Copyright (c) 1988 Time Warner, Inc. Reprinted by permission.

INDEX